Cultural Studies

Theorizing Politics, Politicizing Theory

VOLUME 13 NUMBER 2 APRIL 1999

Special issue:
Chicana/o Latina/o Cultural Studies: Transnational and Transdisciplinary Movements

Edited by
Angie Chabram-Dernersesian

Editorial Statement

Cultural Studies continues to expand and flourish, in large part because the field keeps changing. Cultural studies scholars are addressing new questions and discourses, continuing to debate long-standing issues, and reinventing critical traditions. More and more universities have some formal cultural studies presence; the number of books and journals in the field is rapidly increasing. *Cultural Studies* welcomes these developments. We understand the expansion, reflexivity and internal critique of cultural studies to be both signs of its vitality and signature components of its status as a field. At the same time, cultural studies has been – and will no doubt continue to be – the subject of numerous attacks, launched from various perspectives and sites. These have to be taken seriously and answered, intellectually, institutionally and publicly. *Cultural Studies* hopes to provide a forum for response and strategic discussion.

Cultural Studies assumes that the knowledge formations that make up the field are as historically and geographically contingent as are the determinations of any cultural practice or configuration and that the work produced within or at its permeable boundaries will be diverse. We hope not only to represent but to enhance this diversity. Consequently, we encourage submissions from various disciplinary, theoretical and geographical perspectives, and hope to reflect the wide-ranging articulations, both global and local, among historical, political, economic, cultural and everyday discourses. At the heart of these articulations are questions of community, identity, agency and change.

We expect to publish work that is politically and strategically driven, empirically grounded, theoretically sophisticated, contextually defined and reflexive about its status, however critical, within the range of cultural studies. *Cultural Studies* is about theorizing politics and politicizing theory. How this is to be accomplished in any context remains, however, open to rigorous enquiry. As we look towards the future of the field and the journal, it is this enquiry that we especially hope to support.

Lawrence Grossberg
Della Pollock   *January 1998*

Contents

VOLUME 13   NUMBER 2   APRIL 1999

Articles

Angie Chabram-Dernersesian[1]

INTRODUCTION
CHICANA/O LATINA/O CULTURAL
STUDIES: TRANSNATIONAL AND
TRANSDISCIPLINARY MOVEMENTS

> So I simply want you to know that my own feeling is that the explosion of
> cultural studies along with other forms of critical theory in the academy
> represents a moment of extraordinarily profound danger.
>
> (Stuart Hall, 'Cultural studies and its theoretical legacies')

Chicana/o cultural studies: marking the conjuncture
and an institutional context

IT HAS BEEN ALMOST a decade since the publication of 'Chicana/o cultural
representations: reframing alternative and critical discourses' (*Cultural Studies*
4, 3, 1990).[2] Since then, Chicana/o cultural studies have flourished, incorporating new cultural practices, political interventions, transnational movements, and
transdisciplinary gestures that inscribe vital conversations with Chicana Feminism, Chicana/o critical (racial, legal, gender, sexual, historical) studies, border
studies, hemispheric Latina/o and indigenous (cultural) studies, Mexican cultural studies, Boricua studies, the feminist legacies of women of colour, African
American studies, Asian American studies, Women's studies, American studies,
postcolonial studies, and, of course, cultural studies. While these gestures have
yet to be translated into the other set of practices generally referred to as 'cultural studies' *per se*, there is no doubt that the critical interventions that I refer
to here as 'Chicana/o cultural studies' or 'Chicana/o Latina/o cultural studies',
which interface a cultural studies practice or conjuncture, are here to stay.
Locally, evidence of this type of affiliation/alliance can be found in the appearance of cultural studies courses and sub-fields within Chicana/o Latina/o studies
departments and programmes; the proliferation of conferences that link
Chicana/o studies to cultural studies; and the publication of anthologized

volumes which thematize a connection to Chicana/o and Latina/o subjects through a rearticulation of disparate cultural studies practices and traditions within the Americas.

However, this very convergence between Chicana/o cultural studies and cultural studies is not without its own particular set of internal and external contradictions and tensions that must be openly acknowledged and engaged within a politically accountable as well as socially nuanced cultural studies practice that is attentive to the cautionary note which accompanies Hall's 'gut-feeling' about the dangers of the proliferation of cultural studies in the academy. Only from this type of critical engagement is it possible to envision a productive relationship between Chicana/o cultural studies and cultural studies which fosters an 'understanding of the specific ways cultural practices operate in daily life and social formations' and which is devoted to 'intervening in the processes by which existing techniques, institutions and structures of power are reproduced, resisted and transformed' (Grossberg and Radway, Editorial, 1994).

For this reason, I inaugurate this second special issue by examining the kinds of institutional dynamics that can emerge around the selected denomination, Chicana/o cultural studies, which inscribes a strategic affiliation to not only cultural studies, but also to Chicana/o studies itself. As I see it, this denomination involves a symbolic rearticulation of these fields, emerging from an interpretation of the 'radically contextual, historically specific character of the production of knowledge'[3] within Chicana/o studies, cultural studies as well as other intersected fields of study[4] targeted in this volume through specific transnational and transdisciplinary movements implicating the hemispheric context of the Americas.

Some of the institutional dynamics undergirding this type of cultural studies affiliation surfaced on the West Coast when university administrators at our campus proposed to institutionalize cultural studies through a college-wide re-organizing initiative that ultimately resulted in the formation of HACS (Humanities, Arts, and Cultural studies, formerly The College of Letters and Science). Initially, this initiative faced strong opposition from a number of constituencies, including Chicana/o studies constituencies in particular, who variously critiqued the measure as a top-down 'administrative' construction, as an instance of 'restructuring' and 'downsizing', and as an example of the intrusion of a capitalist-driven, corporate model within the academy. The vocal opposition to this administratively driven construction of cultural studies stemmed as well from the suggestion of an 'unproblematic' incorporation of Chicana/o studies (and, by extension, African American, Native American and Asian American studies) into 'ethnic studies' for 'administrative' and 'bureaucratic' purposes.

Within the collective oppositional dialogue, it was also argued that the administration's proposal implied a forced deterritorialization of Chicana/o studies – the loss of its autonomy and possible disintegration, and the erasure of its 'particular' constituency-based social mission. In addition, it was proposed that this construction – cultural studies? – failed to address the organic relationships between the different programmes and the department associated with 'ethnic studies', especially since no such ethnic studies configuration existed on our campus and had been vigorously opposed with the idea of a 'coalition' incorporating women's studies. While many important issues emerged from the collective scrutiny of cultural studies on our campus, what was largely discussed on the periphery of the debate was the fact that what was being proposed was not only a mainstream and conservative construction of Chicana/o studies (and some other programmes as watered down ethnic studies programmes), but of cultural studies itself. To many of those who were not actively involved in broader cultural studies' networks and interventions, the equation of cultural studies, cultural pluralism and assimilation seemed logical, and within administrative framing, cultural studies generally appeared as an interdisciplinary and 'sexy' mix of traditions that housed 'diversity'.

The debate around cultural studies on our campus involved not just the academic community but other communities at large. And the question most often raised in this mix of academic and public constituencies was not the singular: 'What is cultural studies?' (the question that occupies the attention of a number of scholars these days). Rather the burning questions were: What is its political subtext? Who is its political subject? Who does it own? disown? promote? manage? entitle? shield? reorganize? What are its connections to other intellectual formations that are invested with the power to make a generic claim to knowledge?

For those of us who witnessed firsthand this institutional construction of cultural studies, linked as it was to the university's economic restructuring and administrative reorganization, it was painfully clear that cultural studies did not operate outside of 'local' pre-existing social and institutional identities, relations and conflicts. It was painfully clear that cultural studies could not just move into the socially and politically charged academic arena without addressing its impact on other alternative knowledge formations and practices that did carry the marks of race, class, gender and sexuality at the level of the social and intellectual body – or without delineating its affiliations to these fields whose presence in the academy involved institutional struggles, not institutional mandates.

Given this context, it was necessary to reconnect cultural studies to its cutting-edge radical politics and intellectual formations, and to confront the manner in which these fields (cultural studies, Chicana/o studies and Chicana/o cultural studies) could be made to intrude upon one another in a way that forever marked their separation from one another and sealed an inevitable mutual antagonism. Most importantly, it was necessary to rise above this hegemonic incorporation of cultural studies and to forcefully honour the struggles for self-determination of historically subordinated social and ethnic communities (Chicanas/os, African-Americans, Asian Americans, Native Americans) within the US that lacked both the ability of cultural studies to proliferate and its institutional legitimacy and 'chic' status. Finally, it was necessary to vigorously support their ongoing and current struggles to participate in academic policies, and to face the reality that this participation often came late, after the fact, when the possibilities of a proactive stance were greatly limited.

To be sure, navigating beyond this problematic birthing of cultural studies, which 'speaks to the distinctive conditions and circumstances in which cultural studies is practiced' in the US context, 'means recognizing that those very convergences which bring cultural studies and these area studies together (interdisciplinarity, the objects of analysis and methodological approaches – race, gender, sexuality, and class,) can be used "to pit" these area-studies programs and cultural studies against each other in games of intellectual justification and legitimization.'[5] In this sense many of us share Herman Gray's concern that 'without critical intellectual reflection and active political engagement both within the university and beyond, cultural studies could be enlisted to help to displace and marginalize those very quarters of the university (e.g. area studies) and public life with whom productive alliances might be made.'[6]

In addition to this type of political engagement, it is also important to revisit the thorny issue of the formation of cultural studies in a manner which does not reify the field or invite unacceptable canon formations, or circumscribe these 'local communities' within an overarching 'British–American' connection that sidesteps their valuable 'theoretical interruptions' to the ongoing discussion about cultural studies legacies.[7] In our current temporal and spacial context, it is imperative that we acknowledge multiple and even adversarial constructions of cultural studies (on the inside and outside) and that we approach the question of 'formation' from the perspective of underrepresented and marginalized areas studies that subject 'American' cultural studies to a much needed and sustained critical scrutiny from other borderzones of the Americas.

Finally, when reflecting on a conjunctural relationship with cultural studies, it is also useful to anticipate a range of social and institutional (dis)locations, not only of potentially antagonistic but also disparate brands of cultural studies. Here I am referring to brands of cultural studies that *are* cultural studies formations but that might not subscribe to this naming practice; to brands of cultural studies that might speak different hybrid languages, strategically avert the written word altogether, and move in and/or move in and out of 'cultural studies', depending on the context and nature of the intervention to be made. It is also important to acknowledge brands of Chicana/o Latina/o critical enquiry that interface with Chicana/o cultural studies and that politicize intellectual practices without drawing an explicit relationship to cultural studies.[8]

Stuart Hall has suggested that 'intellectual work is deadly serious', and our institutional scenario confirmed this fact many times over.[9] For in this unforgettable instance, questions of power weren't being 'formalized',[10] they were being materialized at the level of an intrusive institutional practice. This is the 'tension' we had to experience when imagining a conjunctural relationship to cultural studies. Only through an array of manoeuvres (that were not always successful) was it possible to move beyond the paralysing and highly contradictory predicament of formulating a critical cultural studies counter discourse in opposition to the institutionalized, mainstream form of cultural studies that was circulating within the academy, and to move beyond the kind of communal violence that attaches a political and moral imperative to the question of whether 'it's either cultural studies or Chicana/o studies'.

In our struggle against the administrative proposal to co-opt and streamline the cultural studies project we found it necessary to subvert what Gloria Anzaldúa has referred to in another context as a 'culture of silence'.[11] This culture of silence amounted to a form of self-mutilation: an *unqualified* affirmative vote in favour of a depoliticized, hegemonic, top-down institutional construction of cultural studies. In its most generous moments, this construction promised to invite a generic (cultural studies?) race, class and gender accent that would 'eventually' emerge from these ashes of misrepresented and politically uprooted native territories born from struggle, and somehow 'represent' Chicana/o Latina/o subjects. This position was equivalent to something we loathed and resisted: a self-imposed erasure of native concerns around Chicana/o studies, and a tacit willingness to at least contemplate a possible demise of Chicana/o studies as an academic and institutional entity that promoted the educational and social interests of underrepresented youth.

Fortunately, through the concerted efforts of a 'coalition' of faculty members (from Chicana/o studies, Native American, American, Women's, and African American and Women's studies – faculty which were not necessarily affiliated to cultural studies) these types of concerns were addressed, and another type of institutional relationship was formulated within the new college structure that foregrounded the continued autonomy and relative self-determination of these area studies programmes (particularly at the level of programme authority and curricular development, and, to a certain extent, staffing), while maintaining important linkages between them. Shortly afterwards, at the graduate level, a programme in cultural studies was designed which incorporated a discussion of these issues in its pre-proposals and offered a very different representation of these cultural studies legacies that cross-referenced racial and gender studies.

But for those of us working at the intersection of Chicana/o *cultural* studies, moving beyond this 'educational' predicament not only meant achieving this type of closure; it also meant pausing to reflect for a moment on troubling internal dynamics: namely the way in which certain native discourses inscribed what appeared to be an impossible schism between Chicana/o studies and cultural studies. (I am referring to a radical project of cultural studies that militates against the kind of opportunistic institutionalization reviewed here and that does acknowledge the political trajectories of people of colour.) Locally, this schism was activated by an incorporation and diffusion of 'institutional' constructions of cultural studies that equated all cultural studies practices and interventions with mainstream cultural pluralism (and a particular construction of whiteness), and that counted with the ever-present and dutiful assistance of a nationalist logic which all too easily separated Chicana/o studies from other alternative fields of political and intellectual contestation, and distrusted any 'foreign' element as negative or intrinsically colonizing. This notwithstanding the different types of native connections to cultural studies from the inside of native legacies of Chicana/o Latina/o cultural studies and the international and multiethnic movements that have nourished Chicana/o studies over time throughout the Americas. In its most pristine forms this type of nationalist logic pays allegiance to the notion that Chicano studies is somehow free of its own brand of political contest, free of any number of internal forced deterritorializations and unacceptable pluralisms, free of the influences of broad, sweeping political or intellectual movements.[12]

This logic has been reappropriated in a recent influential article that faults Chicana radical and lesbian scholars for moving away from the community.[13] In its subtext, the article, which appears in a volume that is entitled *Chicanas Chicanos at the Crossroads*, invites Chicanas to disown the malinche label by asking them to prove just how much they have done for the reproduction of Chicano through a less adversarial construct of Chicana/o. It is not far-fetched to imagine that what is at stake here at this particular crossroads is the idea that Chicanas and Chicanos should do the unthinkable: 'document' themselves within what is constructed to be a nostalgic, ahistorical formation of Chicano studies. This line of thinking cannot provide a path towards the future because Chicana/o studies is not bound by the hegemonic limits of traditional *or* alternative disciplines; by static intellectual or political requirements; or by the logic of racist, capitalist, patriarchal and heterosexist reproduction.

In an effort to offer a different type of articulation – one that challenges these constructions of Chicano studies that would ignore the vital contributions of a multiply positioned Chicana/o critical studies, and challenges the attendant capitalization of cultural studies and its logic of colonization – this second volume is very deliberately entitled 'Chicana/o Latina/o cultural studies'. This articulation does not involve a superimposition or subsumption of existing fields, but rather a strategic negotiation between disparate forms of social and political enquiry; a closed and narrowly defined inventory of cultural practices or intellectual interventions, but rather a dynamic field of imagined possibilities and critical processes that are negotiated through a counter-hegemonic practice that nourishes meaningful connections while acknowledging necessary disruptions.

Following in the tradition of other cultural studies practitioners, it is necessary that I clarify that this type of articulation, which speaks from and to a specific context without attaching a normative value to Chicana/o Latina/o cultural studies, does not offer any guarantees; its value must be critically reviewed in order to assess its ability to explain 'what's going on in our/other worlds' and to figure out how 'to respond'.[14] However, it is my hope that this will encourage these cultural studies formations to do what is suggested elsewhere – to 'push the dialogues' of both traditions (Chicana/o studies and cultural studies) into uncharted territories of resistance and contestation. And perhaps such an articulation can begin to counter what Bill Swarz (p. 387) has deemed as the 'bad side of the institutionalization of cultural studies as a discipline' in which cultural studies 'operates by conformity and closure' instead of 'working through connections with other areas and opening up new fields'.[15]

If the success of cultural studies practices is to be measured by their ability to deliver unexpected or unlikely responses, then our 1990 volume of *Cultural Studies* achieved that goal. As a consequence of the reception we received from other cultural studies practitioners who were organizing their own networks, we literally found ourselves partnered with critical milieux that we had not anticipated while doing the volume. I/we[16] welcome this type of movement across Chicana/o Latina/o cultural studies because, along with others, I/we believe that part of the success of this type of multi-positioned social practice lies in its ability to subvert narrow nationalisms. I do so, even though I recognize that in the late twentieth century, this means 'living dangerously' – responding to the various challenges that are posed to the progressive agenda from various academic, institutional and political constituencies. In the late twentieth century, this also means recognizing and attending to the political forces and social developments that are framing Chicana/o cultural studies in the contemporary period.

Attending to another context: social and political developments or 'otra vez viene la migra . . ./here comes the border patrol again!'

As a way of attending to these developments I find it useful to comment upon a point we made at the end of the introduction to Volume 4 of *Cultural Studies* (1990). We ended by stating: 'it all comes together in LA.' In hindsight, I am struck by how this has been confirmed in ways that we did not contemplate in that introductory note. Since that period, we have witnessed the LA violence, the sharpening of the racial and gender divide as a result of the Simpson trial, the widely publicized incidents of immigrant beatings in Riverside and other locations, and the ongoing efforts to overturn the election of Loretta Sánchez and to scrutinize those who exercised their constitutional right to vote for her.

On a larger scale, voter approval of the horrific Proposition 187[17] and the equally horrific passage of the officially sanctioned California Civil Rights initiative, Proposition 209,[18] and Proposition 227 (English-only in school) has dramatically altered the social possibilities for many residents of the California region. These California-based initiatives have extended into the national arena of public policy, for example, President Clinton's immigration and welfare bills that further curtail the rights of not only the undocumented but legal immigrants as well; UC-Regent Ward Connerly's nationwide campaign against affirmative action; and the numerous English-only proposals.

While recoding and resignifying civil rights discourse in new ways (the new/old racist order), these trends are indebted to the nation's historic racist logic of demonizing and scapegoating social and ethnic 'others'. As we have seen recently, the cultural rhetoric of the white/non-white persuasion finds its formal expression in legal and legislative discourses (propositions, laws, amendments), yet it also shrouds itself in disturbingly 'popular' and 'nativist' language that re-essentializes disparate groups of people through pejorative stereotypes, thus making it impossible to grasp the 'dynamic' vectors of similarity, continuity and difference that they exemplify (Chabram and Fregoso, 1990; Hall, 1989).

It is not by accident that as we approached 150 years after the signing of the Treaty of Guadalupe-Hidalgo (a treaty which reconfigured the geopolitical limits of the nation-state by expropriating Mexican territories and redefining the limits of US citizenship), this framing of national identity was newly orchestrated through a particular transnational connection to Mexico,[19] and a hegemonic re-appropriation of Mexican, Chicana/o and Latina/o bodies. Indeed, they have been targeted and reconfigured, and obligated to mark the outer limits of US citizenship – a formulation of 'Americaness' which takes aim at the traditionally undocumented, the newly documented, and those with documents/papeles. This formulation constructs these groups as archetypal 'illegal aliens' who are not deserving of full participation within American society, notwithstanding their contributions, their documents and their historic claims to the territory.

In this era these brown bodies increasingly carry the weight of a social dynamic which has turned upon other American identities as well, racializing them, disenfranchising them, and enveloping them within problematic immi-grant as well as civil rights legacies that are orchestrated from above. This type of 'American' reproduction depends in part on the separation of Chicana/os Mexicana/os Latina/os and Indígenas from their social discourses of resistance and from those political interventions that rally on behalf of the undocumented and their families and on behalf of civil, linguistic and women's rights. These interventions contest surveillance and repatriation through political action as well as claims to the continental unity of the Americas. In the face of the devas-tating effects of the new (old) world economic order and an aggressive con-servatism that knows no limits, these interventions respond to charges of 'do-nothingism' with an impressive history of labour, public service and cultural practice, and they counter a destiny of growing impoverishment with expressions of social criticism and transformation.

These expressions 'remember' the way that Chicana and Latina bodies and the bodies of other women and people of colour are 'targeted' for state-wide policies aimed at curbing immigrant reproduction in televisual and election cam-paigns; the way a lack of access to bilingual education and affirmative action will result in a narrowing of educational opportunities; the way maquiladora workers are shouldering the transnational economy; the way race, class and gender converge to produce glaring social differences; the way farm workers and their children are subjected to miserable working conditions and toxic substances while producing our food; and the way Mexicans and other groups 'carry the cross of illegality even after having been sworn in as citizens' (McWilliams, 1964:

Figure 1 *Undocumented* by Malaquías Montoya. Reproduced courtesy of Malaquías Montoya

119) and even after having been born in that territory commonly referred to as Nuestra/Our America. Finally, these interventions link the contemporary movements of the peoples of the Americas to 'el norte' to histories of colonization and dispossession that implicate the US and remind us that 'los they/the they (women, immigrants, people of colour) *are* us'.[20]

In 'American cultural studies' Lawrence Grossberg defends cultural studies as a model of 'cheap theory, expensive politics'.[21] Ultimately, the formation of a conjunctural relationship with cultural studies depends on how cultural studies (in the plural) inflects intellectual resources into 'specific contextual politics' that are 'expensive', and thus engages a variety of contemporary dynamics, including, for example, the social, symbolic and material effects of the recent political, economic, racial and linguistic assault on people of colour, women and immigrants; the fate of racialized and gendered workers in the transnational, global economy; the lack of access to higher education and the high drop-out rates; the hopelessness of the youth and the elderly; the upsurge in racial, sexual, linguistic and domestic violence; the widespread incidence of environmental toxicity; the inordinately high levels of incarceration of Chicana/o youth; the eurocentric bent of educational programmes; and the silencing of the liberatory discourses of women – particularly women of colour and feminists – within political narratives referencing the struggles against the new racism and global capitalism.

Of course, as recent events confirm, there are many other areas in which to inflect expensive theoretical and material resources, not the least of which are those underrepresented and marginalized area studies with which I inaugurated this volume – the ones that have been credited for enriching cultural studies formations in the best of scenarios. For those who are tempted to reinscribe a definitive breach between these area studies and the social populations which they represent in the academy, Ward Connerly's recent proposal to 'review' all UC ethnic studies programmes – or any programme of study which probes the issue of identity (Chao, 1998)[22] (women's studies, queer and lesbian studies, for example) – was a sobering reminder that college campuses were not ivory towers, at least not for some of us. In a recent interview, this Regent, who helped spearhead Proposition 209 and threw his active support behind Propositions 227 and 187, admitted that his proposal was motivated by the desire to 'protect tax-payers' dollars' and the desire to 'nudge the university to question why we are using race and ethnicity as a basis for scholarship'(Lempien, 1998).[23] He further explained that the infrastructure created back in the 1970s and 1980s 'as a result of black nationalism and the black power movement' needed to be examined.[24] Among many other things, this line of thinking fails to acknowledge the differences, the internal critical engagements, as well as the dynamic interrelations that have been forged within – and throughout – these area studies in the last twenty years, thus freezing them into a state-generated model of 'American' identity politics.[25]

Bringing it all back home *again*:[26] Re-engaging Chicana/o Latina/o cultural studies

It has been stated elsewhere that cultural studies 'is less propelled by a theoretical agenda than by its desire to construct possibilities . . . out of historical circumstances' (Grossberg and Radway, Editorial, 1994), and in many ways this volume reflects that impetus.[27] At this historical juncture it is particularly fitting to chart transnational and transdisciplinary movements which reclaim those social identities that have been linked to the narrowing of social, political and economic, and intellectual horizons, and to a reactionary narrative of self-victimization and intellectual deficiency. This volume responds to this charge by re-engaging the transnational and the transdisciplinary through Chicana/o Latina/o cultural studies interventions that reference not only the spatial/cultural contexts of the unofficial Mexican and Latino territories on this side of the border, but also a larger continental dynamic involving the peoples and territories of the Americas. The political particularities of this hemispheric context mean that the transnational cannot be apprehended solely in reference to those groups who are often lumped together as the 'Spanish-speaking' or as 'pan-ethnic bilingual Latinos'. A critical transnationalism of this sort must entertain other types of geopolitical and linguistic complexities, complexities that arise from making strategic connections with other people of colour in the Americas (here and there) and from engaging racial, class, sexual and gender dynamics that are often erased when referring to so-called 'Spanish-speaking' groups.

While these types of transnational complexities can propel us towards an appreciation of some of the imaginative possibilities at stake in Chicana/o Latina/o cultural studies, it is important to remember that this critical practice does not only involve mapping new intellectual movements through Chicana/o Latina/o cultural studies or Latin American cultural studies; nor does it just involve formulating new connections between pan-ethnic Chicanas/os-Latinas/os, Latinas/os and Indígenas. This practice also entails 'participating in an on-going theoretical struggle to understand and to intervene into the existing organizations of active domination and subordination within the formations of culture', history and society.[28] For this reason, I am weary of native forms of multiculturalism that respond to the dilemma of living with difference with 'a quick metaphoric fix' or an artificial plurality that ushers in one representative from each 'cultural' grouping. As Lisa Lowe has pointed out elsewhere, 'narratives of multiculturalism that do not make room for oppositional critiques' risk 'denuding racial or ethnic groups of their specificity'. With the type of 'leveling operation' that we see in celebratory forms of multiculturalism, these cultures 'become all the whole without contradiction'.[29]

Even as I deliberately frame Chicana/o cultural studies in relation to specific transnational and transdisciplinary movements and possibilities, I do not want to harness the production of the interpellated identities (Chicana/o 'Latina/o', etc.) within any one oppositional critique or set of cultural representations, or to redraw a pernicious boundary between Chicana/o cultural studies, Latina/o cultural studies, or Latin American cultural studies. There are important convergences, hyphens and tensions and interrelationships registered here that also need to be re-elaborated in a manner that engages critical institutional, social and historical differences.

While such an enterprise is not undertaken here, this volume does incorporate some of the social, political and intellectual movements of area studies that have historically replenished Chicana/o Latina/o cultural studies by referencing essays which address Latina/o (Mexican, Cuban, Puerto Rican) and Latin American cultural studies next to essays that reference a transnational Chicana/o cultural studies. Admittedly, such a mode of partnering Chicana/o cultural studies legacies might seem inappropriate to those who are inclined to forget how the hemispheric processes of capitalism and colonialism have enjoined the peoples and cultures of the Americas at the level of social discourse and practice.

However, a path for this type of engagement was set from the very beginning within Chicana/o movement discourses that cultivated important transnational possibilities with their support of progressive feminist and worker movements in Mexico; Third World liberation movements; the revolutionary struggles of peoples from Central, South and Latin America and the Caribbean; and the struggles of women of colour worldwide. These populations were not only strategically linked within the political arena, but boundary-breaking seminal anthologies, posters, music and grass-roots productions framed Chicana/o cultural practices with the works of poets, essayists, and philosophers that engaged legacies of conquest as well as resistance in Nuestra America/Our America. [30] In the early 1980s this type of boundary-breaking work was recaptured and further nuanced with the appearance of *This Bridge Called My Back* (Cherríe Moraga and Gloria Anzaldúa, 1981/1983), which incorporated writings by 'radical women of colour' and proposed to forge links across cultures and regions.

The essays in this volume not only effect these types of disparate transnational movements within cultural productions, but they are variously involved in critical retrospectives of area studies, dialogues with important cultural critics, and projects of theoretical expansion. They 'rework' some of the terrain of Chicana/o Latina/o cultural studies, social, political and class and sexual identities; cultural productions (literature, area studies, political writings, music, dancing); and the movements of cultural productions within the circuitry of capitalist production and consumption.

They further nuance social identities, often thinking them in their 'detotalized or deconstructed'[31] and vernacular home-grown forms, and they reroute social identities through alternative theoretical paradigms and cultural productions that reposition cultural theories and practices within a Chicana/o Latina/o, Mexican or Latin American context. They deploy 'concepts of identity that are strategic and positional' and that are 'multiply constructed across different, often intersecting and antagonistic, discourses, practices, and positions'. They provide fertile ground for making important horizontal affiliations between Chicanas/os and other women and people of color at the same time that they address the manner in which these affiliations have been thwarted. They not only engage social identities, social differences and borders that 'matter', but they 'stage' intellectual and conceptual movements within essays which, in the tradition of a self-reflective cultural practice, also render the need for further discussion, elaboration and analysis.

In this vein Michelle Habell-Pallán's essay examines the inter/national appeal of Chicano popular music through a spirited introduction of the Chicano El Vez, otherwise known as 'an Elvis translator', and 'a good will ambassador of Latin culture in the US and Europe'. Habell-Pallán discusses how this dynamic performance artist 'embodies the seemingly contradictory desires of a subject politicized by the Chicano movement as well as the irreverent 1970s punk and 1980s new wave aesthetics'. For Habell-Pallán Robert Lopez's translation of Elvis into El Vez 'opens up a discursive space on the terrain of popular music' that 'enables both critique of the status quo and dialogue concerning progressive social transformation'.

These dimensions of his performance aesthetics are examined in his songs 'Immigration Time' and 'Taking Care of Business'. For Habell-Pallán these songs call into question the criteria by which human rights and citizenship are granted or withheld in a US national space, and respond to the scapegoating of Mexican and Central American workers that was prevalent in the Proposition 187 campaign. She further argues that El Vez's critical multiculturalism works 'over time and over space', generating positive horizontal affiliations with racialized American identities as well as with immigrant Turkish youth in Germany who identify with the plight of Chicana/os and Latinas/os as it is rearticulated in his musical performances.

Rosa Linda Fregoso's reflective account of her travels with Angela Davis also deviates from 'vertical' modes of narrating the 'nation' or 'race' in critical discourse. However, she highlights the 'horizontal affiliations among women moving across the intersections of culture, race, nation, class, and sexuality'. In this way, rather than follow the 'familiar road' which might be expected of her ('a path through a specific genealogy of Chicana feminist recovery'), Fregoso carefully outlines the manners in which Angela Davis' groundbreaking book, *Women, Race, and Class* provides a foundation for what we call 'multicultural feminism', 'women of color feminisms', or 'Third World feminism', and anticipates many of the urgencies of the feminisms 'that are required in this era of transnational capitalism in which there are connections between the deteriorating conditions in communities of color and the restructuring of global capitalism' (Lowe, 1997: 304). Fregoso examines how this text 'resists a unitary history of feminism . . . instructing us that each feminism has its own critiques'; 'partakes in all feminisms' critique of masculinist ideologies, but, also advocates the transformation of all forms of social inequality, the dismantling of oppressive power relations'; 'bridges the distinction between feminist theoretical writing in academia and feminist political theorizing'; and provides an anti-essentialist critique early on, 'including a rejection of the unified and transhistorical category of woman'. Fregoso's full discussion of this work, which continues 'to inspire movements for social justice throughout the world', is a tribute to Angela Davis' legacy – a legacy that inspires us to re-examine how her intellectual contributions as well as her activism have carved out a road for a politically engaged cultural studies and feminist practice.

Frances Aparicio focuses critical attention on the performance of (trans)nationalism by Celia Cruz, an internationally renown figure – often referred to as 'the Queen of Salsa' and the 'Apostle of Latinity' – who has entertained Chicanas/os, Latinas/os and Latin Americans for decades. In her essay, Aparicio 'traces the tensions between Cruz's public ideological position on Cuba and the multiple identities – including blackness – that she assumes and performs through her musical repertoire, professional history and construction of herself as a tropical diva.' Aparicio argues that, while Cruz has promoted afrocubanismo, embraced musical genres from different Latin American regions (often 'tropicalizing them') and used Spanish as a vehicle for 'vocalizing and constructing a Latin American identity', her performances are mediated by a strategic form of essentialism (trans/nationalism) that is rooted in her Cuban exile position.

Aparicio provides an example of the contradictory nature of Cruz's musical positioning in her discussion of how the image of Azúcar Negra/Black Sugar surfaced in one of Cruz's performances in Ann Arbor, where 'Celia's black body, Afro-Cuban rhythms, and voice indexed the cultural survival of slaves in Cuba while she simultaneously vocalized the discourse of a pro-capitalist white Cuban bourgeoisie, also embodying colonial desire with her blonde wig'. Clearly, Aparicio's discussion of the influence of Celia Cruz's music in an international context suggests that her contributions are complex articulations which can best be understood through an appreciation of the relational nature of nationalism and transnationalism.

Lisa Sánchez González also investigates the importance of a transnational musical genre within Latina/o cultures, but this time within the context of the colonial Puerto Rican diaspora. Sánchez González proposes that within this community salsa music helps its listeners and practitioners to 'maintain an intimacy with the past and a living connection with the present, orchestrating a coherently embodied sensibility that can only be fully understood somewhere beyond the purely discursive dimensions of Puerto Rican and Afro-Caribbean cultural history'. While attending to discussions of 'how salsa has been transferred, translated, transculturated and sold all over the world via multinational corporations', Sánchez González proposes that 'salsa still performs a (kin)aesthetic function irreducible to a commodity fetish, a function that promotes and rearticulates embodied forms of knowledge and desire'. Sánchez González describes how this salsa 'calls and agitates you' to 'become part of the music, 'moving p'aca' y p'alla' (right here, over there and everywhere in between)'. In this way salsa marks the 'diaspora's struggle to survive in style', often providing a home away from an 'island that is, and is more than, a metaphor for eviction'. Even while reclaiming salsa in this way Sánchez González examines the entailments of contradictory desires and social practices that converge around salsa upon comparing and contrasting the works of two socially conscious salseros (Willie Colón and Ruben Blades) and upon contrasting her own encounters with salsa music in the home and in LA salsa clubs through an ethnographic reflection.

Saldívar-Hull's essay examines a literary articulation of 'transfrontera' (trans/border) feminism within a socially engaged production that maintains the spirit of earlier Chicana feminist productions of the 1980s and highlights the 'connections' between the material and gendered conditions that are imposed on

Mexican women in the United States and those which are imposed on them in Mexico. In particular, Saldívar-Hull proposes that Cisneros' cuento, 'Women Hollering Creek', offers a feminist reading which illustrates 'how telenovelas (soap operas) and (Tellardo) romances join to coerce Mexican women into accepting patriarchal arrangements', including feminized renditions of the American dream.

In this analysis 'Women Hollering Creek' 'disarticulates' this 'hegemonic immigrant narrative that is restaged and rescripted for Mexican Women within popular televisual culture' through a Chicana feminist revision that offers the possibility of another type of subject formation and another type of narrative – one that incorporates a practice of feminismo popular which puts theory into practice and forges alliances between Chicanas and Mexicanas in their struggles to overcome various forms of domination. Saldívar-Hull's analysis suggests that this practice exceeds representations of literary coalitions, that changing the subject within this transnational arena also entails engaging those feminisms which emerge from the ranks of women from the exploited classes.

Chabram-Dernersesian offers a critical retrospective of the manner in which Mexican 'populations, classes, genders and nations' travelled – or failed to travel – within a home-grown transnationalist discourse that referenced an essential Chicano–Mexican difference through a series of historic exchanges with Octavio Paz and *The Labyrinth of Solitude*. Aside from calling attention to the manner in which these exchanges were effected with the idea of providing the foundation for a local Chicano tradition that could respond to dominant culture's historic nullifying gestures, this article calls attention to the manner in which this emergent Mexican American tradition was invested in transnational racialized patriarchal kinship arrangements that promoted male dominance and male privilege within the intellectual and the domestic sector, in addition to promoting exclusionary notions of identity that impacted not only Chicanas/os but also other women and people of colour.

However, Chabram-Dernersesian argues that these exclusionary transnationalist theories and knowledge formations were themselves 'interrupted', cut across and disclaimed by a wide range of social, political and cultural practices in circulation during this period which contested this type of political and intellectual familism, at once exposing its anti-feminist subtext and providing the foundation for the emergence of another type of social, political and intellectual movement. This multi-sited analysis provides a context for an understanding of how far many of our predecessors travelled in the early 1970s, and cautions against 'celebrating transnational frameworks simply because they are Mexican or because they are mobile'.

Rosaura Sánchez and Beatrice Pita map and contexualize cultural and political debates in Latin American cultural studies from 1989 to 1994 in a wide-ranging article that targets the 'theorization of postmodernism'. They argue that in 'the rush to accept First World theoretical frameworks' there has been 'a collapsing of economic, political and cultural categories' by 'some critics who are quick to label cultural production in Latin America as "postmodern"'. They examine and specify the scope and application of terms and categories employed in discussions of postmodernism that circulate within the US as well as abroad, and engage the cultural debate on postmodernism in Latin America in relation to other debates on development, social movements, democratization and alliance politics, as well as in relation to local debates which concern a global context of restructuring and transnational capital. Finally, they critique the tendency of influential cultural critics and postmodernists to retreat from social class and macrosocial realities, and to ignore or dismiss the historical dimensions of indigenous Latin American cultural productions as well as Latina/o productions in the US.

Clearly, Sánchez and Pita's entry is more than an article on postmodern hermeneutics. They engage social horizons that are framing debates on postmodernism and argue for the importance of creating models that address the issue of 'substantive material change'. Without it, they argue, 'the working class, growing and changing, not only in Latin America but everywhere, will have left to it only a plurality of choices at the market place, without the means to consume most of them, and most importantly, still remain enmeshed in exploitative relations of production.'

María Soldatenko's study of 'Latina' garment workers in Los Angeles calls attention to the existence of these exploitative relations of production in her ethnographic study of garment workers in the Los Angeles sweat shops who labour under Third World conditions of work. However, Soldatenko's article is geared towards problematizing renditions of Latino identity that would construct it as a universal, classless and genderless pan-ethnicity, and/or suggest that this type of originary Latino identity can be the rallying point for organizing workers. Soldatenko's description – of the organizational structure of the garment industry, the ethnic, gender and immigrant specific nature of 'Latina' garment work, and her ethnographic portraits of 'Latinas' – counters these facile assumptions. Far from providing the possibilities for organizing an effective culture of resistance, Soldatenko argues that these 'Latina' identities are 'disarticulated' and 'differentiated' within a capitalist workplace that promotes intra-ethnic and inter-ethnic conflict. She proposes that, given these realities, 'Latina' garment workers need to form collaborative relations which attend to the way ethnicity and gender are rearticulated in the capitalist workplace, and to negotiate – not erase or downplay – their specific ethnic and national differences as they struggle to survive as Latina Americanas, immigrants and workers.

Yvonne Yarbro-Bejarano's article opens with a vivid description of the hostile social climate and the difficult institutional conditions and obstacles that we face as Chicana/o studies practitioners (faculty, students and staff) within US universities where 'everything we achieve has to be struggled for', and where 'if we stop pushing . . . the hard won ground we have gained begins to erode from beneath our feet'. Yarbro-Bejarano argues that these realities have obliged us to see the population of Chicana/os in the university as an embattled community and to undertake a critical analysis of the lived experiences of Chicanas/os in their multiple sites. However, she posits that this type of analysis is thwarted within nationalist formations of the race as family which cast our self-imaginings in 'patriarchal and heterosexist moulds'. Given this context, Yarbro-Bejarano argues that '[o]ur task for what remains of the 1990s and into the twenty-first century is to retain the critique of US state domination, while exercising increased vigilance over the way our narratives can dominate and exclude'.

Yarbro-Bejarano proposes that we make 'the study of sexuality central to Chicana/o Studies, using it to rethink the whole field rather than just adding it in, which would continue its marginalization'. It is further suggested that this type of enquiry involves tackling not only a certain ghettoization in Chicana/o studies, but also engaging Chicana/o identities as 'dynamic' processes that 'recognize and interrogate the heterogeneity of racial and sexual identities'.

From the aesthetic sensibilities of a grass-roots coalition composed of ethnically diverse writers and critics, Alvina Quintana's article invites contemporary readers and critics to reflect once again on the 'subversive' pleasures that emerge from outwitting those patterns of social and literary association dictated by hegemonic academic institutions that 'police, discipline, and ultimately separate artistic endeavours and ethnically complex communities'. Inspired by Jessica Haggedorn's own unique rendition of 'Borders be Damned', Quintana launches the question: 'What types of literary affiliations and analyses are warranted or not warranted by these critical approaches, warranted or unwarranted by these pleasurably subversive cultural productions?' Quintana proposes that contemporary critics need to 'avoid reactionary compartmentalizing aesthetic practices that merely serve to suppress the political lines of affiliation between women (and other writers of colour)', reducing them to 'essentialized, one-dimensional subjectivities'. Quintana's own comparative analysis of the works of Sandra Cisneros and Hisaye Yamamoto calls attention to the way in which these 'Third Wave' feminist writers have employed a process of creolization that reworks and transforms some of the cultural patterns of social, historical and cultural identities and that effectively 'undermines an academic or political aspiration for unitary origins and authenticity'.

Tamara Dukes re-engages the issue of 'border crossing' and 'border subjects' – and Gloria Anzaldúa's discussions of hybridity in *Borderlands* – within a review essay of Ruth Behar's *Bridges to Cuba*. She highlights the importance of a volume such as this which facilitates a transnational connection to Cuba from the US in the midst of the blockade that would 'erase Cuba from the map'. Duke proposes that the richness of this 'collection of essays, interviews, poetry and prose' lies in its articulation of a Cuban identity and experience that goes beyond 'binary' or 'rift of identity'; 'bridges Cuban communities'; 'moves away from essentialized notions of what it means to be Cuban'; and explores the complex hybridities of Cuban culture across shifting geopolitical locations. Even as she calls attention to the way this volume draws on 'the creative liberating power of articulation' for redrawing 'maps of self, nation and culture' and for 'healing', she also argues that the 'extent to which this book can help close wounds depends on the impact of its circulation and readership'. Insofar as this discursive articulation continues to be shaped by larger systemic antagonisms, and what Dukes characterizes as the 'significant power differential between US and Cuba', this type of healing and nuancing of social identities – including Cuban feminist identities – also depends on wide-ranging social transformations.

Together, these articles engage some of the issues that are being taken up through a Chicana/o Latina/o cultural studies process or practice. There are more that need to be re-engaged in a social formation such as ours in which the 'channels for debate' are barred to the vast majority and in which the very idea of a Chicana/o Latina/o or Latin American tradition is itself questioned or characterized as 'foreign', 'non-existent' or 'scant'. Given this context we cannot afford to ignore the significance of picking up the pen and re-entering the world through print,[32] not as dismembered generic social identities or bodies that are voiceless and lack social agencies, but as cultural practitioners who are actively committed to reconfiguring social, political and intellectual legacies, notwithstanding the terrible backlash. As the articles in this volume demonstrate, these cultural studies practices and interventions are not homogenous; important differences are registered here which need to be engaged and considered as we endeavour to articulate other types of imaginative possibilities and as we remember in the late part of the twentieth century that 'yes, it can be done' (Sí se puede) – that it will be done – through a variety of social engagements, and that yes, we do have a stake in articulating this type of poder/power.

Far from exhibiting the political and cultural sensibilities of an intellectual formation that is frozen into a superessentialized model of identity and difference – or that lacks a consciousness of internal critical engagement and developments or is inattentive to the need to forge relations between different social collectivities – this articulation recognizes and reinscribes movements (social movements, cultural movements, political movements). This articulation also responds to the need to affiliate with local, global and hemispheric processes and populations, as well as the need to push the limits of disciplinary formations, even within the 'alternative sector'. Insofar as the challenges that lie ahead, Gloria Anzaldúa's words to women are particularly instructive here. In the 'Forward' to the second edition of *This Bridge Called My Back* she says: 'let's not let the danger of the journey and the vastness of the territory scare us – let's look forward and open paths in these woods' (Anzaldúa, 1983: v).[33]

Notes

1   The volume editor, Angie Chabram-Dernersesian, would like to recognize the substantial input of Rosa Linda Fregoso both in terms of our historic collaborative efforts as well as in terms of her keen insights and editorial suggestions on earlier versions of this introduction, for which I accept sole responsibility. I would also like to thank Richard Chabrán, Zare Dernersesian, Lisa Sánchez-Gonzalez and Soñia Saldívar-Hull for their unwavering support, and the artists and photographers whose work is referenced here. In addition, I would like to thank Lawrence Grossberg, and to recognize the contributions

Figure 2 *Moment of Silence* by Malaquías Montoya. Reproduced courtesy of Malaquías Montoya

of Norma Alarcón, Chela Sandoval, Juan Flores, Alejandra Elenes and Héctor Calderón to the ongoing debates on Chicana/o Latina/o cultural studies in the Americas. Finally, I would like to thank the staff at Chicana/o Studies, UCD, and The Chicana Latina Institute for its financial support.

2   Angie Chabram-Dernersesian and Rosa Linda Fregoso, 'Introduction: Chicana/o cultural representations: reframing alternative and critical discourses' (*Cultural Studies* 4 (3), October 1990).

3   I am drawing from Lawrence Grossberg and Janice Radway's (1994) 'Editorial statement' (*Cultural Studies* 8 (3), October 1994).

4   I am referring to: Latina/o cultural studies, Mexican cultural studies, Latin American cultural studies and the feminist cultural legacies of women of colour.

5   For more on this development, see Herman Gray, 'Is cultural studies inflated: the cultural economy of cultural studies in the United States', in Cary Nelson and Dilip Parameshwar Gaonkar (eds) *Disciplinarity and Dissent in Cultural Studies* (London: Routledge, 1996), pp. 203–16.

6   Ibid., p. 204.

7   Stuart Hall describes the unfolding of cultural studies through a metaphor of theoretical work as 'interruption'. See 'Cultural studies and its theoretical legacies', in David Morley and Kuan-Hsing Chen (eds) *Stuart Hall: Critical Dialogues in Cultural Studies* (London: Routledge, 1996), p. 268.

8   Lawrence Grossberg addresses the inflated claims of cultural studies in his essay, 'Toward a genealogy of the state of cultural studies', in his *Bringing it all Back Home: Essays in Cultural Studies* (Durham: Duke, 1997), pp. 273–4. He also contests the idea that cultural studies aims to displace its competitors in 'Cultural studies: what's in a name (one more time)', in his *Bringing it all Back Home: Essays in Cultural Studies* (Durham: Duke, 1997), p. 246.

9   Hall, 'Cultural studies and its theoretical legacies', p. 274.

10   See Josel Pfister's 'The Americanization of cultural studies', in John Storey (ed.) *What is Cultural Studies: A Reader* (London: Arnold, 1996, p. 293) for further discussion on formalizing power in cultural studies.

11   Gloria Anzaldúa, 'Movimientos de rebeldía y las culturas que traicionan', in her *Borderlands, La Frontera: The New Mestiza*. San Francisco: Aunt Lute, 1987), pp. 15–23.

12   I do not in any way mean to suggest that the position of Chicana/o studies is equivalent to those mainstream cultural representations promoted by dominant culture in the US. It is also important to specify that there is another legacy of Chicana/o studies which counters this line of thinking through an appeal to continuous critical self-reflection.

13   Ignacio García, 'Juncture in the road: Chicano studies since "El Plan de Santa Barbara"', in David R. Maciel and Isidro Ortiz (eds) *Chicanas Chicanos at the Crossroads: Social, Economic and Political Change* (University of Arizona Press, 1996), pp. 190–1.

14   I am rephrasing Grossberg who took lines from Marvin Gaye's song, 'What's Going On' in order to discuss the charge of cultural studies.

15   Bill Swarz, 'Where is cultural studies', *Cultural Studies* 8 (3), pp. 377–93; p. 387.

16   Here I have drawn on the collective voice as a way of calling attention to my discussions with Rosa Linda Fregoso about this thematic.

17   This Proposition denies educational and health benefits to undocumented workers and their children.

18   This Proposition ends affirmative action for women and minorities.

19   I am referring here to a redrawing of the US and Mexican borders.

20   I am paraphrasing this famous verse, 'Los they are US' from José Montoya's poem of the same name which appeared in his *Information: Twenty Years of Joda* (San Jose: Chusma House, 1992), p. 163.

21   Lawrence Grossberg, 'American cultural studies', in his *Bringing it all Back Home: Essays in Cultural Studies* (Durham: Duke, 1997), p. 291. He elaborates: '[i]ts theory is "cheap" in the sense that you use whatever gives you a better understanding of the context so as to open up new possibilities.'

22   Julie Chao, 'Ethnic professors mount defense', *San Francisco Examiner*, 19 June 1998.

23   Edward Lempien, *San Francisco Chronicle*, 17 June 1998.

24   Connerly said the review of the programmes would require the approval of the regents' eight-member educational policy committee. If such a review was to be approved, he said, it would take at least six months to carry out.

25   This partnering of the university with the conservative policies of the state also provides another context for rethinking the advisability of continuing to circulate cultural studies representations that would delimit these area studies within a superessentialist notion of 'identity politics' and/or 'freeze their' dynamic movements within static models of 'identity and difference' that fail to account for the wide spectrum of anti-essentialist critiques within these area studies and their strategically placed, multi-positioned 'politics of location'.

26   I acknowledge that this return gives a different twist to that which is suggested in Lawrence Grossberg's critical endeavour by a similar name. His endeavour provided a semantic path with which to dialogue.

27   'Editorial statement', *Cultural Studies*.

28   Lawrence Grossberg makes this point on several occasions.

29   Lisa Lowe, 'L.A. in the production of multiculturalism', in Avery Gordon and Christopher Newfield (eds) *Mapping Multiculturalism* (Minneapolis: University of Minnesota Press, 1996), p. 421.

30   Only recently, in an attempt to outline the ongoing productive dialogues between Chicana/o and Latin American studies, a local hemispheric group suggested that Chicana/o has 'embodied inherent multiple critiques of Latin American studies: defying the foundational north-south boundary; upsetting power-laden relationships between the experts from the north and the subjects of research from the south; aligning academic research with transformative political agendas . . . offering explorations of the multivalent notions of the borderlands' (Proposal for a Hemispheric Initiative of the Americas, HIA Group, UC Davis).

31   Stuart Hall, 'Introduction: who needs "identity?"', in Stuart Hall and Paul Du Gay (eds) *Questions of Cultural Identity* (London: Sage Publications, 1996), p. 1.

32   I draw inspiration here from Michael Hanchard's reading of Said in 'Cultural politics and black public intellectuals' (*Disciplinarity and Dissent in Cultural Studies*, p. 262) and from César Chávez's grito, 'Sí Se Puede!'

33   Gloria Anzaldúa, 'Forward to the Second Edition', in Anzaldúa and Moraga (eds) *This Bridge Called My Back*.

References

Anzaldúa, Gloria (1987) *Borderlands, La Frontera*. San Francisco: Aunte Lute.

Chao, Julie (1998) 'Ethnic Programs Mount Defense', *San Francisco Examiner*, 19 June 1998.

Fregoso, Rosa Linda and Chabram, Angie (1990) 'Chicana/o cultural representations: reframing alternative critical discourses'. *Cultural Studies*, 4(3).

García, Ignacio (1996) 'Juncture in the road: Chicano studies since "El Plan de Santa Barbara"', in Maciel, D. and Ortiz, I. (eds) *Chicanas Chicanos at the Crossroads*, Tucson: University of Arizona Press.

Gray, Herman (1996) 'Is cultural studies inflated? On the cultural economy of cultural studies', in Nelson, C. and Parameshwar Gaonkar, D. (eds) *Disciplinarity and Dissent in Cultural Studies*, New York: Routledge.

Grossberg, Larry (1997) *Bringing it all Back Home: Essays in Cultural Studies*, Durham: Duke University Press.

Grossberg, Larry and Radway, Janice (1994) 'Editorial Statement', *Cultural Studies*, 8(3).

Hall, Stuart (1989) 'Cultural identity and cinematographic representations', *Frame Works*, 36: 48–81.

—— (1996) 'Cultural studies and its theoretical legacies', in Morley, D. and Chen, K. H. (eds) *Stuart Hall: Critical Dialogues in Cultural Studies*, London: Routledge.

—— (1996) 'Who needs identity', in Hall, S. and Du Gay, P. (1996) (eds) *Questions of Cultural Identity*, London: Sage.

Hanchard, Michael (1996) 'Cultural politics and black public intellectuals', in Nelson, C. and Parameshwar Gaonkar, D. (eds) *Disciplinarity and Dissent in Cultural Studies*, New York: Routledge.

Lempien, Edward (1998) 'Connerly Calls for Review of UC Ethnic Studies', *San Francisco Chronicle*, 17 June 1998.

Lowe, Lisa (1996) 'Imagining Los Angeles in the production of multiculturalism', in Gordon, A. and Newfield, C. (eds) *Mapping Multiculturalism*, Minneapolis: University of Minnesota Press.

—— (1997) *Immigrant Acts*, Durham and London: Duke University Press.

McWilliams, Carey (1964) *Brothers Under the Skin*, Boston: Little, Brown and Company.

Montoya, José (1992) 'Los They are US'. *Information: Twenty Years of Joda*, San José: Chusma House.

Moraga, Cherríe and Anzaldúa, Gloria (eds) (1981/1983) *This Bridge Called My Back*, New York: Kitchen Table.

Pfister, Joel (1996) The Americanization of cultural studies', in Storey, J. (ed.) *What is Cultural Studies?: A Reader*, London: Arnold.

Swarz, Bill (1994) 'Where is cultural studies?' *Cultural Studies* 8(3).

Michelle Habell-Pallán

EL VEZ IS 'TAKING CARE OF BUSINESS': THE INTER/NATIONAL APPEAL OF CHICANO POPULAR MUSIC

Abstract

This article introduces El Vez, an important performance artist and musician, whose translation of Elvis extends far beyond local audiences. In our historical moment of shrinking public outlets for the circulation and discussion of alternative and oppositional perpectives, his creator, Robert Lopez, has opened up a discursive space – on the terrain of popular music, in the unlikely genre of Elvis impersonation – that enables both critique of the status quo and dialogue concerning progressive social transformation. This article investigates Lopez's artful superimpositions of Chicana and Chicano realities and cultural icons on to the iconography, soundings and lyrics that cluster around Elvis, and claims that Lopez subverts both the myth of 'Elvis as the embodiment of the American Dream' and the reactionary assumption that American national identity and cultural belonging are (or should be) equated with exclusionary representations of whiteness. This article also argues that the content of his live and recorded stage shows (which are part strip-tease, part Chicana/o studies, part labour history, and part history of popular music course) respond to hegemonic discourses that fault racialized immigrants and working-class people for the consequences of global economic restructuring, and that his aesthetics of resistance subvert both dominant and subaltern dictates for strict, unyielding definitions of identity, sexuality and citizenship. Finally, it suggests that the positive reception of Lopez's performances by racialized, marginalized, displaced and economically outcast youth in Germany speaks to an identification with Chicana/o struggles that is not based on a specific ethnicity, but instead on an articulation of oppositional politics. In this context, Lopez's music enables the possibility of building coalitions beyond the constraints of the nation-state.

Keywords

> popular music; El Vez; performance studies; Chicano studies; nationalism;
> immigration

¿Quien es El Vez?/ Who is El Vez?[1]

EL VEZ HAS SEVEN compact disks and several 45 rpm singles, a book con-
tract offer, and is the subject of an in-progress independent film. He has
'r-o-c-ked across the USA and all over Europe', and is referred to as both a
'modern multicultral hybrid of Americana and Mexicano' and a 'Cross-Cultural
Caped Crusader singing for Truth, Justice and the Mexican American way'.
Rolling Stone Magazine considers him to be 'more than an Elvis Impersonator . . .
He is an Elvis translator, a goodwill ambassador of Latin Culture' in the US and
Europe. He is the long lost Chicano punk rock hero who has found his way home
to Graciasland, Aztlán, USA; the Pocho Elvis, one who can't speak Spanish, but
'loves la, la, la raza'; the revolutionary Latin lover who makes alienated Hispan-
ics proud to be MexAmerican. He is the thin brown duke who makes explicit
the connection between Elvis Presley, David Bowie, César Chávez and Ché
Guevara in Las Vegas inspired espectáculos (spectacles).

Undulating in a skin-tight red vinyl jumpsuit that provocatively hugs the contours of his well-toned body, or strutting in his gold lamé charro suit, El Vez
embodies the seemingly contradictory desires of a subject politicized by both the
Chicano movement, and irreverent 1970s and 1980s punk and new wave aesthetics. Part strip-tease, part Chicana/o studies, part labour history and part
history of popular music course, El Vez's stage shows incite women to howl and
young men (gay and straight) to growl, with a minimum of six 'rip-away' costume
changes per show. Not only does he shake his money maker in honour of James
Brown (El Vez's 'I'm Brown and I'm Proud' won first prize in the music video
category of the 1998 International San Francisco Film Festival), he and the
Memphis Mariachis (his band) rev up their frenzied multicultural and multiracial
audience to get down for the UFW and the Zapatistas' cause in Chiapas. He
carries the namesake of his London-based fan club – 'El Groover'; he is regularly
referred to as 'the thinking man's Elvis', one who follows his Chicano movement
and British punk roots and routes 'back to a place we've never been'. He is an
exuberant Chicano sex-symbol saviour, a rock and roll superstar persona created
in the late 1980s by musical genius Robert Lopez.

Born to a family of civil servants that included a loud and brown Chicana
activist – despite having no formal musical training – Lopez is a virtual walking
encyclopedia of rock and punk rock of the 1970s, alternative popular music of
the 1980s and 1990s, and Elvis Presley's extensive gospel, rockabilly and ballad
repertoire. He is one of a kind. Who else could turn 'Suspicious Minds' into

Figure 3 El Vez. Photo/Randall Michelson. Reproduced courtesy of El Vez Co

'Immigration Time', and make it clear that it is Mexican immigrants who are 'Taking Care of Business' in the transnational economy? Who else could fuse Adam and the Ants and Santana with Rod Stewart's 'Maggie Mae' or turn the international hit of the British band Oasis 'Champagne Super Nova' into 'Souped-up Chévy Nova' and improve on the original?

In many ways this multifaceted performance artist – whose father worked as master of ceremonies for the Jai-alai games in Tijuana – is a child of 'our extended Borderland culture: the frontera culture stretching from the shanty barrios of Tijuana/San Diego to the rich surf and turf of Santa Barbara (dominated by the megaspace of Los Angeles in the middle)' (Saldívar, 1997: 95). Significantly, Lopez grew up in Chula Vista, California – then a predominately Anglo middle-class suburb of San Diego. Performing in the punk band The Zeros and

Catholic Discipline during the late 1970s and early 1980s, teenaged Lopez participated in the development of oppositional punk music in Los Angeles. Lopez was drawn to this scene, like many other disaffected Chicano youth (myself included) who experienced alienation from both the dominant and Chicano culture, because it was a site where identities outside of ethnic stereotypes could be embodied. By the mid-1980s, Lopez curated for the Luz de Jesús folk-art gallery located on the then low-rent Melrose Avenue in Hollywood – at the time a favourite site of congregation for punk youth. In the process of organizing a folk-art exhibition honouring Elvis Presley, which included Elvis impersonators, he was inspired to develop his own translation of Elvis Presley: El Vez.

But what is it that makes Lopez's translation of Elvis into El Vez so impressive? The answer lies in his abilities as a transculturator of popular culture.[2] With relative ease, a serious dose of playfulness and the well-developed critical arsenal of a camp artist supreme, he morphs Elvis into El Vez, thus enabling multiple layers of cultural hybridity and promoting complex instances of cross-cultural translation. Not only is Elvis reborn as a Chicano/Mexicano on the US Mexican border, but Elvis's music – whose early rock'n'roll embodied a mixture of rhythm and blues and country music – is now partnered with Mariachi, Caribbean, punk and Latin punk rhythms. If this were not enough, with the strategic use of humour, rock'n'roll and a dash of T. Rex and New York Dolls glam rock (with its explicit exploration of gender subversion), El Vez's performance also calls into question traditional definitions of nationhood, masculinity, and the criteria by which human rights and citizenship are granted to or withheld from subjects of the nation.

Given that our historical moment is one of shrinking public outlets for the circulation and discussion of alternative and oppositional perspectives, Lopez's translation of Elvis into El Vez is significant in that he opens a discursive space – on the terrain of popular music, in the unlikely genre of Elvis impersonation – that enables both critique of the status quo and dialogue concerning progressive social transformation.[3]

Through spectacular live and recorded musical performances, El Vez subverts the myth of 'Elvis as the embodiment of the American Dream (and thus, by extension, as the embodiment of America itself)' (Rodman, 1996: 40), and interrogates the reactionary assumption that American national and cultural belonging and identity is (or should be) equated with exclusionary notions of whiteness. Overlaying Chicano cultural myths on top of the iconography, soundings and lyrics that cluster around Elvis, El Vez's performance visually and viscerally demonstrates that Chicano history *is* American history and vice versa. Hence, many of El Vez's lyrics – inflected by a Chicana and Chicano movement politics that adolescent Lopez learned from his aunt – narrativize why immigrant and non-immigrant populations in the US who are racialized as non-white should be recognized as part of American national culture.

Lopez's own engagement with pop culture is subversive to the degree that he has hope for an America that has yet to live up to its democratic possibility, and to the degree that he places much of his music in the service of this ideal.[4] His performances entice an audience's interest with a 'flash', the image and soundings of Elvis. El Vez appropriates the signs of American pop culture to critique American society, but to accomplish this he must 'do' Elvis with a difference.

Elvis as trace, El Vez as screen

Lopez's self-described strategy of 'superimposing' Latino culture on to popular culture allows others, including non-Chicanos, to recognize and identify with the difference that El Vez makes, even as it engenders contradiction. In an interview I conducted with him, Lopez explains the positive reaction of non-Latinos to his performance of El Vez and irreverently draws on Chicano cultural nationalist discourse:

> Everyone's different, but you still have to be proud. It's the old idea, people will come and say, 'I come to your show and I walk away proud to be Mexican, and I'm not, and I'm white' [which is no small feat in a state that constantly constructs Mexicans as inferior]. It's the idea of instilling pride, and you could fill in the blank. I mean I am El Vez, the blank Elvis, black, gay, straight, Asian or whatever.[5]

However, El Vez could never be the blank Elvis – he has overwritten Elvis with Chicana and Chicano culture.[6] Notwithstanding this fact, the body of El Vez on-stage, with its costumes and physical postures, acts as a projection screen where traces of multiple and different cultures and practices are made visible. He projects a critical multiculturalism that hails subjects to identify with the struggles of those most villified by anti-immigrant campaigns. His statement, 'I am the blank Elvis, the Black, Gay, Straight, Asian, whatever' might sound like a simple endorsement for a liberal pluralism or a watered down nationalism that advances the ideology 'that in the United States everyone is equal no matter their colour, religion, or sexual orientation'; however, in this case El Vez implies something very different. By positing a 'family of resemblance' that links the history of many Chicanos – a working-class past and/or present – to Elvis' own childhood of poverty, El Vez's performance subsequently connects Mexican American working-class histories to those of most other Americans, and highlights the fact that any notion of multiculturalism is incomplete without understanding how class and racial position make some residents of the US more equal than others. Furthermore, El Vez does not equate social constructions of racial and class difference with inferiority or superiority. Instead, he suggests that one can be proud of difference, that one should not suppress it, and that one should not have to pay for the consequence of being different.

In addition, by superimposing images of Che Guevara, La Virgen de Guadalupe and César Chávez on to the trace images of Elvis Presley, James Brown and David Bowie, El Vez enacts complex strategies for getting people from different walks of life interested in Chicano history and progressive politics, in this case a politics not based on an assumed biological identity. Lopez's re-presentation of Elvis is important, then, because El Vez embodies an aesthetics of resistance grounded in popular culture and music, yet does so in no simple terms. To incorporate the iconography of Elvis (as a supreme icon of Americana) into the milieu of Chicano culture disrupts the demand of Chicano nationalism for a return to an uncorrupted mythic indigenous past.[7] On the other hand, non-Chicano Elvis fans rarely associate Elvis with Mexican or Chicano culture (or understand how Chicano culture has affected 'white' America) although few can deny Elvis' connection to southern black culture. Enacted on the accessible terrain of popular music, his aesthetics of resistance is double-edged, for it transforms the dominant culture's imposition of social codes that attempt to define 'Mexican immigrant' or 'Mexican American' identity and place in society, as well as subaltern demands to reduce Chicana and Chicano identity to an essentialized fixed form. His aesthetics of resistance disrupts both the dominant and subaltern dictates for strict, unyielding definitions of identity, sexuality and citizenship,[8] and they suggest that breaking with Chicano nationalism does not signify a break with Chicano politics.

It's 'Immigration Time'

These dimensions of Lopez's performance aesthetics can be found in the song 'Immigration Time' which substitutes the lyrics of Elvis' version of 'Suspicious Minds'(a song that thematizes emotional entrapment within a dysfunctional relationship) with a contemporary immigrant narrative that recalls the predicament of displaced Mexicans. Included on the compact disk *Graciasland* (El Vez's reappropriation of Paul Simon's *Graceland*), the lyrics of this song highlight inherent contradictions in official myths that frame a 'melting pot' democracy in the US:

> I'm caught in a trap, I can't walk out/Because my foot's caught in this border fence/Why can't you see, Statue of Liberty/I am your homeless, tired and weary/We can grow on together, it's Immigration Time/And we can build our dreams, it's Immigration Time/

> Yes I'm trying to go, get out of Mexico/The promised land waits on the other side/Here they come again, they're trying to fence me in/Wanting to live with the brave and the home of the free/We can grow on together, it's Immigration Time/And we can build our dreams, it's Immigration Time/

All that I have I will share, I'm not asking a lot,/You're the one that's supposed to care, we're the melting pot/But you lied to me/Woe – my, my/Woe – yeah yeah/I'm caught in a trap, I can't walk out/Because my foot's caught in this border fence

This is the land of opportunity/An American Dream/That can be shared with everyone/Regardless of race, creed, national and sexual origin/Anything/This belongs to everybody.

(1994)

In changing Elvis' lyrics 'I'm caught in a trap/I can't walk out/Because I love you too much baby' to 'I can't walk out/Because my foot's caught in this border fence', the song conjures Elvis' version – the back-beat remains the same[9] – yet thematizes the increased militarization of the Mexico–US border.[10] 'Immigration Time' thus highlights the nation's contradictory immigrant policy and its connection to an economy fundamentally based on hyper-exploited undocumented workers.

In addition, by imagining a conversation between an undocumented immigrant and the Statue of Liberty from the perspective of the former, El Vez's lyrics also provide an oppositional image of the plight of undocumented racialized immigrant workers. This hypothetical conversation is significant, given that the song circulated in California at the same time as the Proposition 187 television and its attendant propaganda campaign. The Proposition's advertisements portrayed immigrants as dehumanized invading 'aliens' and ignored studies proving that undocumented workers boost California's economy[11] to justify its call to further reduce the basic human rights of undocumented immigrant workers and their children (Lowe, 1996: 174). Within this context, El Vez's performances (live and recorded) enabled and enable a site where counter-representations of undocumented racialized immigrant voices (voices rarely, if ever, consulted in national or international debates) are be considered.[12]

In 'Immigration Time' the immigrant voice boldly asserts his humanity by evoking 'our dreams' to 'build' and 'grow on together'. At the same time he indicts the inhumane forces that make his dream impossible today and he alludes to the cyclical deportation of Mexicans by 'la migra', the Immigration and Naturalization Service (Border Patrol), which polices the border and literally chases, corrals and deports racialized immigrants and citizens like animals. With his images of border entrapment El Vez evokes remembrances of internal colonialism and proposes that immigrant workers – economic refugees – are literally trapped behind the fences erected along the transnational border San Ysidro, thus implicating as well the global economic structure of labour exploitation that requires cheap, alienated labour to maintain prosperity.

El Vez thus employs the master's tools to 'dismantle the master's house'. In this song, the singing subject stakes his claim to inclusion in the national body along the lines of a modified Civil Rights discourse by invoking the traditional symbol and ideology of 'Lady Liberty'. He reminds the Statue of Liberty of her obligation to accept all the 'tired and weary', regardless of their point of entry, be it Ellis Island or San Diego county, and, if this were not enough, he condemns her for her deception, thus drawing attention to both the tragedy of her 'conscious' differential treatment of Mexican immigrants and the tragedy of those who are 'fenced in' and forced out. This critique is strengthened by their contradictory positions in the song; unlike Lady Liberty who selectively opposes the American Dream for Mexicans, he offers to 'share all that he has' with America. Equally important, the racialized immigrant protagonist recognizes a shared experience of displacement with other US citizens, and suggests that she is either blind or indifferent as well to members of US citizenry who are also 'homeless, tired' and dispossessed. Finally, as a retort to the position of arch conservatives who would deny him his place in the US, he triumphantly employs their own arguments against them by exclaiming, 'This is the land of opportunity / An American Dream / That can be shared with everyone / Regardless of race, creed, national and sexual origin / Anything / This belongs to everybody.' Yet by embracing the equating of American identity with ability to spend within the parameters of capitalism, 'I got my green card, I want my gold card', the immigrant runs the risk of falling into another trap: that of reproducing the ideology that excluded him in the first place.

'Taking Care of Business', everyday

El Vez's version of 'Taking Care of Business' also disrupts recent national constructions of Mexican, Latina and Latino immigrants as a dehumanized army of social parasites that are 'invading' the nation and depleting resources and employment opportunities.[13] He achieves this by translating the original version of 'Taking Care of Business' into a tribute offered to those racialized immigrants who have been structurally relegated to service positions, jobs that literally take care of business. When El Vez performs 'Taking Care of Business' live, against the backdrop of the North American Trade Agreement (NAFTA) and Proposition 187, he usually prefaces it by asking, 'What would happen if all the Latinos and all the immigrants in the United States decided not to work, what if they all went on strike? Business would shut down, because no one would be around to take care of business, vegetables would rot in fields, parents wouldn't be able to go to work because they'd have to take care of their own children.' For those in the Southwest who have never considered their own reliance on immigrant labour, the song illuminates the everyday contributions of Latinos:

> We get up every morning, from the alarm clock's warning / do the menial jobs that run this city / there's a whistle up above and we're cleaning and we scrub / do your lawn, to make you look pretty / and if our bus is on time,

getting to work way before nine/to stock and slave, $2.15 is our pay/and you're getting all annoyed/blaming us for unemployed/they're jobs you wouldn't take anyway/

and we're TAKIN' CARE OF BUSINESS – everyday/TAKIN' CARE OF BUSINESS – oralé/TAKIN' CARE OF BUSINESS – we're the maid/TAKIN' CARE OF BUSINESS – and getting under paid!/work out!/

for an easy addition you get workers for your kitchen/paid under table, they won't tell'o/If you need a handyman, you can go to Standard Brands/and get one of those stand around fellows/you see us slaving in the sun, from la migra we must run/you tell us that you like it this way/and you're getting all annoyed, blaming us for unemployed/they're jobs you wouldn't take any way/

all we want is good job/so we can stand on our own two feet/we crawling up from the bottom, we're proud labour that just won't hide/You wouldn't want to be a farm worker and be sprayed with pesticide/Oww/

and we've been TAKIN' CARE OF BUSINESS (TCB) – everyday/TCB – oralé/TCB working fields/TCB – and cooking all your meals/TCB – kitchen crew/ TCB – nanny's too/TCB – blowing leaves/TCB – no green cards up our sleeve.

(1996)

For those who are not aware of who is 'taking care of business', El Vez clarifies that it is Mexican or Central American working-class undocumented immigrants. He makes it clear that these workers, who enable a middle-class lifestyle for some, are the ones who are persecuted by 'la migra' (Border Patrol). El Vez also targets the impact of their lack of class privilege upon singing that it is those workers, who are making their way up 'from the bottom', who get scapegoated for social woes. In addition, his description of the real life 'cleaning and scrubbing' of undocumented and documented labour defies the right-wing ideology that criticizes, attacks and belittles Latino, working-poor immigrants as do-nothing social parasites. This description also rebukes the argument of conservatives, of various economic classes and ethnicities, who contend that undocumented immigrants 'take' jobs way from citizens and permanent residents, upon reminding us that the jobs that are made available to undocumented workers by business are the 'menial' ones without benefits and decent pay, jobs they (those who criticize) 'wouldn't take anyway'.

'Taking Care of Business' also targets the unfair and exploitative labour practices of owners and managers who decide that the vital jobs that maintain social survival – childcare, construction, food harvest – only deserve $2.15 per hour – this for hard labour and exposure to lethal toxic chemicals. The lyrics also outline the dependence of overdeveloped economies on hyper-exploited labour to maintain low-cost comforts, services and products (including manicured lawns, somewhat affordable housing for the middle class, cheap dining and so on). In essence, whereas the Proposition 187 campaign created an ideological difference between 'Americans and Mexicans', the song highlights the inter-dependence of citizens and undocumented immigrant workers in the US in socio-economic terms, and exposes the hypocrisy of annoyed middle-class citizens who object to granting basic human rights to individuals who are not recognized by the state: these bothered citizens want the financial benefits of cheap immigrant labour, but they do not want the immigrants themselves, nor their children; they want their own business taken care of quickly and cheaply, but do not care if the workers have time to take care of their own personal business of survival.

Ambassador of Latin culture? El Vez 'n Germany

It is important to note that 'Immigration Time' speaks to an audience far outside of the Chicano and Latino immigrant community as it addresses the effects of transnational capital on low-wage workers in general. The song narrates what is happening to employees at the bottom of the economic tier: they are being told to work harder, work overtime, take care of business, all the while losing employ-ment protections. Of course, when business cycles decline, workers without proper documentation are harassed and deported. El Vez's ability to superimpose issues of immigration, labour and national belonging on top of songs associated with Elvis resonates well abroad in performances that sustain his artistic produc-tion in the US; it also takes Chicana culture and his critique of the status quo out of a local context and situates it within an international one. El Vez's performances thus enable the possibility of building alliances, communities 'with and between others . . . who are subject to and subjects of the state' based on 'horizontal affiliations' – a process by which marginalized groups 'recognize shared stakes in the struggle to create counter-hegemonic practices and communities' (Lowe, 1996: 36). It is worth noting that Lopez is well aware of these repercussions of his music. In our interview, for instance, he reflects on how and when Turkish youth in Germany are attracted to his music. He relates that performing in Europe

> is great. [Ethnic] Turkish kids [who speak English] come to me and go, 'I love when you sing about "Immigration Time" because I know what you are. My family came here and we're immigrants and we're just trying to be here, we're in Berlin here trying to make a living and trying to be part of this society.' It's something . . . we were in Slovania, and the people, some Croatian kids, say 'I know when you sing about Zapata because that's hap-pening now, too'.

In theorizing about the international reception of his performance, Lopez recognizes that even though his performance originated in 'Southern California', 'it took on a whole new meaning in Europe, because the song has something to do with their lives. As he elaborates: 'it's lost something in the translation and gained something else, too. It's the whole process of changing and meaning something else to someone else.'[14]

Although the specificities of Chicana and Chicano cultural symbols and experiences may be lost in the translation, what is gained is the possibility of a recognition that young Turkish Germans are positioned similarly to Chicanas and Chicanos by capitalism and nationalism. Hence, 'Immigration Time' and 'Taking Care of Business' speak to the frustrations of many ethnic-Turkish young people who are also dealing with issues of transnational immigration, citizenship, labour, social mobility and cultural diversity in a contentious social ambient (Caglar, 1991a, 1995b; Phillips 1993; Vertovec, 1996). Of course, there are historical circumstances that allow for these identifications to take place. After the Berlin Wall was built in the early 1960s, West Germany lost access to the cheap labour pools available in East Germany. Thus Turkish temporary guest workers were invited to fill labour needs (Mandel, 1993). Like the Bracero programme launched in the Southwest in 1942, which contracted Mexican nationals under temporary work arrangements, only Turkish men were granted work visas. In this way, Turkish workers were excluded by processes that were similar in structure to the Mexican Bracero policy (Gamboa, 1990; Hondagneu-Sotelo, 1996). Nevertheless in the late 1960s, wives of guest workers were granted work visas as well. The children of the Turkish guest workers – although they were born in Germany – did not receive automatic citizenship since criteria for German citizenship is literally based on German ancestry (Faist and Häubermann, 1996; Smith and Blanc, 1996). As these children came of age in the 1980s and 1990s, they began to question their relation to the nation-state. Although they were considered to be foreigners and had experienced anti-immigration violence, they had grown up in Germany, not Turkey.[15] Many felt that they should be recognized as part of German culture.

We hear the echo of 'Taking Care of Business''s theme concerning immigrant labour in the US in the words of a Turkish working woman in Germany. In commenting on the recent anti-Turkish tension in Germany after the fall of the Berlin Wall, Sasian Ozakbyiyik bitterly explains that 'we were welcomed with open arms . . . none of the Germans wanted to do the jobs we did and now they don't want us'. In the same article, her daughter continues, 'we were the builders of Germany's economic miracle. So we have a right to live here' (Cowell, 1995: A6). Though Turkish-German specific, these sentiments are expressed in El Vez's 'Taking Care of Business'.

'Working over time' and place, orale!

The popularity of El Vez's music in Europe, though it may play into Western Europe's fascination with so-called exotic others, demonstrates that oppositional

forms of Chicana and Chicano culture (including the related form of rock-
'en'español) have a role to play in cross-cultural contestatory musical practices
of racialized immigrant European youth (Kaya). Though not an immigrant
worker himself, Lopez's performances help to humanize the struggle of racialized global immigrants who are displaced by global restructuring and hostile
immigration policies. When young Turkish-Germans recognize the social and
political resemblance between their situation and that of many Latinos in the US,
the progressive potential of subversive forms of popular culture is revealed.
While identities are questioned regularly by the nation-state (who is a citizen, a
worker), and while capital increasingly needs identities to be as fluid as possible
in order to make labour more pliable from which to profit, artists such as Lopez
open up the possibility of creating the newest links of resistance by mixing histories and aesthetic styles within a progressive and pro-democratic performance
form. This form, as it travels, tells racialized immigrants within different communities that they are not alone. This is no small feat; it can be the first step
towards solidarity.

El Vez's performances manipulate the affective power of Elvis-as-icon to
advance the discourse of a renovated Chicano cultural politics that is not bound
to the closures of cultural nationalism; El Vez harnesses the ability of the figure
of Elvis in order to travel (out of the South) across socially constructed boundaries and to attract and forge a mixed audience, one in particular that may have
never been exposed to an oppositional politics. Ultimately, the performance of
Lopez's El Vez translates and transforms nationalist codes (both dominant and
Chicano) that insist on cultural and racial purity. As they recycle forms of mass
popular culture, El Vez and his fans, both here and abroad, make visible the possibility of a new understanding of community – one that responds to an exploitative transnationalism – and the possibility of an international political agency and
musical sensibility of social subjects that, because of their unique histories and
social predicaments, do not posses the luxury of ethnic or national absolutism.

Notes

1   It has been my great pleasure to introduce the performance of El Vez to a community of serious scholars, including my Ph.D. mentor José D. Saldívar, my
professor George Lipsitz, and my colleague Angie Chabram-Dernersesian.
This article, which 'introduces' El Vez and was a natural outgrowth of my
initial research conducted in 1994, has helped to widen Chicana and Chicano
studies' field of analysis. I am also pleased that this current research allows me
to fulfil the charge of cultural studies to take seriously issues and objects 'which
critical work has excluded' (Grossberg 1992: 18). The power of a live performance I attended in January of 1995 of El Vez and the Memphis Mariachis,
while I was a graduate student at University of California, Santa Cruz, convinced to continue this project. I presented an early version of this article at

the 1996 Annual California Studies Association Meeting. I presented subsequent versions at the New Perspectives on Chicana and Chicano Culture Conference, Center for Chicano Studies, University of California, Los Angeles, in May 1997; The Third International Conference on El Vez, Institute for the Living South, Memphis College of Art, Elvis Weep Week, in August 1997; The Annual American Studies Association Meeting, Washington, DC, in December 1997; and 'The Shifting Boundaries: Place and Space in the Romance Cultures of North-America' Conference, at Centro de Estudios Mexicanos, University of Groningen, The Netherlands, in May 1998. I send my whole-hearted thanks to Jaime Cardenas, George Mariscal, José D. Saldívar, Lisa Lowe, Angie Chabram-Dernersesian, Maylei Blackwell, Scott Davis and Christopher Breu for insightful comments on multiple drafts of this piece.

2   El Vez's transculturation of American mass culture is an analogue for the current transformation of the dominant culture engaged by Latinos. Diane Taylor, elaborating on Cuban anthropologist Fernando Ortiz's definition of the term, explains that transculturation 'suggests a shifting or circulation pattern of cultural transference' that is not necessarily based on equal power relations. She continues, 'Transculturation affects the entire culture; it involves the shifting of socio-political, not just aesthetic borders; it modifies collective and individual identity; it changes discourse, both verbal and symbolic' (Taylor, 1991: 90).

3   See George Lipsitz (1994), Herman Gray (1995), and Grossberg (1992) for compelling discussions of popular music and culture as a site where cultural struggles are staged.

4   See the inset of *G.I. Ay, Ay! Blues: Soundtrack for the Coming Revolution* (El Vez, 1996) for a visual representation of Lopez's reappropriation of the signs of Latin American revolution, especially Che Guevara as revolutinonary icon. Citing folksinger Phil Ochs, the inset proclaims: 'If there is any hope for America it lies in a Revolution. If there is any hope for a Revolution it lies in Elvis Presley becoming Che Guevara.' However, juxtaposing symbols of an anti-imperialist history of armed struggle (leaving Che's torture and assassination unspoken) with the pleasures of rock and roll history certainly does not alone advance social change, and does leave Lopez open to criticism that he his diminishing and disrespecting the efforts of armed revolutinary struggle. Yet, by locating his aesthetic strategies between multiracial punk-rappers Rage Against the Machine, and 'just fun and parody', his music and performance wage a conscious negotiation between utter opposition and utter complacency. Through his negotiation, openings are formed that lead to the discourse of a different, progressive set of social possibilities, openings that can occur when people are not on the defensive.

5   Lopez, personal interview, 27 September 1996. A version of this interview is forthcoming in a special edition of *Americas Review*.

6   In this statement El Vez employs the metaphor of the 'blank Elvis' tongue-in-cheek, as he has chosen to embody the Chicano Elvis. Although his provocative statement around Elvis and sexuality needs to be teased out, space

considerations prohibit me from addressing them further in this article. See Gilbert B. Rodham (1996) for an extended discussion of how fans come to themselves reflected by the image of Elvis. While Rodham admits that the figure of Elvis engenders multiple interpretations, he argues it is not an 'empty signifier' that can mean absolutely anything at all. On the contrary, 'Elvis is an incredibly full signifier, one that is already intimately bound up with many of the most important cultural myths of our time. Elvis is not (and never has been) merely a blank slate on to which fans and critics can write their own stories' (Rodman, 1996: 40). Vernon Chadwick's *In Search of Elvis* (1997) serves as a wonderful source for discussions of Elvis' many symbolic functions.

7   Inevitably, Lopez's style of superimposing Chicano and the dominant culture on to each other is a form of cultural politics that is not acceptable to those who are still heavily invested in Chicano ethnic nationalism. Chicano nationalist identity politics demands a rupture from the dominant culture – so the pleasures of 'white' rock and roll could never be openly indulged. Contrary to this nationalist position, El Vez's performance turns on the crossing of cultural and racial lines; more precisely, it is through the humorous reworking of the signifiers of the nation, both American and Chicano, that El Vez can speak to multiple marginalized communities affected by shifts in the global economy. El Vez's work suggests that cultural nationalism must always be surpassed by a mestizo politics of transformation in order to avoid imitating the trappings of the exclusionary model of nationalism of the dominant culture. Thus, in El Vez's work, both Chicano and mainstream national icons take on an international significance and become a site where the possibility for political alliance based on an identity beyond the constraints of the nation-state is imagined.

8   Political complexity is not limited to Lopez's performance and music: El Vez's still-frame assemblages can be as complicated as his stage shows. A photo included in the inset of *G.I. Ay, Ay! Blues* (1996b) appears as a homage to Elvis, Che and the Zapatistas, and provides an excellent example of his transculturation of important signs. This image visually represents his break from traditional Chicano aesthetics and his invention of one that uses old signs in new ways. Here, El Vez's image of manhood subverts traditional representations of masculinity. Traditional masculinity, especially as embodied by a revolutionary soldier, and usually represented as sombre, impenetrable, intimidating and aggressive, is undercut by the photo. Within the frame El Vez's body is staged as the object of the desire in this image; the viewer is implicated (male or female) because El Vez points back to us with his index fingers. His posture is open – hips loose, and his arms, up and away from his body, suggest that he might be vulnerable to attack or pleasure. The gun, symbol of war, conquest and masculine power, an extension of phallic power, does not threaten us, it is not pointed towards us. Unthreatening, it rests behind his neck. Instead of communicating intimidation, his gaze, focused beyond the camera, has an erotic charge with its come hither beckoning. For those invested in traditional representations of manhood, then, this image is unsettling, and is evident in the complex reception of, and even resistance to, El Vez.

9   However, the introductory musical phrase of El Vez's version that superimposes the 'who, who' soundings of both the Rolling Stones and Jane's Addiction's version of 'Sympathy for the Devil' signals Lopez's general engagement in American popular music.

10   See Verhovek (1998).

11   See Fix and Passel (1994).

12   The graphic artist Lalo Alcaraz also employed his weekly comic, *L.A. Cucaracha*, as a public site for the counter-hegemonic discussion of immigrant bashing in California.

13   See Kevin R. Johnson (1996) for an in-depth analysis of rhetoric used against undocumented immigrant labour.

14   See Interview with Habell-Pallán (forthcoming).

15   Public discourse about the place of working immigrants throughout Europe has intesified during the last ten years; see e.g. Jenkins (1989) and Phillips (1993).

References

Caglar, Ayse S. (1990a) 'The prison house of culture in the study of Turks in Germany'. Series Title: Sozialanthropologische Arbeitspapiere, No. 31, Berlin: Das Arabische Buch.

—— (1995) 'German Turks in Berlin: social exclusion and strategies for social mobility', *New Community*, 21(3): 309–23.

Chadwick, Vernon (ed.) (1997) *In Search of Elvis: Music, Race, Art, Religion*, Colorado: Westview Press.

Cowell, Alan (1995) 'Turks seek acceptance of culture in Germany', *New York Times* (International edition), 14 December: A6.

El Vez (1994) 'Immigration Time', *Graciasland*. Sympathy for the Record Industry.

—— (1996) 'Taking Care of Business', *G.I. Ay, Ay! Blues*. Big Pop Records.

Faist, Thomas (1993) 'From school to work: public policy and underclass formation among young Turks in Germany during the 1980s', *The International Migration Review*, 27(2): 306–31.

Faist, Thomas and Haübermann, Hartmut (1996) 'Immigration, social citizenship and housing in Germany', *International Journal of Urban and Regional Research*, 20(1): 83–98.

Fix, Michael and Passel, Jeffrey S. (1994) *Immigration And Immigrants: Setting the Record Straight*, Washington, DC: Urban Institute.

Gamboa, Erasmo (1990) *Mexican Labor and World War II: Braceros in the Pacific Northwest, 1942–1947*, Austin: University of Texas Press.

Gray, Herman (1995) *Watching Race: Television and the Struggle for Blackness*, Minneapolis: University of Minnesota Press.

Grossberg, Lawrence (1992) *We Gotta Get Out of This Place: Popular Conservatism and Postmodern Culture*, New York: Routledge.

Habell-Pallán, Michelle (forthcoming) 'Interview with El Vez', *Americas Review*.

Hondagneu-Sotelo, Pierrette (1996) 'The history of Mexican undocumented settlement in the United States', in Mary Romero *et al. Challenging Fronteras: Structuring Latina and Latino Lives in the U.S*, New York: Routledge.

Jenkins, Jolyon (1989) 'Taken to the cleaners: Germany has its Turks, Kuwait has the Filipinos, and the British have their Nigerians', *New Statesman and Society*, 29 December 1989: 10–11.

Johnson, Kevin R. (1996–1997) '"Aliens" and the U.S. immigration laws: the social and legal construction of nonpersons', *Miami Inter-American Law Review*, 28(2): 263–87.

Kaya, Ayhan (1997) 'Construction of diasporic cultural identity: Berlin Turks and Hip-Hop youth culture', unpublished manuscript.

Lipsitz, George (1994) *Dangerous Crossroads: Popular Music, Postmodernism, and the Poetics of Place*, New York: Verso.

Lowe, Lisa (1996) *Immigrant Acts: On Asian American Cultural Politics*, Durham, NC: Duke University Press.

Mandel, Ruth (1993) 'Foreigners in the Fatherland: Turkish immigrant workers in Germany', in Camille Guerin-Gonzalez and Carl Strikwerda (eds) *The Politics of Immigrant Workers: Labor Activism and Migration in the World Economy Since 1830*, New York: Holmes and Meier.

Phillips, Andrew (1993) 'The gates slam shut', *Maclean's*, 14 June: 18–22.

Rodman, Gilbert B. (1996) *Elvis After Elvis: The Posthumous Career of a Living Legend*, New York: Routledge.

Saldívar, José D. (1997) *Border Matters: Remapping American Cultural Studies*, Berkeley: University of California Press.

Smith, David M. and Blanc, Maurice (1996) 'Citizenship, nationality, and ethnic minorities in three European nations', *International Journal of Urban and Regional Research*, 20(1): 66–81.

Taylor, Diane (1991) 'Transculturating transculturation', *Performing Arts Journal*, 38: 90–104.

Verhovek, Sam Howe (1998) 'Border patrol is criticized as abusive; human rights group reports "Cruel" Acts', *New York Times*, 21 May: A12+.

Vertovec, Steven (1996) 'Berlin multikulti: Germany, "foreigners", and world openness', *New Community*, 22(3): 381–99.

Rosa Linda Fregoso

'ON THE ROAD WITH ANGELA DAVIS'[1]

Abstract

Twenty years ago Angela Y. Davis wrote *Women, Race and Class* — a critical history of the women's movement dating to the nineteenth century. This article traces the theoretical legacy of Angela Davis' work and looks at how her theoretical contributions anticipated the concerns of 'Third World' feminists and shaped the feminist practices the so-called 'third wave' of feminism. My critical assessment of *Women, Race and Class* breaks away from 'vertical' modes of narrating the 'nation' or 'race' in feminist theoretical discourse and highlights instead the 'horizontal' affiliations among women moving across the intersections of culture, race, nation, class and sexuality. Already in the late 1970s, Davis' influential text provided a framework for this type of engagement and for theorizing from the epistemological position of racialized women. In its critique of the universalist underpinnings of 'hegemonic' feminist theory, *Women, Race and Class* is a foundational text for theorizing across a wide range of communities, geographic locations and feminist traditions.

Keywords

Angela Y. Davis; feminism; racialized women; gender and globalization; 'Third World' feminism; Chicana/Latina studies

> Caminante no hay camino
> Se hace camino al andar
> (Antonio Machado, *Proverbios y Cantares*)

I BEGIN MY CRITICAL REFLECTION on the significance of Angela Davis' work for the critical and cultural legacies of feminists of colour by translating my selected epigraph: 'Traveller there is no road/One constructs a road by

Figure 4 Angela Y. Davis. Photo/Philip Gallow. Reproduced courtesy of Angela Y. Davis

walking.' With this quote from the Spanish poet, Antonio Machado (Generación del 98), I would like to clarify that the 'road' in my title is a metaphoric one. When Antonio Machado says, 'Traveller there is no road/One constructs a road by walking', he is referring to the relationship between theory and practice, a relationship so sacred that it has to be the guiding principle, the number one commandment of progressive intellectuals in the late twentieth century. Angela Davis, in particular, has shown us that theory must be practised or better yet that there is a false opposition between theory and practice, that 'social theory is historic practice'.[2] For this reason it is not surprising that in many ways, Angela Davis has been 'on the road' with many of us who work and struggle in the alternative sector. As she has carved out a road for a politically engaged intellectual practice, she has also inspired us to think and to take action.

For example, in my militant days in South Texas during the 1960s and early 1970s, Angela Davis influenced my formation in Chicano nationalist, anticolonialism, anti-imperialism and antiracism struggles. She was one of the handful of militant, public figures – a woman warrior – whom I sought to emulate. Though I never became the brave woman warrior she did, Angela Davis was someone I aspired to be like. Her ideas and her practice travelled with me, guiding me in many of the choices I have made throughout this road, which is my life.

Other racialized women of my generation, including Chicanas, have reaffirmed to me how they have been impacted by her legacy in similar ways. Yet as we approach the end of the twentieth century, it is clear that there is much more 'unfinished business' in scholarship pertaining to the study of 'power, identity and culture'. In this historic moment of intense globalization and widespread fragmentation, we need to revisit the critical apparatus which informs her theoretical contributions and consider how it has shaped our own feminist practice. In many ways, this type of theoretical 'congregation' and 'conversational' practice implies a break with a dominant mode of feminist recovery – even prevalent within circles of racialized women – organized around specific national, racial or ethnic identities and feminist traditions. Breaking away from this vertical mode of narrating the 'nation' or 'race' in feminist theoretical discourse implies refashioning and redesigning what Lisa Lowe (1996) terms 'horizontal' affiliations that have been occulted and making them visible, legible and audible across a wide range of communities, geographic locations and feminist traditions embedded in the intersections of gender, sexuality, nation, race and class. Given the tendency to valorize the works of scholars and activists along a singular racial or ethnic axis, recovering these horizontal affiliations also implies a multi-accented and multi-sited repositioning of Angela Davis' work.[3] For this reason, rather than follow the 'familiar' road which might be expected of me, a path through a specific genealogy of 'Chicana' feminist recovery, I will engage her work directly, even as I would like to make my readers aware of the fact that these horizontal connections that I seek to recover among feminists are themselves informed by my own grounding in a Chicana feminist practice and social experience. This recovery is, after all, consistent with the works of other Chicana critics, such as Chela Sandoval, who proposes that an understanding of 'U.S. Third World feminism' entails 'naming and describing the practices that comprise its methodology' if we are to truly valorize the works of figures whose contribution to feminism and cultural studies 'continues to slip away' from '[inter]disciplinary understanding and recognition' (Sandoval, 1998: 354).

As I initiate my discussion about Angela Davis and how her work is a road map for the feminism which many of us have travelled, I would like to clarify that I do not begin this journey by relating how I 'encountered' Angela Davis while coming into political consciousness. Instead I begin by describing how I re-encountered her and engaged her as a professor at UC Davis in the Autumn of 1997. In that quarter, I co-taught a course on gender and globalization with Lisa Lowe, a professor of literature at UCSC, through distance learning technologies – technologies which produce a video conferencing effect, temporally bridging two or more spatial sites, seemingly simultaneous, but with anywhere from a quarter- to half-second delay (thus compromising its so-called simultaneity). The title of our course was 'Interdisciplinary approaches to gender and globalization', and we taught the graduate seminar in two interdisciplinary sites – women's studies at Davis and ethnic studies at San Diego. Our aim was to conceptualize a common set of research questions, focusing on the scholarly paradigms generated in two of the most important interdisciplinary sites to emerge within the university in the last two decades. We sought to link these two fields of women's studies and ethnic studies together through the study of 'women' within an international and interdisciplinary context. As we stated in our course description: 'Our interdisciplinary approach to the study of "women" – both as an object of study within a variety of academic disciplines and within different national cultures and traditions – [was] comparative in nature, beginning from the notion that "woman" is a different object of knowledge within the paradigms of the academic disciplines but also across different national and cultural mileux and in various sites of immigrant diaspora.'[4] We focused on the problem of globalization in order to tackle the differences (and points of articulation) between a formal mode of colonization (produced by empire and the nation-state) and what Alexander and Mohanty term the 'process of recolonization' (Alexander and Mohanty, 1997: xvii) of women's labour and subjectivities in this new international division of labour. All our readings dealt with the effects of historical, political, economic, social and psychic processes on the bodies of women. Which is where Angela Davis comes in. We began the seminar by reading Angela's *Women, Race and Class*, originally published in 1981.

Women, Race and Class was written nearly twenty years ago. Within the context of our graduate seminar I was struck by how contemporary it read in 1997; with how prophetic it must have read in the late 1970s, already prognosticating the concerns of what is referred to in 'women's studies' as 'the third wave of feminism'. This is what I would like to address here – the kinds of feminisms Angela Davis' groundbreaking book, *Women, Race and Class*, enables. In fact I propose that this is a foundational text for what we now call 'multicultural feminism', 'women of colour feminisms', 'Third World' feminisms, or racialized women as a 'political project'.

This text resists a unitary history of feminism, pluralizing the notion as 'feminisms', instructing us that each feminism has its own specific critiques, its own historical location within and against the political context of variable social formations.[5] While her analysis partakes in all feminisms' critique of masculinist ideologies and regimes of power circumscribed by patriarchy, *Women, Race and Class* is much broader in scope, advocating the transformation of all forms of social inequality, the dismantling of oppressive power relations based on inequality, and the critique of a singular notion of 'patriarchy'.

What makes Angela Davis' book even more extraordinary is how she bridges the distinction between what Katie King identifies as feminist theoretical writing in academia and feminist political theorizing (King, 1994)[6] through a recovery of an alternative history of black women's theory-making practice; interventions into the public sphere of politics on behalf of black women; activism and/or writing; and political theorizing that addresses labour unionism, women's clubs and anti-lynching campaigns.

While her book rewrites the history of the women's movement, exposing its turbulent and disconcerting paths, as theoretical writing in the academy it is very much grounded in the poststructuralist or anti-essentialist critiques in philosophy which are said to fracture the second wave of feminism – a brand of feminism that was indebted to the legacy of modernity, to a conceptual apparatus underwritten by the binary division of gender, male versus female, and the Enlightenment notion of woman as a universal, transhistorical subject; that is, woman viewed as the reversal of the equally unified and transcendental humanist subject of Western, liberal epistemology: the white, propertied male.

US feminist historiography[7] partially credits French feminism for the ruptures in the essentialism of 'the second wave' feminism[8] for a shift in theorization of the social category of 'woman'; a deconstruction of the unified object of feminism; the rejection of the notion of woman as 'essence', and for an understanding of a notion of 'woman' that is provisional and contingent. However, embedded in *Women, Race and Class* we already find a critique of the binary structure of gender, a rejection of the unified and transhistorical category of woman – which is its fundamental linkage with 'Third World' feminisms. Lisa Lowe elaborates on the theoretical dimensions of these feminisms upon explaining that 'the cultural production of racialized women seeks to articulate multiple, nonequivalent, but linked determinations without assuming their containment within the horizon of an absolute totality and its presumption of a single subject' (Lowe, 1996: 164–5).

In keeping with the spirit of contemporary feminisms, Davis provides us with an alternative notion of femininity, an embodiment of black womanhood that is not genetic, but socially produced. The anti-essentialism implicit in her construction of gender identity is grounded in a Marxist materialist understanding of how consciousness is produced. Here, in this early work, gender appears as a form of embodied/corporal subjectivity, produced by objective economic and historical conditions, including labour, language, social practices and discourses of power knowledge, and networks of social relations and institutions like the family and the state. Moreover, *Women, Race and Class* gives voice to the development of racialized woman as a political subject which, at least in the United States, pre-dates its periodization in the so-called 'third wave'.

Along with French feminism, Third World feminists and lesbians are also credited with dismantling the epistemological ground of the concept of woman, envisioned by the social formation which Gaytri Spivak called 'hegemonic feminist theory' (Spivak, 1985: 147), for deconstructing the assumptions of Western feminism-based binary categories; unveiling its imperial, racist and homophobic underpinnings, and insisting on multi-valence, multi-axes variability and difference in social categories and relations of subordination and domination. While feminist historiography traces the emergence of 'third wave' feminism in the US to 1981 (a date that coincides with the publication of Moraga and Anzaldúa's *This Bridge Called my Back*), Angela Davis proposes an alternative genealogy for the development of women of colour as a political subject upon citing a rich and unexplored history of political projects by racialized women and radical feminisms dating as far back as the Civil Rights era of the early 1960s (Lowe, 1997: 310–11).

It is precisely this kind of foundation that *Women, Race and Class* provides with its carefully positioned examples of women like Elizabeth Gurley Flynn who, already in the 1940s, forty years before the so-called 'third wave', wrote about 'the triple-exploitation' of black women, as racialized, gendered and class subjects within the nation-state (Davis, 1983: 165). For those of us who track the footprints of racialized women in history, Davis' book is like a road map that charts a history of racialized gender consciousness back to the nineteenth century, back to women who knew that 'race is always gender'.[9] In *Women, Race and Class* we can also locate the tracks of the 'collective' politics of women, including not only black and white women but also 'Latina' women. One of the activists who Angela Davis writes about, Lucy Parsons, may have hidden her black identity because of anti-miscegenation laws, but let us not forget that her maiden name, González, is also indicative of a Latina heritage. This is why early Chicana feminists such as Ana Nieto Gómez embrace Lucy González Parsons as a foremother for Chicana gender consciousness.[10]

Twenty years ago, *Women, Race and Class* also interrogated the exclusive focus on gender within the social hierarchy, identifying 'common grounds upon which [US feminists of colour] made coalitions across cultural, racial, national, class and gender differences', instances where, in the words of Chela Sandoval, struggles against sexism were profoundly marked by 'struggles against class, race and cultural hierarchies' (Sandoval, 1991: 10). *Women, Race and Class* tracks the fault lines of the US women's movement and alerts us to the importance of a historical consciousness, for lacking a consciousness of history, the women's movement of the late twentieth century was possessed by its racist and classist heritage. *Women,*

Race and Class also challenges the prevailing historical amnesia and ideology of 'presentism' in society, illuminating how past histories (in this case the history of classism and racism in the women's suffrage movement) weigh incessantly on present circumstances. Finally, *Women, Race and Class* calls attention to the contradictions in political goals, for instance, in black male and white female enfranchisement[11] at the same time that it acknowledges that the demands for the production of new citizen-subjects were both racialized and gendered, for the legitimate citizen-subject of the modern nation-state was/is premised on specific types of racial and gender exclusions.

While *Women, Race and Class* does not explicitly target the sexism in the black liberation movement, Davis' attention to gender consciousness among the black intelligentsia and working class does offer us the feature identified with US Third World feminism in general; that is, it 'represents a new condition of possibility' (Sandoval, 1991: 16) for critiquing the sexist, classist and homophobic subtext of patriarchal nationalisms, 'a new condition of possibility' for unmasking unreflective masculinist patriarchy, and a 'new condition of possibility' for building bonds of solidarity across racial, gendered, sexual, cultural, class and national borders and divisions.

Women, Race and Class anticipates feminist studies on whiteness,[12] exemplified in the work of Ruth Frankenberg (*White Women, Race Matters*, 1993) who looks at the traces of colonial discourse in white women's thinking and, in order to dislodge the normativity and invisibility of white identity, names whiteness as a racial category engendering subjects in discourse and everyday practices.

The abjection of black female bodies, evident in Davis' discussion of racialized female labour in the slave economy and under capitalist formation (as both unpaid and paid labour), complicates the universal definition of the sexual division of labour. Her nuanced attention to the domains of material and symbolic production and reproduction masterfully illuminates various sites where the subjection of racialized female bodies takes place, including the domestic sphere of unpaid household labour, the market sphere of domestic wage-labour, sterilization campaigns and reproductive rights, lynchings and rape, re-codified by Davis as 'a pattern of institutionalized sexual abuse' (Davis, 1983: 175).

Women, Race and Class pre-dates the feminist critique of the gendered subtext in Habermas' notion of public–private spheres, in particular Nancy Fraser's critical rereading of Habermas (Fraser, 1994). Extending this feminist rereading of the public–private sphere, Davis' account of the racialized nature of female labour under capitalism adds to feminist insights and understandings about the gendering of the subject in discourse and social practices. Her description of racialized female domestic workers in the spheres of production and reproduction provides a framework for contemporary empirical research undertaken by scholars such as Mary Romero (1992), whose study of Chicana domestic labour unveils the racial hierarchies and contradictions among women in the private, domestic sphere; and Evelyn Nakano Glenn (1983), who elaborates upon feminist critiques of gender oppression under capitalism by examining the racialized character of the sexual division of labour.

In this era[13] of an intensified assault on female bodies, moral panics about the hyper-fertility of welfare mothers, unwed mothers, immigrant women – all code words for women of colour – Davis' chapters, 'Rape, racism and the myth of the black rapist' and 'Racism, birth control and reproductive rights' are as pertinent today as they were twenty years ago. Both are blueprints for women's international activism, at the level of governmental as well as NGOs, for global organizing efforts to have 'rape officially designated as a war crime', to eliminate sterilization campaigns, and for efforts to elevate women's rights as human rights in movements which redefine domestic abuse as a violation of human rights. That *Women, Race and Class* continues to inspire movements for social justice throughout the world is the best indicator of its profound legacy. Her work is the hope for this business of 'unfinished liberations'.

Angela Davis' theory and practice inspires us to think globally and act locally, to reject the oppositions between the local and the global, to grapple with local as well as global manifestations of power, to develop an anti-racist, radical feminism in the face of planetary capitalism. Angela Davis constructs a path – hace el camino – for the new kinds of feminism that are required in this era of transnational capitalism in which there are 'connections between the deteriorating conditions in communities of color and the restructuring of global capitalism' (Lowe, 1997: 304). Given this context, feminism can no longer remain parochial or bound to the nation-state; it must think beyond singular axis, single race, single nation or single gender. The development of this feminism requires linkages to worldwide movements for the structural transformation of repressive regimes, structures and technologies of exploitation, which in each context demand culturally and historically specific responses.

Today, variable and multi-axes analysis are already informing the feminisms exemplified in the works of Ella Shohat (1997), Lisa Lowe (1996), Zillah Eisenstein (1996), Alexander and Mohanty (1997), Inderpal Grewal and Caren Kaplan (1994) – feminisms that centre the exchange of women's bodies in transnational capital, feminisms which rethink their strategies of feminist activism in a transnational framework, within the context of a globalized economy, recognizing that globalization is part of a longer history of colonialism and imperialism which, as Ann Stoler indicates, is already embedded in gender issues and discourses of sex, race and the nation (Stoler, 1995); feminisms which re-imagine the subject of global capitalism differently, less in terms of the universal subject of hegemonic, global sisterhood, and more in terms of a range of multi-accented and multivariable gendered and sexualized subjects, which move across the registers of sexuality, nation, race, class and gender; feminisms which point to global asymmetries, uneven and contradictory linkages in the gendered flow of capital and labour.

Twenty years ago, *Women, Race and Class* illuminated the road for these transnational feminisms. As I write this article I am reminded that the anniversary of

International Women's Day is marked in *Women, Race and Class*. Last year we celebrated the ninetieth anniversary of International Women's Day (8 March 1998), commemorating the socialist organized mass demonstration in support of suffrage. Davis' lifelong work is elegantly sprinkled with an internationalist spirit which alerts us to the fact that transnational feminisms need to be relational and engaged in a comparative feminist praxis if they are to respond effectively to post-cold war capitalism.

In mapping feminist genealogies for racialized women, Jackie Alexander and Chandra Mohanty write: 'Conceptualizing the people and citizenship within the framework of a specifically anticolonialist feminist understanding of democracy . . . requires theorizing from the epistemological location and experiences of Third-world women' (Alexander and Mohanty, 1997). This is precisely the type of labour that *Women, Race and Class* performs. Angela Davis' theorization from the epistemological position and experience of racialized women is a road map for recent feminist interventions into the realm of cultural politics, for this work of unfinished liberations. It is a signpost for the work that needs to be done.

I would like to underscore this fact, especially at this point in time when it is commonplace to denounce the 'identity politics' of the so-called 'cultural left', particularly in the writings of those on the New Right, those in the centre, and those on the New Left.[14] Despite our best intentions to move beyond grounding our critiques in social identities, we are currently witnessing a resurgence of neonationalist politics on university campuses and at the grass-roots level, particularly in geographic regions where the state practises its own brand of 'identity politics'. How are we to respond to the state's efforts to regulate and discipline racialized, gendered and sexualized subjectivities? to the state's newest forms of surveillance designed within a prison industry intended to incarcerate poor and racialized communities? to the 're-racialization of immigrants . . . as the most highly targeted object of a U.S. nationalist agenda' (Lowe, 1996: 174), evidenced by the passage of racially coded Propositions in California (187, 209 and 227) crafted to deny racialized immigrants access to the most basic medical, educational and social services? or to the rise of new (old) forms of racism on a global scale as in the anti-immigrant xenophobia practised in Britain, France and Italy, the ethnic cleansing in Bosnia, Kosovo and Ruwanda, the massacres of indigenous groups in Mexico? Are these not forms of policing, genocide, extermination, repression, surveillance and regulation aimed at racially and ethnically 'distinct' social identities?

It may perhaps be easier for intellectuals who are far removed from the trenches of these ruthless barbarisms to denounce the 'excesses of identity politics'. But for many of us on the front lines of a battle that polices and disciplines citizenship and membership in the nation-state, for those of us inhabiting what Lowe (following Benjamin) calls the 'site of a contemporary state of emergency' (Lowe, 1996: 174) (and I would emphasize that California is a trend-setter in this regard), the issue of 'identity' may be more entrenched in the everyday lives of people and therefore more relevant to them than the debates in theoretical and public discourses will acknowledge.

As a Chicana feminist living in California, witnessing the devastation of our planet (as the wrath of El Niño avenges our excesses), coming to grips with the decimation of the rights of racialized immigrants (in the wake of the passage of Proposition 227),[15] and facing the very real possibility that my Latino son will come of age in the prison system as opposed to the school system, my thinking continues to be enriched by the racialized, gendered, sexualized and classed dynamics of my experience. This mode of theoretical engagement is clearly indebted to the legacy of Angela Davis' intellectual and political practice. Hers is a mode of understanding and social theorizing that favours politicizing identity, or in Angela Davis' own words, 'basing identity on politics rather than politics on identity' (Lowe, 1997: 318). Which is why Angela Davis' work is a cartography for feminist practices in the new millennium.

Notes

1 An earlier version of this article was delivered at the 'Unfinished Liberation: Power Identity and Culture' Conference in honour of Angela Davis, in Arizona State University, March 1998. I would like to thank Angie Chabram-Dernersesian for her help in revising this article. My thanks as well to Lisa Lowe for her inspiration and generosity during our sojourn in co-teaching through distance learning technologies.

2 In evoking the legacy of Herbert Marcuse during the 'Unfinished Liberation' Conference, both Gina Dent and Avery Gordon noted that 'social theory is historic practice'.

3 My aim in this regard is to go beyond contemporary representations of Angela Davis that construct her as an 'activist' rather than as an activist who is also a highly accomplished scholar and theorist. I am thus highlighting her 'intellectual' contributions to feminist theory and practice, which are also 'political'.

4 The course, 'Interdisciplinary Approaches to Gender and Globalization', was taught in autumn 1997.

5 Throughout the text, Davis situates her readings of women's activism in the context of their specific class and racial locations. Not only does she attend to the racial differences among women activists/scholars, but she pays careful attention to the class differences among women; for instance, middle-class suffragists and union activism among working-class women (see chapters 4, 5, 7, 9 and 10).

6 For even though 'woman' emerged as an object of disciplinary knowledge in the late nineteenth century, it was not until the creation of women's studies programmes in the late 1960s and 1970s that the concept of woman was centred as an object of study in an institutional formation and in the context of the interdisciplinary site that came to be known as women's studies/feminist studies.

7   See Linda Alcoff (1988).

8   And here I am referring to the periodization of the women's movement in terms of waves, with the first wave corresponding to the nineteenth and early twentieth century; the second wave to the 1960s and 1970s, and the third wave to the 1980s and 1990s.

9   Zillah Eisenstein, 'Global phallus/ies: the cyber real of racialized gender', paper delivered at the 'Unfinished Liberation' Conference.

10   See the documentary *Chicana* (1979, director Sylvia Morales) which is based on the research of Ana Nieto Gómez.

11   In her account of racism in the women's suffrage movement (Chapter 4), Davis calls attention to the articulation and disarticulation of political goals, particularly in black male enfranchisement, due to the infusion of racist ideologies in the women's suffrage movement.

12   See her description of the social geography of the suffrage movement.

13   As many of us read in March 1998, the Kerner Commission's prophesy about the racialized structure of class inequality has become even more pronounced in the US than earlier anticipated. (See Michael A. Fletcher, 'Report: poor poorer and minorities suffering', *San Francisco Examiner*, 1 March 1998: A6.)

14   For a critique of the New Left's assault on 'identity politics' see Robin Kelley's chapter, 'Looking extremely backward' (1997). As the globalization process accelerates it has rekindled attention to issues of 'class', which in turn has sparked a necessary corrective to the reductionism in single-axis modes of analysis. Along with the contemporary global restructuring of capital, neo-liberalist policies continue to chip away at the public sector and the social responsibilities of the state, thus creating the social conditions for a 'class war'.

However, even more frightening is the fact that this 'class war' will in all probability be inflected by race. For, instead of an inter-class war of proletariats against the bourgeoisie, in the United States, at least, the class war will take the historic form of an intra-class, inter-race war, rather than Marxism's predicted 'inter-class war', as the rise of disenfranchised, working-class males involved in domestic terrorism and racist-inspired militias seems to indicate.

15   Proposition 227 was passed by California voters in June 1997. It will make it illegal for Californian schools and teachers to instruct non-English speaking students in their native language beyond a one-year basis (Latino/as, who voted in record numbers, voted 2–1 against the initiative). Currently, Proposition 227 is being challenged in the courts.

References

Alcoff, Linda (1988) 'Cultural feminism versus post-structuralism: the identity crisis in feminist theory', *Signs*, 13(3): 405–36.

Alexander, M. Jacqui and Mohanty, Chandra Talpade (1997) 'Introduction: genealogies, legacies, movements', in Alexander and Mohanty (eds) *Feminist Genealogies*, New York: Routledge, xv–xlii.

Davis, Angela (1983) *Women, Race and Class*, New York: Vintage Books.

Eisenstein, Zillah (1996) *Hatreds: Racialized and Sexualized Conflicts in the 21st Century*, New York: Routledge.

Frankenberg, Ruth (1993) *White Women, Race Matters: The Social Construction of Whiteness*, Minneapolis: The University of Minnesota Press.

Fraser, Nancy (1994) 'Rethinking the public sphere', *Social Text*, 25: 56–90.

Glenn, Evelyn Nakano (1983) 'Racial ethnic women's labor', *Review of Radical Political Economics*, 17(3): 86–108.

Grewal, Inderpal and Kaplan, Caren (1994) *Scattered Hegemonies*, Minneapolis: The University of Minnesota Press.

Kelley, Robin D.G. (1997) *Yo Mamas DisFUNKtional! Fighting the Culture Wars in Urban America*, Boston, MA: Beacon Press.

King, Katie (1994) *Theory in its Feminist Travels*, Bloomington and Indianapolis: Indiana University Press.

Lowe, Lisa (1996) *Immigrant Acts*, Durham and London: Duke University Press.

——— (1997) 'Interview with Angela Davis: reflections on race, class and gender in the USA', in Lisa Lowe and David Lloyd (eds) *The Politics of Culture in the Shadow of Capital*, Durham and London: Duke University Press.

Romero, Mary (1992) *Maid in the U.S.A.*, New York: Routledge.

Sandoval, Chela (1991) 'U.S. Third World feminism: the theory and method of oppositional consciousness in the postmodern world', *Genders*, 10 (Spring): 1–17.

——— (1998) 'Mestizaje as method: feminists of color challenge the canon', in Carla Trujillo (ed.) *Living Chicana Theory*, Berkeley, CA: Third Woman Press, 352–70.

Shohat, Ella (1997) 'Post-Third-Worldist culture: gender, nation, and the cinema', in M. Jacqui Alexander and Chandra Talapade Mohanty (eds) *Feminist Genealogies, Colonial Legacies, Democratic Futures*, New York: Routledge, 183–209.

Spivak, Gayatri (1985) 'The Rani of Sirmur', in F. Barker (ed.) *Europe and its Others*, Vol. 1, Essex: University of Essex.

Stoler, Ann Laura (1995) *Race and the Education of Desire*, Durham: Duke University Press.

Frances R. Aparicio

THE BLACKNESS OF SUGAR: CELIA CRUZ AND THE PERFORMANCE OF (TRANS)NATIONALISM

Abstract

Studies on transnational cultures have shown that local, national identities are not necessarily subordinated to, or erased by, the globalizing forces of the economy. Rather, the local mediates transnational cultures as well as it is transformed by the crossing of cultural boundaries. Likewise, emerging interdisciplinary and cultural studies approaches to Latin(o) popular music examine the ways in which musical production, circulation and reception create cultural spaces that challenge hegemonic notions of national identity and discrete cultural boundaries. This article examines the figure of the Queen of Salsa, Celia Cruz, and the tensions among the multiple, transnational subjectivities that are constituted through her musical repertoire, her performances on stage, the aesthetics of her body, and her public statements in interviews. Having spanned more than sixty years of performances and recordings, Celia Cruz's diverse repertoire and musical selections have served as a performative locus for the negotiations of her Cubanness (her exile and national identity) and a hemispheric, Latin American identity that also includes the United States. Likewise, her construction of blackness as an Afro-Cuban woman transforms and is transformed by her collaborations with African-American musicians and singers, from jazz to hip-hop. Celia Cruz has also crossed racial and cultural boundaries by collaborating with Anglo musicians and by tropicalizing rock music. Her staged persona and her body aesthetics also reveal the fluidity with which the Queen of Latin music assumes diverse racial, national and historical identities while she simultaneously asserts her Cubanness through the use of Spanish on stage. Celia Cruz serves as a complex and intriguing icon of the relational nature of nationalism and transnationalism.

CULTURAL STUDIES 13(2) 1999, 223–236

Keywords

Latin popular music; Latino studies; Cuban nationalism; transnationalism; Celia Cruz; race

O N 16 OCTOBER 1997 the Cuban singer Celia Cruz, known as the Queen of Latin Music, donated a bright orange traditional Cuban rumba dress, a blonde wig and a pair of her unique stage shoes to the permanent collection of the National Museum of American History. What could be seen merely as an entertainer's accessories, these objects point to the unique ways in which Celia Cruz uses her body, in addition to her voice and songs, as a site for performing transnationalism. Together, the three personal accessories serve as icons for the ways in which Celia Cruz has negotiated heterogeneous musical and cultural systems throughout sixty years of making music in Cuba, Latin America, the United States and internationally. The traditional rumbera dress, which suggests her years of singing with La Sonora Matancera, has served to visually construct Celia as a symbol of Cuban national identity and of *afrocubanismo*. For many years, the curious platform shoes without heels were custom-made for her by a Mexican shoemaker, thus indexing her affective and professional ties to Mexico and the larger sense of *latinoamericanismo* (Latin Americanism) that Celia has created through her music. Finally, her blonde wig metonymically reminds us of her incursions into Anglo music, her entry into the international entertainment scene and mainstream Hollywood.

These specific props, however, are only three out of an innumerable repertoire of dresses, shoes, wigs and songs that well illustrate the versatility with which Celia Cruz has entered diverse markets and created different audiences at particular historical moments. If her fame rests on her unique 'deep, metallic contralto' voice and her improvisational skills in the soneo, it is also the result of the diverse repertoires and styles that she has performed and literally embodied (Sabournin, 1986: 553). In an interview with Raúl Fernández (1996), she commented that 'yo me meto en todo; lo que a mí me piden yo canto', adding that she even sang La Macarena at an event in New Orleans [I get into everything; I'll sing anything people want]. This versatility is, to be sure, due to the Cuban singer's genial musical talents that allow her to perform songs without having to rehearse. As Larry Harlow has commented, 'Esa señora es un genio' [That lady is a genius] (Rondón, 1980: 136).

Celia Cruz's repertoire is indeed vast. Her performances and recordings include, among many others, traditional Cuban santería music, pregones, guajiras, Afro-Cuban rumbas, guarachas, mambos and cha-cha-cha, boogaloo and salsa in the 1960s and 1970s, rock en español with Los Fabulosos Cadillacs, Brazilian music, Peruvian folkloric songs, Mexican rancheras, Puerto Rican bombas, and collaborations with Wyclef Jean and David Byrne in the United

Figure 5 Celia Cruz. Photo/Ricardo Betancourt. Reproduced courtesy of RMM Records

States. The stylistic and musical fluidity, coupled with her ever-changing bodily aesthetics, easily wins her audiences out of widely diverse communities. This versatility, facilitated by her musical talent, illustrates the multiple subjectivities that Celia Cruz has constructed for herself. Yet it does not diminish Celia Cruz's subject position which is strongly rooted in the Cuban exile experience. As George Lipsitz (1994: 5) notes, 'even under circumstances of global integration, local identities and affiliations do not disappear. On the contrary, the transnational economy often makes itself felt most powerfully through the reorganization of spaces and the transformation of local experience'. In this short article,

I will trace the tensions between her public ideological position on Cuba and the multiple identities – including blackness – that she assumes and performs through her musical repertoire, professional history, public interviews, and the aesthetic construction of herself as a tropical diva.

As the singer of La Sonora Matancera during the 1950s, Celia Cruz was the female embodiment of Afro-Cuban music and música tropical in Cuba and throughout Latin America. Since her exile in 1961, she has served as the voice of Cuba in a different way. In her song, 'Yo soy la voz' (Cruz and Puente, 1969), the singing subject enumerates the evocative meanings that her voice carries. She is the voice of the Cuba of the past, 'el sabor tropical' [the taste of the tropics], the symbol of the Cuban son, of coffee and of sugar cane. In this song, the Queen of Salsa defines her voice as the vehicle for imagining pre-socialist Cuba and as a tool for articulating a metaphor between the singing subject and the national body of Cuba. If the voice is 'the locus of articulation of an individual's body to language and society' (Furman, 1991: 303), then Celia Cruz's performative Cuban grito, 'azúcar' [sugar] takes on added meaning. The performative use of this signifer emerged at a restaurant in Miami and it has become her universally recognized trademark.[1] Yet it carries within it the history of Cuba's plantation culture, the economics of slavery, and the racial and gender dynamics from which Cuban national identity and popular music emerge (Benítez-Rojo, 1996; Ortiz, 1947 [1995]; Rivero, 1989). Given these subtexts, the symbolic reiteration of the word 'azúcar' reaffirms the role of Celia Cruz's voice and body as an icon of Cuba's African-based heritage and mestizaje. Yet it also serves as a vestigial reminder of the US-dominated capitalist economy that was transformed by socialism, a nostalgic signifier given Celia Cruz's subject position as a Cuban exile.

Her 1998 recording, *Azúcar negra*, and its title song, render the single utterance of 'azúcar' much more complex. While sugar is white, the seemingly oxymoronic metaphor of 'black sugar' foregrounds the traces of slavery behind the national economy of the plantation, a blackness that is indeed reaffirmed in the title song 'Azúcar negra'. The initial, ritualistic African-style drumming in this cut composed by Mario Díaz indexes the genealogy of blackness in Afro-Cuban music. Again, this song establishes a metaphor between Celia as a singing subject and Afro-Cuban culture. When she states that her blood is black sugar and that her skin is marked by the rumba and the bongó, this discourse inscribes Africanness and black agency on her body, the traces of slavery that facilitated the economy of the island. Significantly, the lyrics also identify the singing subject as the daughter of a rich island, foregrounding the association between slavery and capitalism and simultaneously suggesting the nostalgic discourse of the Cuban exile subject.

Celia Cruz's musical repertoire is indeed an expression of afrocubanismo. Afro-Cuban vernacular poetics, including popular religious beliefs such as santería, popular oral traditions such as pregones and street slang, are the stylistic and discursive substance of many of Celia's songs. From the early hits with La Sonora Matancera, such as 'El yerberito moderno' and 'Burundanga' to the famous two-volume recording, *Homenaje a los santos*, which anthologizes some authentic African santería music with modern arrangements of songs dedicated to particular saints, Celia Cruz's music has consistently foregrounded the African legacy in Cuba's music, rhythms and cultural heritage. Her singing in African languages, particularly in lucumí, as in 'Lalle lalle' (Cruz, 1991) and 'Changó "ta veni"' (1989), her rhythmical dialogues with the drums, as in 'Quimbo Quimbumbia' (1969), and songs such as 'Azúcar negra' (1998), 'Bembelequá' (1994), and 'La cumbanchera de Belén' (1989), which foregrounds the figure of the black rumbera and her dancing movements, are all traditional expressions of afrocubanismo at multiple levels. Salsa hits such as 'Quimbara', according to Mayra Santos, 'are basically a call to the dance floor, where the purpose of rhyme, rhythm, and lyrics is to bring to consciousness the act of salsa itself, an act of bonding where audience, dancers, musicians, and singers come together as a community of "entendidos"' (1997: 184). As the Afroboricua writer Mayra Santos suggests here, this particular song by Celia Cruz enacts the ritualistic task of creating a translocal, mulatto and black working-class community through the Afrocuban vernacular poetics and rhythms that inform many of her songs.

If Mayra Santos proposes a 'translocal' definition of salsa anchored in a working-class, mulatto, pan-Caribbean cultural semiotics, Celia Cruz's own definitions of salsa music, on the contrary, have served to reaffirm a pre-socialist Cuban national identity racialized as white. In the continuing debate about the origins, authenticity and ownership of salsa music, Celia's definitions of salsa coincide with many who insist that it is only Cuban music recycled for an international market. In this vein, she has proposed that 'El yerberito moderno', which is a traditional Cuban pregón, is now called salsa. Salsa, for her, is a commercial label that has created a larger audience for Cuban music, for which she is very happy. And while Celia Cruz publicly recognizes the talents and collaborations of Puerto Rican and other Latino musicians in the development of salsa, she insists on conflating it with Cuban music. In an interview with Alberto Nacif (1997), Celia Cruz reveals the connection between this Cubanist definition of salsa and her own experience of exile:

> I have 37 or 38 years outside of my country, and the longing for it is precisely what allows me to conserve that feeling and never lose it. Today that thing that you call, or rather we call (because I'm also doing that) salsa, is nothing more than my Cuban music, variations of the son, but it needed another name so that it could be actualized and be successful. It was around that time that the great Cuban orchestras, which were the truly great exponents of Cuban music, were not allowed to travel to the United States any longer. When that happened, Cuban music was starting to get pushed to the side. This was, of course, because the bands that were playing it were

not around. So then the name salsa came along, and nothing really changed. It was still Cuban music. One of the few things that has changed is perhaps the addition of electronic instruments. In fact the Sonora Matancera didn't use electronic instruments until the very last minute, at which time they incorporated the electric bass. Also there is the fact that a lot of the musicians and the arrangers from today were born in other places like Puerto Rico or New York, for example, Tito Puente, who have also been influenced by jazz, are playing salsa. However, that's not my style. I'll continue with my Cuban music until the last day. You can call it 'salsa' or 'sulso' or whatever you want to call it, it's still Cuban music. I will always have it present within me. I can be here in Mexico or in Venezuela or in Spain or Argentina, and my accent is still a Cuban accent.

(Nacif, 1997: 2)

This lengthy reply is worth quoting since it suggests that Celia Cruz's definition of salsa has more to do with her own cultural deterritorialization than with wanting to deny the musical, stylistic and instrumental innovations of New York Puerto Rican salsa since the 1970s. When she distinguishes her style from that of Tito Puente, she is in fact contradictorily acknowledging that there are diverse styles of salsa under the rubric and that not all music labelled salsa is Cuban music. Yet this statement also reaffirms the fact that one of her most important contributions to the Latin popular music scene in the United States was to bring back, so to speak, the 'Cuban son aspect' (Rondón, 1980) during the salsa boom, what she refers to as her 'Cuban accent' in more metaphorical ways. César Miguel Rondón (1980: 92), in fact, speaks of Celia Cruz as 'la propia guaracha personificada' and calls her influence on salsa 'matancerización salsosa'. Celia's musical style and performances have tropicalized (Aparicio and Chávez-Silverman, 1997) or, to be more specific, 'cubanized' songs and musical numbers from other national traditions, such as 'Cucurrucucú paloma' (1981). Yet Celia's reply, in itself, evinces the ambivalence between the discourse of Cubanness for and by the exiled subject, and the transnational audiences and musical styles that have emerged, ironically, out of her own political and geographical displacement.

Celia Cruz has been very vocal about her exile politics both in interviews and in her own musical repertoire and performances on stage. In interviews she has acknowledged her painful departure from the island and the personal repercussions that the exile status has imposed on her (Fernández, 1996; Nacif, 1997; Rath, 1995). In her recordings, she has consistently included songs that either evoke a pre-socialist Cuba or imagine a post-socialist Cuba, a lyrical and desired reclaiming that has musically vocalized the hegemonic political agenda of the Cuban exile community in Miami.[2] Her stance has been overtly expressed in public performances and has informed, for example, the controversy over the visit of Silvio Rodríguez to Puerto Rico. As the opening act for the Concierto de las Américas in 1994, Celia Cruz sang José Martí's verses and publicly exhorted all presidents to bring Fidel Castro down. This appropriation of José Martí's discourse in the context of liberating Cuba from its socialist state is not unique to Celia Cruz, but a discursive strategy common to many Cuban singers in exile, such as Gloria Estefan and Willie Chirino (Guevara, 1997). With regard to class and race, it is interesting, although not necessarily contradictory, that despite Celia's urban, working-class black origins, she was to become a central spokesperson for the politics of the early, white bourgeois, landholding Cuban exile community. The fact that in Cuba she sang to white audiences helps to explain this stance, since the revolution initially dismantled the economic infrastructure of the music clubs in which La Sonora Matancera performed (Fernández, 1996).

Her exile politics were clearly illustrated during her concert in Ann Arbor, Michigan, in November 1997. Celia responded to the presence of the Cuban community signalled by a large, Cuban flag in the audience. Following the dialogic modes of Afro-Caribbean music and exemplifying the power of her vocality, that is, the 'vital interrelationship between vocalization and audition' (Dunn and Jones, 1994: 2), Celia sang predominantly Cuban music: guajiras, sones, guarachas, mambos, many of them expressing a nostalgic and national sentiment towards Cuba. She picked up a little Cuban flag, which she held in her hand throughout the long performance, and enveloped herself in the large Cuban flag that the Cuban listeners offered her. Interspersed among songs and commentary, Celia would utter in Spanish comments against socialist Cuba and coded allusions about Fidel Castro. Speaking in Spanish during the whole concert in a region where Spanish is far from being a public language, these comments served as coded messages that privileged a particular Cuban exile ideology. Yet they were also received by a Hispanophone or bilingual public who may not have been politically in agreement with her, but who nevertheless enjoyed the politically imbued rhythms and the sonorous arrangements. Indeed, this particular concert established an unprecedented carnival-like environment, a dialogue between the singer and the audience, that fostered free and communal dancing in the aisles, listeners standing up and clapping, and some angry audience members who expected to see the show from their seats undisturbed by a participatory auditorium. Celia Cruz's unique musical style and collective performativity truly tropicalized Hill Auditorium in Ann Arbor, yet this transculturative event was mediated by the discourse of the Cuban exile. Perhaps the Queen of Latin Music felt safe and comfortable expressing her nostalgia for a pre-revolutionary Cuba to a highly responsive, warm and heterogeneous audience in a small, midwest college town far from the Latino politics of either coast. Yet ironically, her political and politicized performance, like her traditional rumbera dresses and the new digitalized recordings of her performances with La Sonora Matancera, serve as visual and sonorous re-creations of that Cuba of the past. The image of 'azúcar negra' comes to mind, as Celia's black body, Afro-Cuban rhythms and voice together indexed the cultural survival of slaves in Cuba while she simultaneously vocalized the discourse of a pro-capitalist, white Cuban bourgeoisie while embodying colonial desire with her blonde wig.

As was recently observed in the *New York Times* (Ojito, 1998), '[I]n an era of crossover pop stars and the relentless Americanization of almost everything, Ms. Cruz . . . is an oddity. She has seen her popularity in this country grow even as she has clung resolutely to her roots, her language and her style.' This contradiction is significant in understanding the relational nature between national and transnational identities. Celia Cruz's insistence on retaining her Spanish after thirty years of residing in the United States, and despite her international fame, also illustrates a strategic nationalism that has not, interestingly, limited her access to a global market that advertises itself as English-only. When she comments publicly that her 'English is not good-looking' in a Caribbean, hispanicized English and insists on using Spanish on stage, she is indeed contributing to the increasing visibility of Spanish as a public language in the United States. Simultaneously, however, Spanish is also a dominant paradigm for *latinidad* that does not always include Latino younger generations nor Anglophone Latinos. In this regard, it can well function as a dominant marker of identity within the larger, Latino community.

Yet Spanish is also Celia's vehicle for vocalizing and constructing a Latin American identity. Her first song, which she performed for a radio amateur show in Havana and which won her a prize, was an Argentinian tango entitled 'Nostalgia'. As the singer for 'Las mulatas de fuego', a group of Cuban dancers who travelled to Mexico and other Latin American countries, Celia Cruz was a key figure in the initial dissemination of the mambo throughout Mexico and, eventually, of música tropical. She toured Mexico with Toña la Negra in 1961 and brought Cuban rhythms and musical genres to many parts of that country (Fernández, 1997). Likewise, her travels with La Sonora Matancera during the 1950s created audiences for Afro-Caribbean music in Colombia, Haiti, Venezuela, Costa Rica and Panama. Her recordings also circulated her vocal and improvisatory talents to all regions of Latin America. Significantly, these early tours cemented the intergenerational popularity that Celia Cruz is currently enjoying in the United States among Latino audiences. Not only US Latino adults who grew up listening to Celia Cruz in their respective countries constitute her Latino market but, as Mirta Ojito (1998) well observes, 'the more recent immigrants, who tend to be younger, attend her concerts buoyed by their own interest in her music but also by curiosity over a woman whose music their parents and grandparents danced to back in the 1950s' (Fernández, 1996; Walsh, 1988). Thus, Celia Cruz's vocality and song repertoire literally create a hemispheric community of Latino and Latin American listeners that crosses generations, national borders and cultural divides. It serves as a vehicle of cultural memory that unifies Latinos, at least temporarily, across age and national borders. In the United States, her performances in Spanish also serve, like Latin popular music, as public spaces where a colonized cultural identity is performed decolonizing itself, reaffirming its presence. That Celia

Cruz's construction of *latinidad* within the United States has been facilitated by her past Latin American appearances reveals how the transnational circulation of music, in its production, performance and audition, is already always embedded in local experiences of national identities.

If within salsa music Celia Cruz's performances and recordings represent the traditional, Cuban sound, she has also embraced musical genres from diverse Latin American regions and folklores, such as Peruvian waltzes, Mexican boleros, Uruguayan songs, Dominican merengues and Puerto Rican bombas, thus hybridizing her own Cuban music with other Latin American folkloric rhythms and tunes. It was Celia who took Chabuca Granda's 'La flor de canela' into Mexico in 1957, where it was first recorded by los Hermanos Silva (Fernández, 1996). She has also interpreted Ismael Rivera's hits (Cruz, 1992), performed 'La cama de piedra' in her Mexican tours, and has two recordings dedicated to Mexico.[3] She has recorded the Argentinian Palito Ortega's Nueva Ola hit, 'Corazón contento' from the 1970s (Cruz and Puente, 1969) and in 1988 she recorded 'Vasos vacíos' with *Los fabulosos Cadillacs*, entering the world of rock en español (Cruz *et al.*, 1997). In her stage appearances, she has played an important role as a cultural ambassador to Latin America throughout the world, having toured Europe, Japan, Greece, Finland, Africa, and most countries in Latin America, including Brazil. When Jean Franco (1994: 19) writes that Celia Cruz is the 'apostle of latinity' and that, as a singer, she has played the role of a Simón Bolívar in unifying Latin American countries, the Latin Americanist critic recognizes the alternative political power of popular culture. Celia's vocality in building a sense of community across national borders exemplifies what George Lipsitz (1994: 17) has described as 'the potential of popular culture as a mechanism of communication and education, as a site for experimentation with cultural and social roles not yet possible in politics'.

Much of this *latinidad* associated with Celia Cruz, however, has been imagined and constructed outside Cuba and the geopolitical borders of Latin America. The years of Celia's growing fame were during the 1970s, when she performed with Willie Colón and Johnny Pacheco. Her record with the Dominican Johnny Pacheco, *Celia y Johnny*, according to Raúl Fernández (1996), has been one of the most anthological Latin American repertoires ever recorded in the salsa industry. It includes the Brazilian hit, 'Usted abusó', Zambúllete, an Uruguayan song that Celia sings to Panama, and other hits such as 'Vieja Luna', the Peruvian 'Toromata', and 'Quimbara' (Rondón, 1980). The dialectics, then, between national and pan-American identities in the salsa industry resist fixed categorizations or boundaries. New York salsa during the 1970s responded both to local Puerto Rican experiences in the barrio as much as it created pan-Latino audiences in the United States and Latin America. New York itself, as Ruth Glasser (1995) has documented, has been, historically, a site of pan-Caribbean and Latin American musical borrowings and collaborations that produced what has been traditionally considered to be Puerto Rican national or even nationalist music. Yet, as the songs

'Pasaporte latinoamericano' (Cruz, 1998) and 'Latinos en Estados Unidos' (Cruz and Colón, 1981) suggest, Celia sings a Latina identity that emerges out of homogenizing the diverse experiences of migration and of cultural deterritorialization of Latin Americans, rendering them synonymous with the Cuban exile and its constructed otherness of the United States and of English. Through these songs, which she ultimately selects, she is resolving some of the ambivalences between her constructions of Cubanness and the transnational dimensions of her audiences and reconciling the fact that the US Latino market paved the way for her growing fame and mainstreaming.[4]

In the United States, Celia's traditional afrocubanismo is transformed in relation to the African-American community, thus extending this nationally based racial identity into hemispheric dimensions. Her hairstyles, for one, suggest these diasporic identities. During the 1970s she wore dreadlocks in a concert in Colombia and on the album cover of *Celia y Willie* (1981). Assuming blackness in the United States context, she also wore an Afro hairstyle in the album *Recordando el ayer* [Remembering the past] (Cruz, 1976) to signal the reaffirmation of the African heritage in her music. The politics of her hair also served as a visual marker of her solidarity with the claims of the black movement and of 'black is beautiful', a solidarity which Salsa music reaffirmed through its articulation with the political and social movements of the Young Lords and the Black Panthers (Pagán, 1997). In the 1960s, Celia performed boogaloos and in the 1990s she collaborated with The Fugees' Wyclef Jean in his hip-hop version of 'Guantanamera' (1997). Celia's prelude in Spanish of the traditional national song based on José Martí's verses assumes solidarity with African-American cultural expressions, yet these lyrics are also radically resemanticized by Wyclef Jean as they are overlaid with the hip-hop song that transforms the signifier Guantanamera into a Latina woman's name in Spanish Harlem and the song into a dialogue of desire between her and the singer. Like the African drumming in 'Azúcar negra', Celia's 'Guantanamera' has become one of the foundational lyrics for hip-hop music, a genealogy that is also evident in Wyclef Jean's own Afro-Cuban heritage.

Celia explained in an interview (Fernández, 1996) that in the Cuba of the 1950s she had heard, at a distance, 'of jazz in the United States, of Cab Calloway, the film Stormy Weather', yet she was 'never too interested'. By 1989 her concert at the Abyssinian Baptist Church in Harlem on 21 October 'underscored the connections between the various outposts of the African diaspora in the New World' (Watrous, 1989: 62). On stage with Mario Bauzá's orchestra, Tito Puente on the timbales and Chico O'Farill, Celia Cruz indeed embodied the historical connections between Afro-Cuban rhythms and African-American jazz.

Perhaps the most illuminating example of the transnational circulation of Afro-Caribbean music is the fact that, from her exile in the United States, Celia Cruz herself has influenced musicians in Cuba. Her role as a musical 'transmigrant' (Basch *et al.*, 1994) is clearly evidenced in her interview with Alberto Nacif, who tells the Cuban singer the following anecdote:

A couple of years ago when I was in Chicago for the last tour of the Muñequitos de Matanzas, I had six of them piled into my car, and as we were going to eat some dinner and then spend some time walking through the downtown Chicago area, I happened to put in a copy of your CD *Azúcar Negra* in the car, and they absolutely went crazy to hear your voice and to hear the quality of music that you were singing. They all asked me to make them copies for themselves, and refused to leave the car, even though we were all hungry, until the CD was done playing. That says a lot about the effect that you still have on the people of Cuba.

(Nacif, 1997: 2)

Celia responded that she has never met Los Muñequitos de Matanzas but that she hears they're very good. Despite the rigid boundaries established by the US embargo on Cuba and Celia's own ideological boundaries, the members of socialist Cuba's most important folkloric Afro-Cuban group listen to Celia's homage to afrocubanismo in 'Azúcar negra' inside a car in Chicago, a city renowned for its jazz and blues. Mediated through CD technology, this musical encounter in Chicago between the music of the two Cubas attests to the diasporic and hemispheric nature of musical migrations.

A final instance of Celia's multiple musical hybridities is her incursion into Anglo music, particularly rock, and her mainstreamed presence in Hollywood and the US entertainment market, a hybridity signalled by her reiterated use of her blonde wigs. Before coming to the United States, her recording with La Sonora Matancera of 'Rock and roll' (1988), a guaracha hybridized with rock and roll rhythms, announces the emergence of rock and its entrance into Cuba, yet it locates it as the new rhythm that follows the mambo and the cha-cha-cha. This musical genealogy and the use of English in the song blurs the binaries that have been imposed between Latin music and rock. If anything, it proposes that rock is part of the musical productions of the African diaspora in the Americas more than a sign of the cultural divides between the imperial Anglo and the colonized Latin American cultures. Celia's participation in the *Tropical Tribute to the Beatles* overtly articulates the connections between rock and Afro-Caribbean musics and the participation of Latino musicians in the development of rock, historically deemed as imperialist music from the perspective of Latin America. As Ralph Mercado (1996) writes in the liner notes, the unquestionable influence of the mambo and of Latin/Cuban jazz and rhythms during the 1950s and 1960s, the use of the clave beat in many of The Beatles songs, and the cha-cha-cha beat in 'And I Love Her' and 'Obladi Oblada', are some of the traces of Latin influence in the compositions of 'the Fabulous Four'. Although this recording was received with lukewarm support by the Latino public, it is an important recognition of the underlying presence of Afro-Caribbean musical contributions to rock music, historically racialized as white from the Latin American perspective. Celia's interpretation of 'Obladi Oblada' shows the cyclical forces of musical migrations, for its Spanish lyrics about the love between Celia and her husband, Pedro Knight, in addition to the salsa rhythms and arrangements, tropicalize the original text. The Spanish, salsified versions of classics such as 'I Want to Hold your Hand' and 'Can't Buy me Love' and the interlingual soneos in the English songs speak to the local, Latino reality, thus repeating rock with a difference.

In terms of her 'spectacular body' (Parker *et al.*, 1992: 12), that is, the ways in which Celia Cruz's bodily aesthetics speak to the dialectics between national and transnational locations, the blonde wigs do not necessarily whiten Celia's repertoire but are, on the contrary, transculturated by her dark skin, her Spanish vocals, and the song repertoires that reaffirm afrocubanismo, a Cuban exile perspective and a hemispheric *latinidad*. Her changing fashions, her flashy style, glamorous, elegant, and, to some, extravagant stage costumes, serve as visual traces of social history since the 1950s. Her tropicalized, baroque and colourful attire serve as a visual reaffirmation of the Caribbean presence in the United States while it simultaneously makes Celia the embodiment of transnationalism. The fluidity with which the Reina Rumba imagines and reimagines herself as Afro-Cuban, Latin American, Latina and international may be easily dismissed as marketing strategies or as an instance of postmodernism. Rather, I propose that these multiple subjectivities and performative identities do not necessarily dilute or preclude national identities, but in fact are interpellated by them. Celia Cruz's singing and bodily aesthetics suggest more complex modes of understanding the cultural implications of the migrations of Latin popular music.

Notes

1   According to Celia Cruz, once, when she was having lunch at a Cuban restaurant in Miami, the waiter asked her if she wanted Cuban coffee with or without sugar. She thought that was very strange given the fact that Cuban coffee is very strong and tastes bitter without sugar. So, she told him, 'With sugar! With sugar, my dear boy!' She told the story to her audience afterwards and she began screaming 'Azúcar, azúcar' during her performances. This information appeared in the Website http://tyrone.hob.com/events/960315cruz/ (3-15-96).

2   Songs such as 'De la Habana hasta aquí' (1998), 'Yo regresaré' (1969), 'Yo soy la voz' (1969), y 'Cuando Cuba se acabe de liberar' (1994), are but some examples of both the nostalgic and utopic discourses around Cuba's liberation.

3   Among her innumerable recordings, see *México qué grande eres*, Secco SCLP 9227, and *A ti, México*, Tico, SLP 1164. No dates were available.

4   Based on his extensive interview with Celia Cruz, Raúl Fernández (1997) writes that Celia has not just been a singer, but that she has personally chosen each and every one of the hits that have become a success, at times against the wishes of composers, musicians and producers. In this light, her personal ideologies highly inform her musical selections.

References

Aparicio, Frances and Chávez-Silverman, Susana (eds) (1997) *Tropicalizations: Transcultural Representations of Latinidad*, Hanover and London: University Press of New England.

Basch, Linda, Glick Schiller, Nina and Cristina Szanton Blanc (1994) *Nations Unbound: Transnational Projects, Postcolonial Predicaments, and Deterritorialized Nation-States*, Langhorne, PA: Gordon and Breach.

Benítez-Rojo, Antonio (1996) *The Repeating Island: The Caribbean and the Postmodern Condition*, Durham and London: Duke University Press.

Cruz, Celia (1976) Celia, Johnny, Justo and Papo: *Recordando el ayer*, Vaya Records, LPS 88722.

—— (1988) *La reina del ritmo*, Peerless, SA de CV PCD-011–3.

—— (1989) *La incomparable Celia con la Sonora Matancera*, Palladium Latin Jazz and Dance Records, PCD-133.

—— (1991) *La dinámica Celia Cruz con la Sonora Matancera*, Seeco Tropical, 0019–2.

—— (1992) *Tributo a Ismael Rivera: Celia Cruz*, Vaya Records, JMVS 110.

—— (1994) *Irrepetible*, RMM Records, CDZ 81452.

—— (1998) *Azúcar negra*, RMM Records, RMD 80985.

Cruz, Celia and Colón, Willie (1981) *Celia y Willie*, Vaya Records, JMVS 93.

Cruz, Celia and Puente, Tito (1969) *Quimbo Quimbumbia*, Tico Records, TRSLP 1193.

Cruz, Celia *et al*. (1996) *Tropical Tribute to The Beatles*, RMM Records, RMD 82011.

Cruz, Celia *et al*. (1997) *Celia's Duets*, RMM Records, RMD 82201.

Dunn, Leslie C. and Jones, Nancy A. (1994) 'Introduction', in *Embodied Voices: Representing Female Vocality in Western Culture*, Cambridge: Cambridge University Press.

Fernández, Raúl (1996) Interview with Celia Cruz, 15 September, Hollywood, CA: Jazz Oral History Project, The Smithsonian Institution.

—— (1997) 'Celia Cruz: artista de América Latina', *Deslinde*, 21, July/September: 102–21.

Franco, Jean (1994) 'What's left of the intelligentsia? The uncertain future of the printed word', *NACLA Report on the Americas*, 28(2): 16–21.

Furman, Nelly (1991) 'Opera, or the staging of the voice', *Cambridge Opera Journal*, 3(3): 303.

Glasser, Ruth (1995) *My Music is my Flag: Puerto Rican Musicians and their New York Communities, 1917–1940*, Berkeley: University of California Press.

Guevara, Gema (1997) 'La Cuba de ayer/La Cuba de hoy: the politics of music in the Cuban-American community'. The Rhythms of Culture: Dancing to Las Américas. International Research Conference on Popular Music in Latin(o) America, 21–22 March , University of Michigan, Ann Arbor.

Jean, Wyclef (1997) *The Carnival*, Columbia Records, 487442–2.

Lipsitz, George (1994) *Dangerous Crossroads: Popular Music, Postmodernism, and the Poetics of Place*, New York and London: Verso.

Mercado, Ralph (1996) 'Introduction' to *Tropical Tribute to The Beatles*, RMM Records, RMD 82011.

Nacif, Alberto (1997) Interview with Celia Cruz (unpublished) 21 October, Ann Arbor, Michigan.

Ojito, Mirta (1998) 'Celia Cruz: longtime Salsa star with rising appeal', *New York Times*, 27 June.

Ortiz, Fernando (1947[1995]) *Cuban Counterpoint: Tobacco and Sugar*, trans. Harriet de Onís, Durham and London: Duke University Press.

Pagán, Adam (1997) 'Indestructible!: Diasporican identity, the Young Lords Party, and the cultural politics of music – a brief synthesis, 1960s–1970s', The Rhythms of Culture: Dancing to Las Américas. International Research Conference on Popular Music in Latin(o) America, 21–22 March, University of Michigan, Ann Arbor.

Parker, Andrew, Russo, Mary, Sommer, Doris and Yaeger, Patricia (1992) 'Introduction' to *Nationalisms and Sexualities*, New York: Routledge.

Rath, Derek (1995) 'Celia Cruz: legendary lady of Latin music', *The Beat*, 14(6): 42–5.

Rivero, Eliana (1989) 'From immigrants to ethnics: Cuban women writers in the U.S.', in A. Horno-Delgado *et al.* (eds) *Breaking Boundaries: Latina Writings and Critical Readings*, Amherst: The University of Massachusetts Press.

Rondón, César Miguel (1980) *El libro de la Salsa: Crónica de la música del Caribe urbano*, Caracas, Venezuela: Editorial Arte.

Sabournin, Tony (1986) 'Celia Cruz', in H. Wiley Hitchcock and S. Sadie (eds) *The New Grove Dictionary of American Music*, London: Macmillan.

Santos, Mayra (1997) 'Salsa as translocation', in C. Fraser Delgado and J.E. Muñoz (eds) *Everynight Life: Culture and Dance in Latin/o America*, Durham: Duke University Press.

Walsh, Michael (1988) 'Shake your body', *Time*, 11 July: 50–2.

Watrous, Peter (1989) 'Celia Cruz takes Cuba to Harlem', *New York Times*, 29 October: 62.

Lisa Sánchez González

RECLAIMING SALSA[1]

Abstract

Recent scholarship on representational politics in popular music tends to dwell on the macropolitical entailments of contradictory desires acted out through the consumerization of culture within the globalized circuitry of supranational capitalism. This article takes a micropolitical look at what salsa means for working-class Puerto Ricans in the colonial diaspora, positing salsa as a musical culture that fuels, and is fuelled by, the organic intelligence of its practitioners. Comparatively analysing the performative content and contexts of two albums produced at the symbolic juncture of the Quincentennial (1992) – Willie Colón's *Hecho in Puerto Rico* and Rubén Blades' *Amor y Control* – and sharing an auto-ethnographical account of experiences with salsa music in the Puerto Rican colonial diaspora, this article explores the cultural politics obtained between mainstream appropriations of Latin musical cultures and salsa within the working-class communities who created it. Thus shifting the critical lens from above to below, the most salient concerns become the ethical dimensions of subaltern (kin)aesthetics and knowledges, which can be charted alongside the overt rejection of consumerist assimilation, the conscious racialization of cultural agency and other articulations of liberatory desire.

Keywords

salsa; critical race studies; colonial diasporas; Willie Colón; Rubén Blades; aesthetics

> Eu não acredito num deus que não dance.
> Não acredito num fiel que não mexa.[2]

SALSA MUSIC WITHIN THE Puerto Rican diaspora helps us maintain an intimacy with our pasts and a living connection to our present, orchestrating a coherently embodied sensibility that can only be fully understood somewhere beyond the purely discursive dimensions of Puerto Rican and Afro-Caribbean cultural history.[3] Salsa was born in the Puerto Rican colonial diaspora during the first half of the twentieth century, and raised among segregated communities of Puerto Ricans, Cubans, African Americans and a variety of Caribbean peoples in and around Manhattan, whose rich aesthetic traditions coalesced in unique performative logics and logistics.[4] In the face (and fists) of brutally dehumanizing pressures, musical performance was cultivated within these communities as a realm of irremediable signification that challenged the whole social fact of racism in the US.[5] Emerging in a moment when disparate but analogous histories of forced relocations, economic hardship and survival met, salsa flourished in the wake of the Depression as a Puerto Rican inflected diasporic praxis in New York City.[6]

At home (so to speak) in the colonial diaspora, salsa creates performative trenches that resist reduction to simple structural frames of feeling or experience. Like other mainland Puerto Rican cultural texts – the rhythmic intertextuality of Miguel Piñero's, María Umpierre-Herrera's and Martín Espada's poetry, the quasi-psychotic dreamwork of novelists Irene Vilar and Ed Vega, or the artwork of Pepón Osorio and Jean-Michel Basquiat – salsa is a singularized visible, audible and sensual aspect of our yearning to construe ourselves as dynamic but integral subjects in subaltern transnational context, instigating articulations of 'poetics and poesis' (aesthetics and the aesthetic process) that ultimately disrespect, perforce, the usual '(pre)occupied' generic borders and criteria drawn by industrial and institutional authorities (Zamudio-Taylor, 1993: 18). On the philosophical plateau, our artists dialogue in modes which contest the Euro-North American modern(ist) rifts between ethics and aesthetics, and between culture and politics (Gilroy, 1993: 136).

Cultural critics in the US have lingered on how salsa as an erstwhile 'authentic' cultural form has been transferred, translated, transculturated and sold all over the world via multinational corporations. For some of these critics, the consumerization of Puerto Rican music is charged with positive 'anti-essentialist' lessons for people of colour around the world (Lipsitz, 1994: 84). For others, this trend induces a plurality of ideological positions among listeners who interpret the music in their distinctive contexts.[7] Still others infer that salsa is merely the Afro-Cuban *son* plagiarized and commodified by Puerto Ricans, who are erroneously presumed to be 'White' and are thus bereft of any genuine virtuosity within the African-diasporic tradition.[8]

This is the context surrounding the proposal that salsa is merely a 'commercial label' that can convert an entire spectrum of local musical contributions and styles into an easily (and perfidiously) marketable commodity (Duany, 1992: 72). Certainly, Puerto Rican salsa is subjected to many of the marketing strategies that Nestor García Canclini (1993: vii ff.) describes in the case of Mexican popular art. These strategies de-emphasize cultural histories and conceal the racial inequalities behind the artwork packaged as 'folk' or 'indigenous' crafts, which are sold as curious commodities for outsiders. The logic here entails the dehumanizing compulsion 'to recognize popular creations but not the people who make them, to rate them only in terms of profitability'. Tellingly, this commodification process is not merely a question of profits, but is also entangled in a type of retrograde cultural voyeuristic looting; a tendency whose popular musical equivalent would be Paul Simon's or David Byrne's pillaging of sounds, rhythms, tonalities and harmonies from Caribbean and African artists as exotic foils for North American pop. Canclini underscores the general method of contorting specific cultural modes of expression into the centuries-old binary of civilization vs. barbarism. 'The popular is another name for the primitive,' Canclini explains, 'an obstacle to be removed or a new category of commodities to help increase sales.' The lure for the consumer-tourist here reads as a subversion and sublimation of cultural traditions s/he refuses to respect, creating a primitivist kitsch commodity fetishism, where buyers purchase 'testimonies to the superiority of their own society' and 'symbols . . . of their own purchasing power'. Indeed, as Yúdice *et al.* point out, the 'ideological veneer of pluralism admits difference' in the Americas, as long as the way in which the Other is articulated does not pose a 'threat to state and market systems' (1992: x).

My take on salsa as a 'native'[9] born and raised within the working-class Puerto Rican diaspora interrupts these macropolitical theories of globalization (if only for a moment), pausing to consider from below the ways in which salsa still performs a (kin)aesthetic function irreducible to a commodity fetish, a function that prompts and re-articulates embodied forms of knowledge and desire that cannot be bought, sold, claimed or learned by proxy. The salsa I know *te agita, te llama*, it agitates you and invites you to become part of the music, part of its whole social fact in a mindful, intimate and powerful spiritual-physical Gestalt. Moving *p'acá y p'allá*, the *clave* (prime rhythm) inspires and is inspired by the syncopated motion between the dancers and the dance, between the lyrical production of meaning and everyday experience, between the subject interpolated by this performative commotion and a collectivized, phenomenal and epiphenomenological colonial community. *P'acá y p'allá* means right here, over there and everywhere in between, marking the diaspora's specific geopolitical struggle to survive *in style*. For this diaspora it can mean a concerted articulation of hope between San Juan and New York or even Los Angeles, our homespun stopovers in exile, homes away from home away from a colonized island that is, and is more than, a metaphor for eviction.

This Gestalt cannot be attained by superficial forms of capitalist tourism, enabled by a few drinks and a dance lesson, a CD and a fine stereo, talking to 'natives', or even decades of research in books, magazines and liner notes: the pleasure and anguish of our music is part of an inimitable intentionality born from the ways in which we negotiate our unique being-in-the-world. Salsa is this community in motion and metaphor, abstracted by lyric and made flesh by rhythm, as it glides between the *p'acá*, the whole context of its immediate interaction – the dancing, improvisations and joy we experience, as well as the racism, exploitation, sorrow and violence we encounter every day – and the *p'allá*, a sociophilosophical projection of past, present and future possibilities, an audaciously hopeful realm that is just beyond reach but so close you can feel it coming. This yearning and the work invested in sustaining it is similar to Paul Gilroy's (1993: 133) discussion of the moral dimensions of music in the Anglophone African diaspora; that is, 'by posing the world as it is against the world as the racially subordinated would like it to be, this musical culture supplies a great deal of the courage required to go on living in the present'. And with courage comes strength, conviction, focus and many other intangible ingredients that are imperative for sustaining liberatory desire.

But this is not to say that salsa can be transparently tagged as a social movement *per se*, whose dialectical friction creates tendencies we can cite as liberatory guarantees. Nor can it be flattened into a map of purely ideological positions that are (meta)discursively at play with and against each other. Rather the music, in all its performative complexity, attests to an organically intelligent aesthetic form, one that gorgeously and hungrily festers on the underbelly of the imperial beast, rhyzomatically reproducing itself on its most receptive hosts, and transforming the body's mind in a powerful will-to-beauty.[10] In this sense and mindful sensuality, the consumerization of salsa may very well prove to be an impotent antidote among those for whom it really matters.

To begin tracing the formal terms and sociorhythmic logistics of these engagements, the next section of this article offers an analysis of the performative content and contexts of two albums marketed in the early 1990s by Miami-based Sony Discos, one of the world's largest salsa distributors. These albums were produced by two salseros who enjoy reputations as socially conscious musicians, Willie Colón and Rubén Blades, whose respective projects respond to the symbolic juncture of 1492/1992. Following this comparison is an auto-ethnographic narrative which, in the scripting of this cultural critique, situates my own diasporically cultivated knowledge of salsa music and my experiential understanding of its consumerization in urban North America.

Y por eso canta Willie Colón (This is why Willie Colón Sings)

Willie Colón is one of the last of the old-school *soneros*. His 1993 album *Hecho en Puerto Rico* (Made in Puerto Rico), explores the current *cuadros* (tableaux) of Puerto Rican life in the US. In the piece entitled '*Por eso canto*' ('This is Why I Sing'), Colón explains his project as one of *denunciando*, or declaring and denouncing, the materially and ideationally oppressive side of life in the Puerto Rican community specifically. In his words, '*hablar al cantar es denunciar y pensar*', or 'speaking in song is to denounce and think'. The lyrics here provide a meta-critical explication of this role of lyric storytelling:

Figure 6 Willie Colón. From Website. Reproduced courtesy of Willie Colón

I can't silence myself and deny what's going on around me,
Nor ignore all those who suffer miserably.
Singing for singing's sake makes no sense;
I want to sing because I feel a responsibility.

I can't silence myself knowing what's going wrong,
Nor look away for fear of what folks may say.
Singing for singing's sake is just repeating a bunch of words,
But speaking in song is to converse with the soul.[11]

To sing, for Colón, is to fulfil an obligation to his people and his conscience. 'Singing for singing's sake,' he explains, is an empty gesture, but giving voice to his audience as a collective is 'to converse with the soul.' As this conversation unfolds, Colón posits the following: that his message reflects the reality of the *barrio* (neighbourhood), that he is singing for his audience *p'acá*, for their '*sentimientos*' – their feelings – and to reach even further *p'allá*, to '*tantas cosas hermosas*' – so many beautiful things – he feels compelled to project. Like the central speaker in the Taíno *areíto* and Afro-Antillean *bomba*, Colón makes music into social commentary, and calls for action with '*echen p'alante, somos latinos*' – 'go for it, we are Latinos'.

This voice presents ideas for consideration, while the music leaves spaces open for vocal and physical response, thereby creating a dialogue. But the success of the communicative act – the declaration, denunciation and analysis – depends on how the audience responds. Ultimately, the audience must carry the song into the dance, as Colón's piece builds to an improvisational break that leads to its closing moment.

As in *bomba*, and other genres that evolved in Puerto Rico's coastal slave communities, the drums here speak to the dancer, punctuating the dialogue, just as the *clave* itself forms a percussive call and response rhythm. Meanwhile the singer, the audience or the chorus will goad the dancer with interjections specific to music. The interjections Colón uses in his breaks – such as *jele* and *yimboró* – are incorporated improvisational elements of this African oral/musical tradition. Importantly, antiphony is not restricted to the vocals, but underlies the performative logic in its totality.

This song reflects not only a strong connection with the syncretic styles of Puerto Rican orature, but also shuttles between the *p'acá y p'allá* of daily life and the hopeful possibilities of collective agency, of the individual's and the community's potential futures, which is conceptualized as a project of resistance.[12] Each song on the album presents thoughtful ideas about things like romantic love ('*Idilio*'/'Idyll'), underemployment ('*Buscando trabajo*'/'Looking for Work'), and problematic relationships ('*Desde hoy*'/'From Now On,' '*Yo te podrí a decir*'/'I Could Tell You'), all of which position the reality of difficult predicaments in quotidian life against creative, hopeful solutions, portraying subaltern subjects with respect and assuming their culturally specific intelligence and knowledge. And most importantly, the aesthetic meanings of the performance depend on the active agency of the audience, whose dialogic and diarhythmic response fuels, and is fuelled by, the music in an elaborate process of embodied communication.

¿Pero por qué, Rubén Blades? (But why, Rubén Blades?)

In striking contrast to Willie Colón, Rubén Blades enunciates a very different sociocultural motivation in his 1992 solo album, *Amor y control* (*Love and Control*). The comparison between Colón and Blades is particularly relevant, because

Colón was in fact Blades' musical mentor; the two collaborated for years (and still do on occasion) though Blades has become more of a commercial success outside the East Coast enclave within which he started his salsa career.[13]

Many of the pieces included in *Amor y control* are rather humorous in the grimmest Latin American mode. In this sense the work does reflect certain oral and written traditions, and many current trends in Latin American fiction as well. We could compare Blades' brand of bitter irony with, for example, the writing of Ana Lydia Vega, Luis Rafael Sánchez, Alejo Carpentier and Gabriel García Márquez. Yet the album has a certain abstracted musical style that disenfranchises the audience, forming a modality quite different from Colón's dialogic and diarhythmic engagement. Likewise, its mode of storytelling evinces an attitude that is arguably complicit with the status quo, resembling the missionary posturing of some strains of First World style liberalism.

For Blades, at least on this album, the *p'acá* is explored in gruesome snapshots of death, despair and hopelessness for the characters in the stories he tells. Consider how, for example, an unemployed man is killed while trying to rob a bank with his child's water pistol ('*Adán García*'/'Adam García') while glowing children die of radiation poisoning after playing with a canister of nuclear waste ('*El Cilindro*'/'The Cylinder'). Unlike Colón, whose songs about daily travail include characters who assess the day's losses but cling to the optimistic hope of a better tomorrow, Blades elaborates tales that evoke images of helpless victims caught in a hemispheric web of poverty and apocalyptic degeneration.

Blades dedicates his album to his mother, whose terminal cancer he discusses in the songs '*Canto a la muerte*' ('Song for Death') and '*Canto a la Madre*' ('Song for Mother'). Here, as in many of the pieces, death represents an oddly liberatory pathos, which underscores the album's reflections on the 500th anniversary of the Spanish Conquest. This broad thematic projects a quasi-historical terrain *p'allá*: The cover photo has three Spanish galleons, presumably Christopher Columbus' *Niña, Pinta* and *Santa María*, approaching what seems to be a Caribbean coastline (in flames), while songs such as '*El Sub-D*' ('The Under-D[eveloped World]') and '*Naturaleza Muerta*' ('Dead Nature') pose as musical assessments of Latin America's current malaise of 'underdevelopment' and ecological disaster.

This musical disengagement and narrative complaisance are most clearly expressed in the album's final song, '*Conmemorando*' ('Commemorating'), which is Blades' catchword for his own project of recuperating the good, the bad and the ugly in his re-evaluation of Latin America's post-Colombian history.[14] In this song, Blades is critical of the exaggerated celebrations that marked *Día de la Raza* ('Columbus Day' in the US) all over Latin America in 1992. Yet here, unlike Colón's antiphonic strategies, the story is downloaded on to the music, with few improvisational breaks, no dialogic motion between voices (except for the sombre repetition of a medieval sounding chorus) and no space for interlocution. Furthermore, the message, like the music, distances itself from the issues it broaches, offering a functionalist reading of power relations in the Americas:

> The positive and negative get confused
> in the significance of 1492.
> Today, and without trying to offend those who disagree,
> I commemorate, but won't celebrate.[15]

The spirit of Blades' remarks are conciliatory. Throughout the song he refers to the atrocities of the 'Conquest', most notably the genocide of the indigenous peoples of the Americas, yet he sketches into the historical panorama a portrait of Christopher Columbus as a man 'made omnipotent by his faith', and rationalizes what he calls Castile and Aragon's imperialism with the mixed intentions – good and bad – of New World mercenaries and colonists. His strategy of con-memorando, of remembering with – and not against – the grain of history, not only lacks the urgency of Willie Colón's *denunciando* strategy, but seems a large step to the right of Blades' own earlier albums with *Son del Solar*.[16]

The creative subversions among Puerto Rican musicians have much in common with the music of a number of other popular Latin American performers. To reference perhaps the most obvious example, Juan Luis Guerra's work has critical trajectories analogous to Colón's. Guerra's apostrophe of the Taíno language in his 1992 *Areito*, along with the album's (metaphorical) claims to an incendiary Black/White/Taíno Caribbean identity, attest to a certain '*pan-Caribeña/o*'[17] sensibility that effectively (and progressively) blends distinct cultural experiences and rhythmic traditions in the Caribbean diaspora *without* losing sight of the historical roots of racism, poverty and Caribbean mal-development in the process.

This renaming and reinvention of a syncretic, diasporic pan-Caribbean subjectivity within music can very easily be erased by corporate interests that have, after all, honed a peculiar expertise in enticing general audiences to recognize Caribbean aesthetics only in terms of bright, exotic tropes that foment tourism. But while this imperial *joyeux tropiques* imaginary is a strong affective lure for cultural cannibals, there is a positive and active desire at work within the Caribbean diaspora that presides over the production of meaning among ourselves. Thus, in closing, my narrative will explore the entailments of contradictory desires and social practices as they erupt in contemporary urban North American salsa venues, offering a glimpse at how, despite awesome forces of over-determination, Puerto Ricans in the diaspora manage to overcome the commodification of our historical selves.

Conclusion: A restless 'native', in the gates, writes home

As a Boricua raised in Los Angeles, I learned salsa in my home and among our extended family. The music itself has been for me another home in what I came to understand as a species of exile, as part of the legacy of the Puerto Rican working-class diaspora. Faced with a confusing and violent melange of racist-sexism[18] in Southern California's public sphere, in which the colonial relationship betwen the US and Puerto Rico was never broached in school books, newspapers and television, and in which Puerto Rico's diasporic culture was never explored or celebrated, what I knew of Puerto Ricanity was always grounded in the relatively unconfusing environment my family cultivated at home. Consequently our familial soundtracks became objective correlatives for love, belonging and a specifically Puerto Rican diasporic aesthetic we could own, perform, share and reshape as circumstances demanded, safely and on our own terms. This kind of aesthetic praxis is a precious improvisational legacy of not only the Puerto Rican colonial diaspora but the majority of this continent's population as well – its working-poor indigenous, black and other definitively racialized castes – attesting to centuries of not merely surviving the terror of conquest, slavery and colonization, but of guarding and revamping our own understandings of aesthetic-ethical desire under the most extreme duress.[19]

In the hope of this kind of aesthetic collaboration, I enthusiastically explored the LA salsa circuit as an adult. But, sadly, here is precisely where the collusion with the logic of transnational capital begins to prevail. These clubs – East Side, West Side, Suburban and Downtown – appear to have highjacked salsa to create an atmosphere of elitism and conservative values. I have rarely run across other Puerto Ricans at these clubs, although the houses bill such events as '*Noche Caribeña*' ('Caribbean Night'), '*Salsa Tropical*' ('Tropical Salsa') and '*Festival Borinqueño*' ('Boricua Festival'). DJs seem to design their play lists for an odd mix of nationalities in the audience, whose most enthusiastic collective responses are elicited by refrains such as '*que se vayan p'al carajo, de Cuba los comunistas*'.[20] These clubs also tend to be racist, barring darker-skinned clientele from entry with a number of policies, while the high cost of admission and selectively enforced dress codes ensure that only those who can afford the charade of bourgeois success can enter. Meanwhile *merengues*, *puntas* and *salsas* with lyrics such as '*el negro allí, el negro sigue allí*' ('the darkie over there, the darkie keeps it up over there') and '*el negro bembón*' ('the darkie with the big bottom lip') are popular standards.

And yet, every few months or so I used to pay cash to enter and dance in these clubs anyway, despite the fact that they disgusted me: the hopeful desire for cultural collaboration in the public sphere overrode my misgivings, and I persisted. Eventually I learned that chances were I would end up at the end of the night piqued and often harassed, but even so I kept going with friends I could trust, motivated in part by a righteous sense of entitlement over the music, often making faces on the dance floor and otherwise mocking and limiting with my body any racist-sexist performance around me, including a few strategic gestures towards the DJ. But by 1995, after years of this ritual in my own home town, I gave up, because the pleasure and desire wore thinner than the annoyance.

Taking Los Angeles as a case in point, salsa venues are often highly exoticized commercial ventures in US contexts that consciously exclude from its clientele the very communities – working-class Puerto Ricans, Cubans and African American people, among others – from whose rich and varied aesthetic arsenals salsa was originally created in New York City. Certain Latin American values that are characteristically marred by latent and not-so-latent racist and bourgeois attitudes seem to have hitched a ride along the northbound lanes of the transcontinental highway, and salsa clubs appear to be a convenient space for conspicuously displaying these attitudes. How else can we explain the way that 'música cocola, plebeian music, lower-class music' (as salsa has been viewed within Puerto Rico's insular upper and middle classes since its inception) is being transformed by Latinas/os outside the Puerto Rican diasporic community into a site for uppity signifying practices (Storm Roberts, 1992)?

In Mexico and other parts of Latin America, as well as within the US, Afro-Caribbean musical styles and songs have been appropriated and toned down to suit the tastes of mainstream audiences, especially the petit bourgeois audiences, for decades.[21] But more recently it seems that this type of appropriation is occurring in Latina/o communities inside the US, among folk who are not necessarily middle class but fervently cling to an illusion of racial and class privilege. Does this attest to a nostalgia for a social status which certain immigrants may have lost after coming to the US, or the hope of achieving it now that they are here, or even among later generations as a conscious rejection of (musical traditions in) their own communities? Has salsa become yet another background tune for a High-Spanic 'American Dream' (-state) pesadilla (nightmare)?

The contours of (neo)colonialism, in the era of NAFTA, GATT and MTV Internacional, have made public aesthetic resistance, in salsa, a precarious process, one which inspires those from within the Caribbean diaspora to contest and subvert the overdeterminations that occur when people in our local environment try to commodify our music as an exotic (hence fundamentally racist-sexist) thrill. Even today, living in Austin, Texas (which has at least four salsa venues), or visiting friends and family in New York and San Juan, I am extremely selective about where and with whom I dance Caribbean music. Other Puerto Ricans from working-class backgrounds usually understand my concerns immediately and intuitively, and we often make a serious effort to analyse the cultural micropolitics of the clubs, to share this analysis with other people of colour and, when we do go to a club, to carve out a little zone on the dance floor where we can make sense of the music in our own way. Non-Puerto Ricans sometimes argue that we are being 'overly sensitive', that we are spoiling the neutralized 'fun' of the music for them by making such a fuss; but that is, of course, precisely our intention.

Notes

1   I would like to thank Angie Chabram-Dernersesian for her gentle but thorough editorial advice on this article, her professionalism as a senior

scholar, her encouragement and her persistence in speaking truth to power at every turn. TKO Boricua!

2   In English: 'I do not believe in a god who does not dance. I do not believe in a believer who does not move.' This is a slogan popularized within Rio de Janeiro's black movement. I would like to thank Julio Tavares for sharing this motto with me and for all the conversations we have had about power, rhythm, aesthetics and embodiment.

3   Building on Jorge Duany's discussion of this sensibility's cohesion in anthropological terms (1992: 85).

4   Puerto Ricans had no choice but to hold public dances in private homes for lack of any access to public venues during the early part of the twentieth century. Later the community attended shows at the Palladium and in virtually segregated venues such as the Taft Hotel. On the insular Puerto Rican reappropriation of salsa as popular music, see Aparicio (1998) and Figueroa Hernández (1992).

5   My usage of the term 'racism' connotes historically sustained lived conditions in which racialized subjects are *de facto* or *de jure* emplotted in radically unequal social spaces. The social fact of racism thus implies an entire panoply of structural inequalities (for example, unequal access to housing, wages, legal options, healthcare, childcare, education, etc.) as well as ideational inequalities (such as discriminatory treatment based on gender, sexuality, idioms, accent, customs, skin tone, etc.), which combine in an insidiously protean matrix of disempowerment.

6   On the problematic urge to render diasporic Puerto Rican music as a stagnant Puerto Rican or (exclusively) Afro-Cuban folkloric practice, see Glasser (1995).

7   Aparicio (1998) includes an ethnographic section examining how Latinas critically listen to (and reinvent) salsa for themselves.

8   This particular diatribe against Puerto Rican musicians is made in Vernon Boggs' essay, 'Founding fathers and changes in Cuban popular music called salsa', in which Mario Bauzá and 'Machito' are celebrated as the seminal Afro-salseros of New York (a claim based on thirdhand information presented in small publications, interviews cited in John Storm Roberts' (1979) *The Latin Tinge* and the anthropological work done in the 1970s by insular Cuban ethnomusicologist Fernando Ortiz). Understandably, given his acknowledged political vision, Boggs' essay leans heavily towards conclusions that corroborate discourses of the Black Power Movement in the US, in which Afro-Cuban religion, arts and music became a reductive metonym for all Afro-mestizo culture in the Spanish-speaking Caribbean. To his credit, Boggs included insular Puerto Rican claims on salsa in the collection as well, but what gets lost in the argument over Puerto Rican and Cuban folklore are the Puerto Rican and Cuban musicians who created salsa, together in the US, for audiences in the New York *colonia*, which had an overwhelming majority of Puerto Rican residents (Sánchez-Korrol, 1983). Furthermore, it is disconcerting to see contemporary scholars citing this polemic as a transparent reportage of the

historical record, in effect perpetuating the wilful historical amnesia the Puerto Rican community suffers at the hands of cultural intellectuals in our colonial metropole.

9   I have reappropriated this term advisedly here, realizing and embracing the over-determinations it suggests. This effort should be read as a Sycoraxean (rather than Calibanistic) recuperation of my colonial I, despite the risks, from the clutches of eternally contingent reinventions so popular today in 'hybrid' and 'postcolonial' studies. On these risks, see Nayarin (1993). For a review of the stakes at play in feminist auto-ethnography by women of colour, see Visweswaran (1994), Chabram-Dernersesian (1994) and Benmayor et al. (1992).

10   Here I am suggesting that, in subaltern colonial context, Nietzsche's (1886/1966) analysis of the relationship between art and power must be turned on its head. On rhyzomatic reproduction see Deleuze and Guatarri (1972–1980/1987).

11   In the original:

> No puedo callar ante lo que me rodea,
> tampoco ignorar a los que sufren mil penas.
> Cantar por cantar no tiene ningún sentido,
> yo quiero cantar porque siento un compromiso.
>
> No puedo callar sabiendo lo que anda mal,
> cambiar la mirada por temor al qué dirán.
> Cantar por cantar es repetir mil palabras,
> hablar al cantar es conversar con el alma.

12   Not uncoincidentally, 'Por eso canto' became Colón's theme song during his (unsuccessful) 1996 Congressional campaign.

13   Colón and Blades have since collaborated on another album, entitled Tras la Tormenta (In the Storm's Wake), which was released in 1995. (Rumours of conflict over their creative differences were reported in trade publications and newspapers during the album's production).

14   For a fuller analysis of symptomatic Latin American paradigms of Hispanic identity in the context of the Quincentennial, see Chabram-Dernersesian (1996).

15   In the original:

> Positivo y negativo se confunden
> en la herencia del 1492.
> Hoy, sin ánimo de ofensa hacia el
> que distinto piensa,
> conmemoro, pero sin celebración.

16   Considering some of Blades' earlier songs – such as 'Pablo Pueblo' and 'Buscando América', among others – the sociopolitical content of Amor y control is as surprising as it is disappointing.

17   The Caribbean's cultural sweep can include the coastal communities of the continent's Atlantic rim, stretching from the Yucatán through central America's port communities all the way to Rio de Janeiro.

18   This term was coined by Ana Nieto Gómez (1974), and implies the inextricability of racial and gendered experience for women of colour in the US.

19   In this regard, as I have suggested throughout the article, my discussion is specific to the *mainland* Puerto Rican community, which is often rendered invisible by cultural intellectuals from or in Puerto Rico who (quite wrongly) convert diasporic Puerto Rican signification into an insular Puerto Rican phenomenon and who, based on racist common sense cultivated on the island, assume a folkloric kind of 'pobre-negrito' homogeneity among those of us whose parents, grandparents or great-grandparents came as underskilled workers to the US. This motif is rooted in insular culturalist apologies for racialized inequalities, in which dwelling on the 'cultural riches' of the racialized poor tends to gloss our denied access to material wealth in Puerto Rico. On the institutional roots of this racial-economic stratification in Puerto Rico, see Sued Badillo (1986), Chapter 1.

20   In English: 'let the communists in Cuba go to hell' – a particular favourite at Pedro's Grill in Los Feliz.

21   On what she terms the 'whitening' of salsa in Puerto Rico, see Aparicio (1998: 176 ff.).

References

Aparicio, Francis (1998) *Listening to Salsa*, Hanover and London: University of New England Press.

Benmayor, Rina, Torruellas, Rosa and Juarbe, Ana L. (1992) *Responses to Poverty Among Puerto Rican Women: Identity, Community and Cultural Citizenship*, New York: Centro de Estudios Puertorriqueños.

Blades, Rubén (1992) (With Son del Solar). *Amor y control*, Sony Discos Internacional, CDZ-80839, 471643-2.

Blades, Rubén and Colón, Willie (1995) *Tras la tormenta*, Sony Tropical, CDT-81498/478354-2.

Boggs, Vernon W. (1992) 'Founding fathers and changes in Cuban music called salsa', in his (ed.) *Salsiology*, New York: Excelsior Music: 95–105.

Chabram-Dernersesian, Angie (1994) '"Chicana! Rican? No, Chicana-Riqueña!" Refashioning the transnational connection', in D.T. Goldberg (ed.) *Multiculturalism: A Critical Reader*, Oxford: Blackwell.

—— (1996) 'The Spanish Colón-ialista narrative: their prospectus for us in 1992', in A. Gordon and C. Newfield (eds) *Mapping Multiculturalism*, Minneapolis and London: University of Minnesota Press.

Colón, Willie (1993) *Hecho en Puerto Rico*, Sony Discos Internacional, DCC-881040, 4-469580.

Deleuze, Gilles and Guatarri, Felix (1972–1980/1987) *A Thousand Plateaux: Capitalism and Schizophrenia*, trans. Brian Massumi, Minneapolis: University of Minnesota Press.

Duany, Jorge (1992) 'Popular music in Puerto Rico: toward an anthropology of salsa', in Boggs (ed.) op. cit.: 72–89.

Figueroa Hernández, Rafael (1992) *Ismael Rivera: El sonero mayor*, San Juan: Instituto de Cultura Puertorriqueña.

García Canclini, Nestor (1993) *Transforming Modernity: Popular Culture in Mexico*, trans. Lidia Lozano, Austin: University of Texas Press.

Gilroy, Paul (1993) *Small Acts*, London and New York: Serpent's Tail.

Glasser, Ruth (1995) *My Music is My Flag: Puerto Rican Musicians and Their New York Communities, 1917–1940*, Berkeley, Los Angeles and London: University of California Press.

Guerra, Juan Luis (1992) *Areíto*, With 4:40, BMG Music, 3456-2RL.

Lipsitz, George (1994) *Dangerous Crossroads: Popular Music, Postmodernism and the Poetics of Place*, London and New York: Verso.

Nayarin, Kirin (1993) 'How native is a "native" anthropologist?', *American Anthropologist*, 95: 671–86.

Nieto Gómez, Anna (1974) 'La feminista', *Encuentro Femenil*, 1(2): 34–47.

Nietzsche, Friedrich (1886/1966) *Beyond Good and Evil: Prelude to a Philosophy of the Future*, trans. Walter Kaufman, New York: Vintage.

Ortiz, Fernando (1975) *La música afrocubana*, Madrid: Ediciones Jucar.

Sánchez-Korrol, Virginia (1983) *From Colonia to Community: The History of Puerto Ricans in New York City, 1917–1948*, Westport and London: Greenwood Press.

Storm Roberts, John (1979) *The Latin Tinge*, New York: Oxford University Press.

—— (1992) 'The roots', in Boggs (ed.) op. cit.: 5–22.

Sued Badillo, Jalil (1986) *Puerto Rico Negro*, Río Piedras: Editorial Cultural.

Visweswaran, Kamala (1994) *Fictions of Feminist Ethnography*, Minneapolis and London: University of Minnesota Press.

Yúdice, George, Franco, Jean and Flores, Juan (Introduction and eds) (1992) *On Edge: The Crisis of Contemporary Latin American Culture*, Minneapolis and London: University of Minnesota Press.

Zamudio-Taylor, Victor (1993) 'Demystifying marginality: identity, tradition and resistance', in his Exhibit Catalogue *In/Out of the Cold*, San Francisco, CA: Center for the Arts Yerba Buena Gardens, 18–21.

Sonia Saldívar-Hull

WOMEN HOLLERING TRANSFRONTERIZA FEMINISMS

Abstract

The publication of texts by Chicana feminists in the 1980s offered an alternative mapping of feminist literary cartographies and subject positions. This article examines the work of contemporary Chicana writer, Sandra Cisneros, whose literary text enacts a practice of Chicana feminism that engages with a transnational, transfronteriza practice of *feminismo popular*, which literally translates as 'popular feminism'. This type of border feminism articulates a feminist materialist aesthetics that enables us to re-examine an emergent formation of feminism on the border, a formation characterized by specific types of movements of Mexican women across geopolitical boundaries and borders. The complex movements of this transnational Chicana feminism are announced in the story 'Woman Hollering Creek', which complicates the binarisms of the metropolitan opposed to the rural, the core and periphery, and militates against a reductionist opposition of First World versus Third World. I argue that armed with a transfrontera feminism, the protagonist Cleófilas and her peers can resist the power of a transnational media. This story changes the subject of dominant, patriarchal discourse and lets readers imagine how Chicana transfrontera feminism and Mexican *feminismo popular* can converge in other spaces and under other circumstances to produce socially nuanced global Chicana Mexicana coalitions.

Keywords

Sandra Cisneros; Chicana feminism; Mexican feminism; transfrontera feminism; popular feminism; Chicana/o literature; Chicana/o popular culture

THE PUBLICATION OF TEXTS by Chicana feminists in the 1980s offered an alternative mapping of feminist literary cartographies and subject positions. For example, in *Loving in the War Years: lo que nunca pasó por sus labios*,

Cherríe Moraga (1983) proposed a global feminism that linked racialized, sexualized women in the US to women engaged in struggles throughout the Americas. What Moraga termed 'third world feminism' was a bold effort to forge political linkages between mujeres, lesbian and heterosexual; this was a feminism that destabilized *hetero*sexuality in a traditionally homophobic community; a feminism that was working-class inspired and working-class identified.

In this article, I examine the work of an internationally acclaimed contemporary Chicana writer, Sandra Cisneros, whose literary text enacts a practice of Chicana feminism[1] that maintains the spirit of this earlier production while engaging it with a transnational, transfronteriza practice of *feminismo popular*, which literally translates as 'popular feminism'.[2] Cisneros' articulation of this brand of 'border feminism' is a practice of feminism that moves beyond abstractions to practices, that engages Chicana feminist theories with social and cultural productions in multiple Chicana and Mexicana locations and that also breaks with Euro-American feminisms' geopolitical racist and elitist mappings.

Sandra Cisneros' short story collection, *Woman Hollering Creek and Other Stories* (1991), articulates a feminist materialist aesthetics that enables us to re-examine this emergent formation of feminism on the border, a formation characterized by specific types of movements of Mexican women across geopolitical boundaries and borders. The complex movements of this transnational Chicana feminism are announced in the titular *cuento*, 'Woman Hollering Creek', which complicates the binarisms of the metropolitan opposed to the rural, the core and periphery, and militates against a reductionist opposition of First World versus Third World.

Rather than glossing over the contradictions embodied and experienced by Mexican immigrant women of colour who live in poverty in the wealthiest country in the world and never really experience themselves as fully constituted citizen subjects in a Mexican or US context, this collection engages them through a fictionalized literary *testimonio*. This testimonial not only speaks, it 'hollers' social and political intersections frequently absent from metanarratives of globalization, mainstream feminisms and Chicano nationalist discourses.[3]

'Woman Hollering Creek' also problematizes an unacceptable dichotomy that US scholars often inscribe between gender conditions in the United States and those in Mexico, a dichotomy that is often supported with the presumption which suggests that 'gender' matters are better over here (in the overdeveloped US) than over there (in an underdeveloped Mexico). This is a story in which Cleófilas, a young Mexican woman, moves from one Third World patriarchal context to another with the hope of escaping economic limitations and fulfilling romantic illusions. In Cleófilas' migrations Cisneros suggests that the material and gendered conditions of domination and exploitation imposed on subaltern Mexican women in the United States are connected to the exploitation and domination from which they seek to escape in the *pueblos*/towns of Mexico.

These connections take shape as the protagonist comes to consciousness

Figure 7 Sandra Cisneros. Reproduced courtesy of Felix Hull, MD

about her oppression and exploitation within a trans/national domestic sphere that is saturated with media images that plot[4] women's destinies according to the designs of time-honoured patriarchal formations. With skilful, elegant language, Cisneros engages her readers with the particulars of a 'gendered' immigration – a feminized Third World rendition of the American Dream – that leads Cleófi-las to anticipate a new life of material comfort and romance with her bridegroom in the United States. Encouraged by love songs, romance novels and *telenovelas* (soap operas), Cleófilas believes that all spaces across the border are lined with gold and dreams of crossing into an entirely different social and geopolitical location:

> *Seguín*. She had liked the sound of it. Far away and lovely. Not like *Monclova. Coahuila*. Ugly.
>
> *Seguín, Tejas*. A nice sterling ring to it. The tinkle of money. She would get to wear outfits like the women on the *tele*, like Lucía Méndez. And have a lovely house, and wouldn't Chela be jealous.
>
> (Cisneros, 1991: 45)

Like other Mexican women who regularly watch Spanish 'novels' in the US and Mexico, Cleófilas is totally immersed within a fully mediatized culture which instructs young women that their goal in life is marriage, and that marriage to a US citizen is synonymous with social mobility and unbridled consumerism. 'Woman Hollering Creek', however, disarticulates this hegemonic immigrant narrative that is restaged and rescripted for Mexican women in the domestic sphere through popular televisual culture.

The narrative opens with Cleófilas and her son, sitting next to the creek referred to in the title, remembering her father's assurance that he would always welcome her back home as she prepared to leave Mexico proper with her new husband, Juan Pedro. Although instructed and socialized that her husband will fulfil all her desires, in practice this does not come about, and as a result, Cleófilas experiences a rude awakening. Instead of romantic love, she finds herself with a child, an abusive husband and another pregnancy. Instead of the comfortable life she believed that the United States would offer her, she lives in isolation from the community of women she had known across the border, and whose subject formations are also actively engaged with – and to a degree complicitious with – hegemonic media representations that 'plot' Mexican women.

This originary community of Mexican women is itself never romanticized; on the contrary, Cisneros calls attention to the cross they must carry as impoverished, engendered women who bear the weight of an unequal and unfair patriarchal contract. In a masterful parody of the *telenovela* and Mexican romance novel, she strategically names Cleófilas' US neighbours Soledad, solitude, and Dolores, pain. In this way, they too are distanced from the unrealistic expectations 'learned' through media lessons which foment the kind of romantic ideals that ultimately lead Cleófilas to cross the border.

What makes 'Woman Hollering Creek' such an important work, however, is that Cisneros makes it clear that Cleófilas' migration to patriarchal domesticity and the north is not the product of a singular engagement with 'romantic' constructions of marriage, but of a lifelong engagement with media representations (the books, the songs and the *telenovelas*) that define and ultimately discipline women's passions in particular ways:

> But what Cleófilas has been waiting for, has been whispering and sighing and giggling for, has been anticipating since she was old enough to lean against the window displays of gauze and butterflies and lace, is passion. Not the kind on the cover of the *¡Alarma!* magazines, where the lover is photographed with the bloody fork she used to salvage her good name. But passion in its pure crystalline essence. The kind the books and songs and *telenovelas* describe when one finds, finally, the great love of one's life, and does whatever one can, must do, at whatever the cost.

> (Cisneros, 1991: 44)

With this literary re-representation, Cisneros coincides with critics such as Virginia Erhart (1973), Jan and Cornelia Butler Flora (1978) and Jean Franco (1986, 1989), who argue that the mass media, specifically through *fotonovelas* (photo-novels), *telenovelas* and *revistas femeninas* (women's magazines), shape women's consciousness and delimit their knowledge of the world. The power of these media practices which generate not only social identities but also consumerism, must be understood within the context at hand. In Mexico, for example, the *fotonovela* and the *telenovela* target the barely literate working poor

– people like Cleófilas – who usually have little more than a grammar school edu-cation. Favourite *telenovela* actresses such as Lucía Méndez also peddle products in the commercials; their hairstyles (and often bleached blonde hair colour), and 'fashionable' attire are indeed emulated in pueblos throughout the Mexican Republic. Cisneros makes the link between the *telenovela*, romantic love, the circulation of commodities and their ultimate consumption by Mexican tele-vision viewers – in this case, a community of Mexican women – in this passage:

> *Tú o Nadie.* 'You Or No One.' The title of the current favorite *telenovela.* The beautiful Lucía Méndez having to put up with all kinds of hardships of the heart, separation and betrayal, and loving, always loving no matter what, because *that* is the most important thing, and did you see Lucía Méndez on the Bayer aspirin commercials, wasn't she lovely? Does she dye her hair do you think? Cleófilas is going to go to the *farmacia* and buy a hair rinse; her girlfriend Chela will apply it – it's not that difficult at all.
>
> (Cisneros, 1991: 44)

The power of the media to plot Mexican women is not only evident in its ability to promote this type of material consumption of commodities and popular icons that allow her to model whiteness, it also nurtures other types of gender performances. Immediately after her marriage and ensuing isolation in rural Texas, Cleófilas is compelled to put into practice the other lessons provided by her *novelas* when her husband asserts his role as head of the family through the power of his fists. Like the heroines of the *novelas* who are motivated by unadul-terated romantic desires but often encounter brutal realities, Cleófilas endures Juan Pedro's blows 'until the lip split and bled an orchid of blood, she didn't run away as she imagined she might when she saw such things in the *telenovelas*' (Cisneros, 1991: 47). She responds exactly as the '*tele*' programmed her to do: she accepts her place and her submission to 'this man, this father, the rival, this keeper, this lord, this master, this husband til kingdom come' (Cisneros, 1991: 49). She puts up with all kinds of hardships of the heart . . . no matter what, because '*that* is the most important thing' (Cisneros, 1991: 44).

At this point in Cisneros' transfrontera *novela*, alternative feminist dis-courses are not readily available to Cleófilas. While she disdains the sexually explicit *¡Alarma! fotonovelas* because they purport to be based on 'real cases', these inexpensive comic book *novelas* seem to be the texts most readily available to her. 'Reality' in Cleófilas' mind is indelibly marred by the image of a 'lover' with 'a bloody fork she used to salvage her good name' (Cisneros, 1991: 44). Instead, to ensure pleasure and a sense of safety, her reading material cannot resemble the foto-reality of the men she knows, men like Juan Pedro's best friend, 'Maximiliano who was said to have killed his wife in an ice-house brawl when she came at him with a mop. I had to shoot, he had said – she was armed' (Cisneros, 1991: 51).

Isolated in Seguín, Texas, Cleófilas faces the violence she witnessed in the *telenovelas*. But she can no longer watch the soap operas for solace with her *tele compañeras*; her husband in the US cannot even afford to buy them a television set. The 'good job' he promised with a tyre or beer company is really a menial position at the local ice-house bar/cantina. Cleófilas, who has experienced a reverse in social mobility evidenced by her inability to consume *telenovelas*, none the less attempts an escape via the pages of Corín Tellado romances which also encourage her to ignore her class limitations.

It is important to note that her 'readerly escape' stands in marked contrast to what Janice Radway concludes in her benchmark study, *Reading the Romance* (Radway, 1984). Radway proposes that for the bourgeois romance readers, escape is in itself an oppositional strategy against the demands of the patriarchy. Thus the mere act of making time to read the romances in spite of derision from husbands and society at large is a performance that 'counter-valuates'. Here she builds on José Limón: counter-valuation is a process of inversion whereby the original socioeconomic limitations and devaluations of a subordinate group are first addressed by the folkloric performance and then transformed within or by it into something of value to the group (Radway, 1984: 211–12).

Radway admits, however, that the women whom she studied never trans- formed anything about their individual middle-class existence nor did they chal- lenge patriarchal rule (Radway, 1984: 212). While I do not place greater value on the subaltern Mexican women's circumstances, I do stress the difference in their situation as women of colour who are at greater risk of economic exploi- tation and domestic abuse as a result of race and class inequalities. In the case at hand at least, Cleófilas' performance as consumer of the *novelas* and Tellado romances never 'counter-valuates' her subjugation as battered wife.

For Cleófilas, who reads the Tellado *novelas* as primers for her future as wife and as self-help manuals that feed her aspirations towards upward mobility, the Tellado romances are most insidious in their denial of race, class and cultural difference. Tellado's tomes, as Virginia Erhart observes, erase national bound- aries as they encourage the reader to assume that their lives and customs in Latin America are universal (Erhart, 1973: 101–2). Tellado's ahistorical narratives urge the reader to imagine that her world is the only one 'possible, a strategy', according to Erhart,

> that distances all troubling questions she may have about the order in which she finds herself; it is not about there being other systems – good, bad, or at least possible – what results is that they are either eliminated or she renders the differences so insignificant that they can be easily disdained.
>
> (Erhart, 1973: 101; my translation)[5]

Faced with the opportunity to marry a man who works in the United States, Cleófilas trusts that '[he] has a very important position in Seguin' (Cisneros,

1991: 45). Her (under)education does not allow her to question 'proper' documentation, their legal status as immigrants to the US; on the contrary, it does encourage her to imagine a life with unlimited economic possibilities and to re-enact media-tized plots. What she gets instead is a man and a life firmly situated within specific types of gender and class limits. As the narrative progresses, the gap between the plot and the reality becomes difficult to overlook to the point that '[s]he has to remind herself why she loves him when she changes the baby's Pampers, or when she mops the bathroom floor, or tries to make the curtains for the doorways without doors, or whiten the linen' (Cisneros, 1991: 49). Cleófilas has reached the point that she has to

> wonder a little when he kicks the refrigerator and says he hates this shitty house and is going out where he won't be bothered with the baby's howling and her suspicious questions, and her requests to fix this and this and this because if she had any brains in her head she'd realize he's been up before the rooster earning his living to pay for the food in her belly and the roof over her head and would have to wake up again early the next morning so why can't you just leave me in peace, woman.
>
> (Cisneros, 1991: 49)

lthough Cleófilas is increasingly aware of her position she believes that she alternative but to stay with this man, regardless of the physical and mental he suffers at his hands. Interestingly enough, she remains in the marriage u ...e day that his actions force her to reanalyse her constructed fantasies of what it means to be a woman:

> He had thrown a book. Hers. From across the room. A hot welt across the cheek. She could forgive that. But what stung more was the fact it was *her* book, a love story by Corín Tellado, what she loved more now that she lived in the U.S., without a television set, without the *telenovelas*.
>
> (Cisneros, 1991: 52)

The dreams that were fashioned by the Tellado romances and the *telenovelas* are literally thrown at her by the man who can never live up to her expectations. But what keeps Cleófilas' story from becoming an unmediated parody of *novelas* is the way that Cisneros refuses to give us a facile, uncomplicated, happy ending. Cleófilas does not magically transform into a self-sacrificing but solid career woman from one page to the next. Her reality is that she is once again pregnant and has nowhere to turn except back to Mexico and 'the chores that never ended, six good-for-nothing brothers, and one old man's complaints' (Cisneros, 1991: 44). Cleófilas' decision to return to Mexico and her father's house does not offer us a utopian reading; nor, however, does it do something even worse: turn to the Third World and to Third World women for quick solutions to what will inevitably be a long historical process.[6] Yet Cleófilas' story undeniably signals an alternative vision: a Chicana feminist revision of powerful cultural plots. This rendition illustrates how *telenovelas*, romances and traditional tales of infanticide by disobedient 'wailing women' who are punished for rejecting motherhood join to coerce Cleófilas into accepting patriarchal arrangements.[7] This *cuento* textualizes a Chicana practice of *feminismo popular* which puts Chicana feminist theory to work and crosses borders (geopolitically and across class lines) when Cleófilas is given the opportunity to meet some women – the Chicanas at the obstetrical clinic – who have the means and the desire to help victims of physical abuse.

This is a transformative experience because at that point, Cleófilas takes control of her *historia* and becomes a producer of meaning rather than merely a consumer of dominant ideology. Resisting the power of the media, she transforms herself from being a passive *object* of dominant discourse to the *agent* of an alternative vision and backs up this transformation with a specific practice: a counter-migration from north to south and a separation from her abusive husband.

Significantly, it is Felice, a Chicana practitioner of *feminismo popular*, who drives Cleófilas to the bus station. On the way, Cleófilas witnesses a different plot of Mexican womanhood and a different type of subjectivity:

> Everything about this woman, this Felice, amazed Cleófilas. The fact that she drove a pickup. A pickup, mind you, but when Cleófilas asked if it was her husband's she said she didn't have a husband. The pickup was hers. She herself had chosen it. She herself was paying for it.
>   I used to have a Pontiac Sunbird. But those cars are for *viejas*. Pussy cars. Now this here is a *real* car.
>
> (Cisneros, 1991: 54)

Cleófilas returns to Mexico, her material conditions relatively unaltered. She returns to her father and brothers, to a patriarchal *familia,* as what Norma Alarcón (1994) calls a feminist 'subject in process' or a 'speaking subject', telling stories that might include the narratives of activist Chicana feminists. Here Cisneros captures the kind of feminist awakening that inspires transformation:

> What kind of talk was that coming from a woman? Cleófilas thought. But then again, Felice was like no woman she had ever met. Can you imagine, when we crossed the *arroyo* she just started yelling like a crazy, she would say later to her father and brothers. Just like that. Who would've thought?
>
> (Cisneros, 1991: 56)

Reading Felice as a woman who transgresses scripted gender roles opens up a radical political trajectory for this text. Felice owns a pickup truck, she is not connected to a husband, and she dares to 'holler' rather than weep. Her willingness to transport Cleófilas signals a woman 'like no woman [Cleófilas] has ever met'. Felice embodies the Chicana feminist that Cherríe Moraga envisioned nearly a decade before this story was published. In Moraga's words, 'this is what being a Chicana feminist means – making bold and political the love of the women of our race' (Moraga, 1983: 139).

As a Chicana feminist reader of the Chicana feminist *novela*, however, I read Felice's difference as lesbian or as a heterosexual woman-identified-woman who, in Cisneros's (1994) poem, 'Loose Woman', rejects homophobic, misogynistic Chicano community roles that naturalize heterosexuality:

> They say I'm a *macha*, hell on wheels,
> *viva la vulva*, fire and brimstone,
> man-hating, devastating,
> boogey-woman lesbian.
> Not necessarily,
> but I like the compliment.

(Cisneros, 1994: 112)

In 'Woman Hollering Creek', Sandra Cisneros skilfully rewrites *la novela*. In this subversive rendition of *la novela*, Felice, a politically active Chicana who defies heterosexual or lesbian labels, flaunts her transfrontera feminist politics. The text hints at the possibility that Cleófilas can cross over to her compañeras in Mexico new, 'hollering' narratives with the power to change the subject of ultimately misogynist plots.

Yet another scenario can be imagined. Perhaps Cleófilas can perform the bridgework necessary to unite Chicana transfrontera feminism to Mexican renditions of *feminismo popular*. I am referring to that brand of Mexican *feminismo popular* that emerged from working-class women's labour struggles. Gisela Espinosa Damián (1987) explains that out of the chaos and suffering which the masses endured in the aftermath of the 1985 earthquake in Mexico City, the *mexicanas* organized as gendered workers with specific problems that required new ways of formulating their needs. Espinosa Damián describes the powerful 'movement of women whose wretched working conditions and high level of exploitation were revealed from the rubble of their workshops and factories: the dressmakers' (Espinosa Damián, 1987: 33). This feminism, which coincides with the publication of 'Woman Hollering Creek' in the 1980s, offers important affinities with Chicana feminism, for this is also a feminism which emerges from the ranks of women from 'the exploited classes' who are 'seeking to incorporate demands and struggles, arising from their own particular forms of exploitation and oppression', and who also seek to 'create their own arenas for discussion and new forms of organisation' (Espinosa Damián, 1987: 33).

Certainly this concept of *feminismo popular* is relevant to the transfronteriza predicament of the Mexican woman who protagonizes 'Woman Hollering

Creek', for this movement is composed of women in the other Mexico who, according to Lynn Stephen:

> are struggling to define popular feminism for themselves [and who] are looking to the harsh realities of their daily lives – economic problems in the household, long days of domestic work made worse by a lack of services and infrastructure, domestic violence, poor health and lack of control over their own bodies, and a life of work which has remained invisible – for tactics and strategies to develop a unified struggle around gender and class, without subordinating one to the other.
>
> (Stephen, 1989: 102)

The links between this brand of *feminismo popular* and the one that inspires a Chicana feminist practice in 'Woman Hollering Creek' are evidenced in the story of how Sandra Cisneros came to write this feminist tale in Central Texas. In an interview I conducted with her, she explained how she identified with a group of popular feminists who struggled and became what one artist hollered: 'mujeres de fuerza', women of strength.[8] These mujeres in fact ran an underground railroad, often from 'home' to a battered women's shelter, for Chicanas and recent Mexican immigrants victimized by their men and by the economic collusion between the US and Mexico on both sides of the border.

In avoiding a predictable closure, Sandra Cisneros leaves the way open for several productive transfronteriza feminist movements and engagements with *feminismo popular*. This story not only changes the subject of dominant discourse, but it lets readers imagine how Chicana transfrontera feminism and Mexican *feminismo popular* will converge in other spaces and under other circumstances. In other words, what social, material and political encounters will enable socially nuanced global Chicana Mexicana coalitions? Another transfronteriza feminist cartography?

Notes

1   This feminist practice is a class-based, transnational construction that insists on the unambiguous use of the political appellation 'Chicana'. The insistence on the label 'Chicana' rather than the homogenizing 'Hispanic' or the more assimilationist 'Mexican-American' underscores the term's grounding in a materialist, politically engaged feminism. It is a feminist practice that grew out of many women's discontent with the unabashedly sexist Chicano power movement of the 1960s and 1970s, a movement sustained, if not nurtured, by women's unacknowledged labour. Further, this Chicana feminism breaks with Euro-American feminisms in its insistence on the dialectical relationship between class and race as well as gender concerns.

2   Stephen (1997) provides an excellent, comprehensive account of popular feminism.

3   For a powerful critique of Chicano nationalist narratives see Chabram-Dernersesian (1992), 'I throw punches for my race' in L. Grossberg, C. Nelson and P.A. Treichler (eds) (1992) *Cultural Studies* (New York: Routledge).

4   I am indebted to Jean Franco's groundbreaking work, 'The incorporation of women' (1986) and *Plotting Women: Gender and Representation in Mexico* (1989), where she examines how 'the feminine is constructed [plotted] in the multinational era' by mass culture narratives of romance fiction and comic strip novels (Franco, 1986: 120).

5   Erhart notes that the Tellado *novelas* pre-date Harlequin romances by about a decade; she fears their 'reactionary and conformist' power (Erhart, 1973: 93). Further, these *novelas* preach absolute moral order and obscure class and marital conflict, and assert that marriage and love serve to level socioeconomic differences as they additionally mask the sexual (Erhart, 1973: 93).

6   My thanks to Barbara Harlow whose words I echo here.

7   See my forthcoming book, *Feminism on the Border* for a discussion of the role of the oral tradition of *la llorona*, the wailing woman, in Chicana feminist literature. I include a reading from a *fotonovela* and a Tellado story in an expanded study of Cisneros' fiction.

8   Saldívar-Hull (1988).

References

Alarcón, Norma (1994) 'Conjugating subjects: the heteroglossia of essence and resistance', in A. Arteaga (ed.) *An Other Tongue: Nation and Ethnicity in the Linguistic Borderlands*, Durham and London: Duke University Press.

Butler Flora, Cornelia and Flora, Jan L. (1978) 'The fotonovela as a tool for class and cultural domination', *Latin American Perspectives*, 5.1: 134–50.

Chabram-Dernersesian, Angie (1992) 'I throw punches for my race, but I don't want to be a man: writing us – Chica-nos (girl, us) / Chicanas – into the movement script', in L. Grossberg, C. Nelson, and P. A. Treichler (eds) *Cultural Studies*, New York: Routledge.

Cisneros, Sandra (1991) *Woman Hollering Creek and Other Stories*, New York: Random House.

—— (1994) 'Loose Woman' in her *Loose Woman*, New York: Alfred A. Knopf.

Erhart, Virginia (1973) 'Amor, ideología y enmascaramieinto en Corín Tellado', *Casa de las Américas*, March–April: 93–111.

Espinosa Damián, Gisela (1987) 'Feminism and social struggle in Mexico', in M. Davies (ed.) *Third World – Second Sex II*, London: Zed Books.

Franco, Jean (1986) 'The incorporation of women: a comparison of North American and Mexican popular culture', in T. Modeleski (ed.) *Studies in Entertainment: Critical Approaches to Mass Culture*, Bloomington: Indiana University Press.

—— (1989) *Plotting Women: Gender and Representation in Mexico*, New York: Columbia University Press.

Moraga, Cherríe (1983) *Loving in the War Years: lo que nunca pasó por sus labios*, Boston: South End Press.

Radway, Janice A. (1984) *Reading the Romance: Women, Patriarchy, and Popular Literature*, Chapel Hill: University of North Carolina Press.

Saldívar-Hull, Sonia (1988) Unpublished, informal interview with Sandra Cisneros, Austin, Texas, July.

—— (1999) *Feminism on the Border: Gender Politics, Geopolitics, and Transfrontera Collectivities*, Berkeley: University of California Press.

Stephen, Lynn (1989) 'Popular feminism in Mexico', *Z Magazine*, December: 102–6.

—— (1997) *Women and Social Movements in Latin America: Power From Below*, Austin: University of Texas Press.

Angie Chabram-Dernersesian

EN-COUNTERING THE OTHER
DISCOURSE OF
CHICANO–MEXICANO DIFFERENCE[1]

Abstract

In this period in which Mexicans in the borderlands are being constructed as aliens and sources of cheap deportable labour (not makes of intellectual traditions which encourage transnational area studies and theoretical reflections in the US), it is important to remember that not only people but also ideas cross Mexican–American borders. It is doubly important to scrutinize those intellectual movements that cross state-sanctioned borders while restricting social possibilities and movements.

  In this article I consciously assume this charge by focusing critical attention on an influential venue of transnational(ist) travel (On the road to Octavio Paz/On the Road to Chicano) within cultural productions that laid the foundation for an 'alternative' Chicano studies epistemology and tradition in the early 1970s. Drawing on disparate cultural studies traditions and the deconstructive insights of Chicana feminists and activists, I encounter the patriarchal dynamics, conceptual idioms, political investments (nationalism/familism) and essentialist difference that undergirded this intellectual formation and its construction of Chicana/o identity. In the process I argue that this formation not only rendered the desired form of political exceptionalism, but also served to distance Chicanas/os from the political and intellectual claims of Chicanas, Chicana feminists and other women and people of colour. However, as my concluding section demonstrates, this circulation of theories was – to use the language of Clifford – 'cut across', interrupted and contested by other theories in circulation during the same period that offered different claims to representation, different forms of transnational travel, and other possibilities for imagining social political and intellectual relations.

CULTURAL STUDIES 13(2) 1999, 263–289

Keywords

Travelling theory; Chicana/o studies; Chicana feminism; familism; patriar-chal connectivity; transnationalism

Introduction: Intellectual, generational and contextual frames

IN THE OPENING PAGES of an issue of *Inscriptions* entitled 'Traveling theory, traveling theorists', James Clifford and Vivek Dhareshwar pose these and other questions: 'What counts as theory in specific traditions?' 'Who counts as a theorist?' (Clifford and Dhareshwar, 1989). Later on in a closing essay Clifford asks: 'How do different populations, classes and genders travel?' 'What kinds of knowledges, stories and theories do they produce?' (Clifford, 1989: 183). In this article I will address some of these questions in relation to a very specific Chicano context by examining an early intellectual and cultural movement that follows a semi-public route; reconfigures the intellectual/theoretical; transports popu-lations, classes, nations and genders 'selectively'; and lays one of the foundations for an emergent authoritative tradition and epistemology in Chicano studies. I am referring here to a circulation of Octavio Paz and his essay, *The Labyrinth of Solitude* (Paz, 1961) within Chicano transnationalist[2] productions that featured an essential Chicano–Mexicano difference.

It is important to clarify that the choice to remember this circulation of theories and theorists was made prior to the news of Paz's death (19 April 1998), which generated worldwide attention as well as a torrent of memorials con-firming his importance as a twentieth-century thinker, poet, essayist and a for-midable spokesman (and translator) of Mexico (and Mexicans) to the world community (Vacio and Buiz Esparza, 1998).

Inspired by transcendental canonical categories, most of these memorials failed to draw attention to what is spoken in this article by way of a partial rep-resentation: the importance of Paz within that Mexican community *en el norte*, the community that delivers back the Mexican national's questioning image from the pages of an essay which is touted as a defining moment in Paz's career and as one of his most important and profound characterizations of Mexican life and thought in the post-revolutionary period.

In fact, one of these memorials, which displayed an unusually high level of irritation at an otherwise well-read US public, went so far as to suggest (by way of a rhetorical question) that his death would not have been noticed at all by *norteamericanos* if it were not for the fact that Octavio Paz won the Nobel Prize (McLemee, 1998: 1). As I read these words I was overtaken by disbelief, then the disbelief was replaced by yet another troubling recognition: the specific cul-tural and historical movement which was etched in my imagination by way of a

Chicano/a discourse, lived experience and programme of study was effectively erased by this author's memorializing, claims to ethnographic and intellectual authority and 'generic' reference to 'norteamericanos'. In his reading not only were we, the inhabitants of *Nuestra América en el Norte*/Our America to the North, simultaneously displaced and subsumed, but so were our other remembrances of Octavio Paz. I am referring specifically to those remembrances that preceded the recognition afforded by the Nobel Prize, and that continue to be fuelled by living memories, conflicting desires and hybrid Chicana/o cultural productions which reroute Octavio Paz through a number of heterogeneous social, political and artistic practices.

Like many of my cohorts I encountered these remembrances during the Chicano Movement while I was coming into political and social consciousness. However, it was not until the 1980s that I became keenly aware of his continued importance for a number of Chicano critics. As I questioned them about their intellectual trajectories, several of these critics went to great lengths to claim Paz as an (intellectual) precursor (of Chicanos) and to establish an uninterrupted 'Mexican' tradition on this side of the US–Mexican border, even though such an appropriation necessarily meant reinventing his political and textual personas.

One of the most memorable conversations that I had about Paz's legacy was with a critic who followed a slightly different tactic: he tried to impress upon me the necessity of contextualizing generational movements and influences when organizing an alternative ethnography of Chicana/o intellectuals. Without taking into account that I myself read *The Labyrinth of Solitude* in an undergraduate Chicano studies course at UC Berkeley in the early 1970s, but fully cognizant of the fact that I pursued graduate study within the Literature Department at UC San Diego, he said: 'Paz was important to us, the way Foucault or Jameson are important to you . . . critics . . . Mexican literature was all the context we had.'[3]

While there are many things that can be engaged and disputed here, this observation is important because it confirms vital shifts in theoretical preferences that are also ignored within US-based 'academic' landscapes of transnational global theories and movements. Within these highly selective landscapes, intellectual and theoretical travels continue to be severely restricted – particularly travels through a Mexico-US-Chicana/o context – even in the midst of the unprecedented reception of a book such as *Borderlands, La Frontera* (1987) and even in the midst of a notable flourishing of cultural productions which orchestrate other types of imaginative border crossings through the hemispheric context of the Americas. As a result, our understanding of the changing idioms and faces of theoretical travel is itself very limited, particularly in the case of transnational cultural theory that migrates through informal, unrecognized or unsanctioned social networks and productions.

At this point in history, where Mexicans in the borderlands are being constructed as sources of cheap deportable labour (not makers of intellectual traditions that encourage theoretical responses and disciplinary formations in the

US) and are once again being subjected to cruel forms of surveillance and impoverishment because their 'Americaness' is suspect, it is important to remember that not only people but also ideas travel across Mexican–American borders and that they have travelled historically along different inter/national routes and within different social political and economic registers. Finally, it is also important to examine those intellectual circuits/pathways that have moved Chicanas/os and Mexicanas/os into particular types of social and intellectual partnerships.

It is this urgency – together with the upsurge of pan-ethnic Mexican and Latino nationalisms within local grass-roots movements – that propelled me to focus critical attention on this early Chicano Mexicano intellectual formation which attempted to counter the effects of a dominant culture's regimes of representation by writing '*nuestra*/our' *diferencia*/difference *chicana-mexicana* from a strategically placed convergence with Paz.[4] From the very beginning I wish to alert my reader to the fact that I do not examine this convergence of *lo chicano/lo mexicano* because it enacts a form of travel that we would do well to emulate in the late 1990s; on the contrary, it crosses state-sanctioned inter/national borders while restricting social possibilities and social movements.[5]

Drawing on the idea that theoretical work can be a form of struggle,[6] I not only unearth but also scrutinize one of the most problematic legacies of this intellectual partnership: the 'collaborative' production of a patriarchal, transnationalist discourse that references an essential Chicano–Mexicano (masculinist, heterosexist) difference. Admittedly, the direction of my multi-sited path of analysis deviates from 'centrist' readings of Chicano, Mexican or Latin American culture that would regionalize Chicana/o productions and/or suppress their alternative venues of transnational travel – the ones that move us from *el norte* (the north) to *el sur* (the south) and within '*el sur en/in el norte*'. At the same time my path of analysis signals an engagement with disparate cultural studies formations to the degree that it directs attention to the loss of 'critical innocence' (Hall, 1987: 170) of the essential Chicano subject by (1) critically en-countering the theoretical and familial underpinnings and power relations associated with early Chicano Mexicano identities and categories, and (2) re-encountering their 'aspirations to potent overview' (Clifford, 1989) from the deconstructive insights and oppositional engagements of leading Chicana activists and theorists (Anna Nieto-Gomez, among others) who ushered in a new 'politics of criticism' (Hall, 1987: 170). Within the scope of my analysis, then, transnational travelling Chicano Chicana/o theories are not only inflected by heterogeneous local interests, movements and contradictory power relations, but also by conflicting interpretations of 'our' intellectual and cultural legacies.

In terms of approach, I part with those who would view conceptual deviations as misreadings or conceptual failures and/or who would link Chicanos to *The Labyrinth of Solitude* or Paz through a comparative, intertextual analysis. In contrast, my article is meant to be a form of critical address that is geared towards examining how particular transnationalist formations were circulated, contested and interrupted as a way to advance particular identities and communities, traditions and agendas. The primary focus of my address is a cluster of texts (a formal essay, a transcribed interview, and travel notes) that were authored, organized and published by José Armas, the managing editor of *De Colores*, a journal of emerging Raza philosophies, in 1975.[7] Together, these texts offer a double-voiced representation of *lo chicano/lo mexicano* (the Chicano/the Mexican): José Armas recovers Octavio Paz (as a precursor) and Chicanos (from the pages of *The Labyrinth of Solitude*) in an introductory essay, and later, Armas and Octavio Paz reflect on Chicano Mexicano social identities and dynamics (including Chicano liberation, women's liberation, La Familia and more) in a transcribed interview that is prepared by *De Colores*. Here, as in the most famous productions of the Chicana/o Movement, the literary and the anthropological converge in a 'quest for our roots'.

See how it all comes together? Transnational(ist) lessons in patriarchal connectivity

Then you are the Chicano
and I am the Mexican.
We form part of one nation, one family,
one barrio, one epoch. See how it all comes together?[8]

At first glance, José Armas' introduction to Octavio Paz appears to be your standard literary biography that once again re-anoints the great (universal) writers of Latin American literature in the US. However, this introduction, which appears in a journal that is defined as a 'forum for controversial ideologies' and proposes to explain 'what it means to be a Chicano', soon lapses into describing Chicano politics, national identity, cultural history, marginalization, border crossings and struggles. This 'submerged' ethnographic narrative is the narrative that surfaces with full force, embarks on the Chicano 'journey' to Octavio Paz, facilitates the encounter between Chicanos and Octavio Paz, and ultimately partners Chicanos and Octavio Paz within a Chicano *movimiento* discourse that references difference.

To be sure, this sixtyish 'travel' narrative deviates from mainstream canonical representations because it refuses to police the borders between the literary, the cultural and the political, and endeavours to lay the foundation for an 'alternative' intellectual tradition via Paz. However, this journey to Paz none the less engages in an all too familiar social and academic practice – patriarchal connectivity. From another context, the anthropologist Suad Joseph (1996: 108) suggests that patriarchal connectivity refers to a 'patriarchal relational construct of the self' and to 'connective relationships' that are organized in the context of patriarchal societies which promote male domination over females and 'the mobilization of kinship structures, morality, and idioms to institutionalize and legitimate these [patriarchal] forms of power'. In the case at hand, patriarchal connectivity manifests itself at the discursive level through a series of exchanges between masculine intellectual figureheads/native ethnographers (José Armas and Octavio Paz) who mobilize patriarchal kinship structures as a way of reconfiguring Chicana/o Mexicana/o cultural traditions, social identities and political contestations.

In his introduction José Armas sets into motion a 'native' dynamic of 'patriarchal connectivity' by reclaiming Paz as a 'surrogate father' of the Chicano intellectual and political movement (Armas, 1975: 6).[9] With this dramatic gesture he reinscribes a cycle of masculine fertility and succession that was widely promoted by early representations of *mestizaje*, which selectively targeted male bodies and identities as sites of masculine 'Chicano' reproduction without attending to the presence of female bodies or the concrete historical realities of female (social, political, economic and cultural) reproduction. Armas' representation of Chicana/o Mexicana/o legacies also incorporates a familiar reversal of traditional Western patriarchal relations. Because of the devastating effects of colonialism, it is the Chicano son who must anoint (give birth to) his Mexican (surrogate) father in the name of the collective and embrace him as the figurehead of a Chicana/o Mexicana/o intellectual tradition/family. However, it is understood that this arrangement is temporary – the successful consolidation of a full-blown intellectual tradition that is Chicano will allow the son to occupy his rightful place at the head of the intellectual 'family' here in Aztlán.

This is of course a highly symbolic reconstruction of the intellectual order that lurks behind José Armas' positioning of Octavio Paz and Chicana/o productions within a patriarchal order. The gut-wrenching postmodern testimony of his failed attempts to set up meetings with Octavio Paz reveals the difficulties of achieving this type of patriarchal connectivity from Armas' particular social and intellectual location. In fact, this testimony, which borders on a confessional, inadvertently exposes a number of glaring social, cultural and political differences and contradictions that almost threatened to disband Armas' carefully forged intellectual and political alliance with Paz, an alliance that was clearly rendered with the aim of lifting Chicanos out of their marginal status within US society and culture.

In practice, the trickle-up theory that provided the impetus for the appropriation a figure of 'great stature' such as Octavio Paz (who purportedly 'flattered' Chicanos with his attention) did not deliver the expected familial connection to Paz or legitimate Chicano studies in the mainstream cultural institutions of the Americas. However, a symbolic connection to Paz did provide a conceptual framework from which to consolidate a Chicano studies intellectual agenda that offered many cultural practitioners a 'Mexican' resemblance to dominant culture's notion of a tradition. Actually promoting this agenda – and reaping whatever cultural and institutional capital that could be derived from this Mexican resemblance – meant cultivating a transnationalist affiliation to Octavio Paz which could link him to Chicanas/os and the Chicana/o Movement.

In his introduction, José Armas achieves this type of connection by activating a series of imaginary disidentifications that were widely popularized within Chicano nationalist movement discourses. After introducing Octavio Paz as a leading Latin American spokesman and informing readers of this non-profit bilingual forum (*De Colores*) that *The Labyrinth of Solitude* is widely read in Chicano studies courses and that it is considered to be a 'modern classic of critical interpretation by the establishment literary community', José Armas provides an impressive list of Paz's 'Chicano' credentials. These include: his residence in the US, organic connection to binational traditions, popularity among Chicanos, and his role as the intellectual precursor who purportedly 'wrote about Raza in this country even before they were writing about themselves' (Armas, 1975: 3).

While the ethnographic dimensions of his travel narrative reveal that this 'Chicanoization' of Paz is largely a product of Armas' wishful thinking, Armas none the less seals a Chicano connection to Paz at the symbolic level by drawing from another popular nationalist strategy: he boldly declares that 'Paz represents our roots, our cultural base and history as a people' (Armas, 1975: 6). In this way Armas proposes a fusion between Chicanos, Paz and Mexicans that conceals geopolitical, cultural, economic and institutional road-blocks, the presence of competing social and intellectual identities on both sides of the border, the monumental effects of 1848, and the differences between the Chicana/o Movement and mainstream intellectuals. If this were not enough, he delivers the necessary 'political' connection to Paz with his own *grito de independencia intelectual* that appears to be lifted straight out of *El Plan Espiritual de Aztlan*:

> We [Chicanos and Mexicanos] are the same people. We are the northern region of a nation of 400 million MESTIZOS; the bronze nation. We are hermanos in blood, culture and language.
>
> (Armas, 1975: 6)

These imaginary disidentifications move an appropriated Octavio Paz from a 'Mexican he' to a 'Chicano we', from Mexico into Aztlan, from a highbrow tradition into the throes of a Chicano nationalist discourse. In the process, Paz is enjoined to Chicanos via a political narrative and he and his *Labyrinth* are enlisted in the local struggles against Anglo encroachment.[10]

Armas' appeal to this type of Mexican similarity does provide an imaginary transnationalist connection to Paz but it does not achieve the complete erasure of all Chicano–Mexicano differences. A number of differences appear through the back door of this narrative which struggles with multiple separations, recognizes that the conquest produced an eclipse in the consciousness of *la Raza*, distinguishes itself within a travel narrative that reaffirms not only geopolitical but also conceptual differences,[11] and privileges Chicano identities and dynamics while editing Mexicans and subsuming them into a transnationalist variant of Chicano: Chicano–Mexicano.

The differences that enter through the front door and are openly celebrated by José Armas in his introduction are those that reposition Chicanos–Mexicanos within a US context in relation to other groups, that 'put form and structure' into a transnationalist definition of the race/*la Raza*, and that are traced directly to Octavio Paz. After all, it is he who receives an acknowledgement for providing Chicanos with a necessary 'intellectual' framework from which to determine 'what were some of the things that made the Chicano a Chicano and *different* from the Anglo, the Black and other peoples' (Armas, 1975: 6).

Though rudimentary and formulaic and overwritten with essentialism, this path of Chicano identity (as a relational difference) is itself a theoretical expression because it provides a group of general propositions, a proposed mode of explanation and a conjectural response.[12] In addition, this expression is a blended one; it strategically incorporates elements from Paz's cultural theory as well as elements from Chicano transnationalist epistemologies. Finally, this path incorporates the desired patriarchal lineage: here the son emerges as the native theorist/pensador. He draws on the intellectual insights of his adopted surrogate father but assumes the charge of determining for himself some of the things that make the Chicano a Chicano and the charge of projecting his own legacy. The question is: What is this early Chicano–Mexicano path to identity? (How does it frame Chicano difference within discourse? How does it differentiate Chicanas/os? How does it incorporate *The Labyrinth of Solitude* as a vehicle for masculine introspection and political affirmation? How does it incorporate or disengage local ethnoscapes? struggles? women?)

The theoretical legacy. Writing ChicanO: long live his (essential) ChicanO–Mexicano difference!

Although there is a tendency to undermine the complexity of nationalist epistemologies, it is clear that arriving at the essence of the Chicano double (some of the things that make the Chicano a Chicano) from Armas' formula of identity is a fairly complicated matter: this means not only answering the question 'Who am I?' but also the question 'Who are We?' As Armando Rendon elaborates in *Chicano Manifesto* in reference to Chicano identity, to pose the dilemma of self-identity is to pose 'not merely a dilemma of self-identity but, of self-in-group identity' (Rendon, 1971: 324). This implies attending not only to a Chicano group identity (men and women), but to other multi-ethnic, multiracial and multicultural contexts.

In the case of Armas' construction of Chicano, this type of reckoning ultimately means determining some of the things that make the Chicano himself and no other – it involves the suggestion of a highly problematic doubling which assumes that all people of colour are similar to the Anglo but different from the Chicano. This construction of Chicano identity threatens to rob other people of colour of their social and political agency as well as of their 'differences' and to submerge them into the dreaded melting-pot. In addition, this notion of identity opens the way to the kind of separatist logic that is apparent in the following passage from *Chicano Manifesto*, although Armas does not mark these particular racial negations:

> The Chicano, to state the obvious, is in essence himself and no other. He is not a Negro and cannot be like a Negro. He is not an Indian in the way native tribesman are in the United States. He is not an Anglo even when he resembles the Anglo in coloring and speech. Thus he should not and cannot act like the black, the red, or the white man, nor does he view his condition in the same way that they do.
>
> (Rendon, 1971: 106)[13]

Like other nationalist formations of identity of the period, Armas' conceptualization of Chicano as relational difference strategically contains and inhibits the dynamic relations between Chicanas/os and other ethnic groups, suppresses the internal differences between Chicanas/os, and assumes that we Chicanas/os are all identical to him (ChicanO). Here masculinity is the visible universal norm. Because of its dominance, this masculinity does not have to name the other brown gender (or other non-hegemonic forms of masculinity, for that matter) in order to constitute itself as a discourse. On the contrary, this masculinity can draw on a patriarchal legacy which is self-legitimating and self-affirming and on a tradition of male intellectuality – the (male-authored) Mexican essay[14] – which incorporates a male prerogative to define thought.[14] Finally, this masculinity can draw on a widely disseminated nationalist epistemology that suggests that 'to be a Chicano is a new way of knowing your brown brother and understanding our brown race' (Rendon, 1971: 320). In retrospect, it is clear that the proposed theoretical construction of Chicano an 'enormous' (race-based, gendered) 'totalization' is itself an impossibility given that Chicana/o is complexly constructed within history with a range of other social, political and (multi)cultural relations and relationships, with classes, genders, races and sexualities, and within the theoretical insights of multiple and competing social, political and intellectual legacies.[15]

Insofar as Armas' notion of Chicano identity is undergirded by culturalist and existentialist dimensions, it also reinscribes the limitations identified with respect to these essayistic representations of Mexican national culture and identity – this notion promotes an idealist and subjectivist notion of history and reduces history to cultural practices and to existential psychodrama (Lomnitz-Adler, 1992: 2). Affirming social and political identities through these early

Mexicanized Chicano traditions often boils down to enumerating or synthesizing 'unique' character traits, cultural practices or profiles, creating larger-than-life mythic prototypes, and delivering a unitary image of political struggle, national culture and identity. In the most popular variants of this type of 'Chicanismo', individual reassessments of Chicano personalities often lead to the 'unanimous conclusion that all Chicanos have traveled the same rough paths', experienced much of 'the same indignities and injustices' – and rebelled in much the same ways – *simply because they are Chicanos* (Rendon, 1971: 113).[16]

In reference to another Mexican context and a very different line of argument, Claudio Lomnitz-Adler has pointed out that the works of the Mexican *pensadores* rarely provoke empirical research, that '[t]hey are synthesis meant to be consumed in particular political conjunctures', and that within these works '[k]nowledge created is knowledge politically used, exploited and (eventually) discarded into a pool of reusable symbols.(stereotypes)' (Lomnitz-Adler, 1992: 9). To some extent his critique is valid within the US context because these essentialist constructions of Chicano identity and the revolt have generated an arsenal of reusable political symbols while allowing for little accumulation of knowledge of the diverse social identities which intersect with Chicanas/os and help to reconstitute them within the social formation and discourse. However, there are different political dimensions attached to the Mexican production of *lo mexicano* and the Chicano production of lo chicano–mexicano.

For instance, Roger Bartra identifies cultural studies of *lo mexicano* with those dominant forms of subjectivity that are circulated within a Mexican hegemonic political culture in the post-revolutionary period (Bartra, 1987: 16–17). Within a US context these dimensions of the narrative of *lo mexicano* are often ignored. The theorists of *lo chicano* often assumed that texts such as *The Labyrinth of Solitude* delivered an authentic representation of the Mexicano (the Mexican, Mexican-ness), although they took issue with its representation of the Chicano (*pachuco*).[17] In contrast to contemporary critics of Mexican nationalism who have linked these forms of (Mexican) subjectivity with 'una voluntad de poder nacionalista ligada a la unificación e institucionalización del Estado capitalista moderno' (Bartra, 1987: 17) these *pensadores chicanos* who dreamed with the idea of a different Chicano nation linked *The Labyrinth of Solitude* to national dynamics on this side of the international border, including internal colonialism, racism, economic oppression, and social and cultural dispossession. These *pensadores* were also responding to other social movements in the US, especially to the towering presence of African Americans in the struggle for civil rights and to the social and political demands of women and other marginalized groups.

In this sense it is of supreme importance that Armas himself prefaces his formulaic discussion of a Chicano difference by alerting his readers that 'the movement of the Chicano in the 1960's' searched to articulate and to identify *Chicanismo* and that '[f]or a long time (and even today in many places) the activist, the vocal Chicano, identified his struggle as the same as the Black man in this country' (Armas, 1975: 5–6). While Armas admits that some of the causes of 'their oppressed and colonized condition' are the same, he none the less marks their distinction upon highlighting 'subtle, yet *definite* differences' that 'began to take Blacks and Chicanos by different paths en route to cultural, political and economic liberation' (Armas, 1975: 6).

It is *The Labyrinth of Solitude* that provides Armas with a necessary conceptual springboard for jumping from what he constructs as an artificial Chicano black similarity to an essential Chicano black difference, which within his particular transnationalist epistemology is tantamount to a Chicano-double. For Armas *The Labyrinth of Solitude* complies with this function because it provides Chicanos with *intellectual* 'insights into the makeup' of the Mexicano that are relevant for the Chicano, including his 'familiar traits' and 'the existential nature of la Raza' (Armas, 1975: 6). Here *The Labyrinth of Solitude* functions as a substitute for a socially grounded analysis of Chicana/o Mexicana/o relations and subjectivities; it is none other than the 'artificial entelechy' that Bartra refers to within another context which 'exists primarily in the books and discourses of those who describe and exalt it' (Bartra, 1987: 17).[18] Nevertheless, at the hands of Armas, *The Labyrinth of Solitude* offers a constructed Chicano–Mexican identity that renders the desired form of political exceptionalism and the desired Chicano–Mexicano familial resemblance.

In and of itself, Armas' introduction does not offer the type of pseudo-scientific ethnographic support for this type of familial resemblance that is commonly found in the literature of *lo mexicano* with regard to other ethnic contexts and national dynamics. While he breaks with his Mexican forefathers on this count, this type of ethnographic support is supplied in an important interview that features another appropriation of Paz that may or may not correspond to what was actually voiced in the exchange between Paz and Armas. Within this interview Armas assumes ethnographic authority: he organizes the interview, serves as the authenticating voice, incorporates an unruly form of Chicañol, and uses the opportunity to ask Paz to elaborate on the differences between Mexicans, Anglos and Chicanos. After multiple setbacks, Paz graciously accepts the invitation to elaborate.

Rotating essential Chicano–Mexicano differences. Speaking in the name of the familia: The interview with Octavio Paz[19]

In contrast to what occurs with the Chicano *pachuco* in *The Labyrinth of Solitude*, in this interview Octavio Paz identifies Chicanos on the basis of a number of relational differences that assign to the Chicano a much desired and apparently positive Mexican resemblance. Paz rejects the assimilationist framework that mediates his vision of the *pachuco* as a *pocho* (a whitened half-breed) in this famous essay and qualifies any identification of the Chicano with the Anglo as a stupid form of ignorance. If this were not enough, Paz reaffirms difference as a highly prized form and structure for speaking 'Chicano' upon suggesting to Armas that the Chicano is not only different but *very* different. In addition, Octavio Paz finally satisfies Armas' nationalist appetite for ethnic and national difference by affirming that there is more likeness between a Chicano and a Mexican than between a Chicano and an Anglo-American (Armas, 1975: 12).

It is within this context that an essential Mexican resemblance surfaces as Paz elaborates on the survival of Mexican culture – especially the Spanish language – in the United States. Paz explains that what enables this linguistic survival is the *familia* and not just any *familia*: one that upholds 'la moral tradicional mexicana'. This morality is described as being so uniquely Mexican that it conserves 'certain values' that are not even apparent in Mexico's cities (Armas, 1975: 12–13). Here Paz espouses a 'Mexican' rendition of familism that finds its complement in a local nationalist ideology on this side of the international border once Armas jumps on the family values bandwagon and links Paz directly to his own communitarian interpretation of familism. Armas seizes the moment and intervenes in this way:

> This is the concept that we want to advance. The concept of the family and the values that can be found in the family have maintained us while we live in an Anglo American society.
>
> (Armas, 1975: 13)[20]

Armas enlists the traditional patriarchal heterosexist family in the struggle against further Anglo encroachment without confronting the disturbing contradiction that historically stable marriage systems of this nature have rested upon coercion and upon inequality, without redressing marital inequality, and without taking into account the fact that women bear disproportionate responsibility for their children (Stacey, 1996: 68–72). In addition to the fact that this 'political' construction of the family leaves gender roles and economic divisions intact and reinscribes compulsory forms of heterosexuality, this construction also sidesteps larger social conditions in its formulation of domination and resistance to domination. [21]

Finally, Armas' notion of 'the traditional family as shield' incorporates many of the most regressive elements of cultural nationalism, elements that can also be found in a more elaborate form in his own Chicano manifesto, *La Familia de la Raza* (Armas, 1972). Here a 'cultural concept of la Familia' not only provides Chicanos with an emerging identity and a unique stability that is purportedly absent among blacks, Jews, Indians, Italian-Americans and Anglos, but also with a ready-made base from which to side-step more drastic social transformations. As Armas himself proposes: '[t]he Chicano Movement today does not need to look to revolutionary models nor radical changes and philosophy' (Armas, 1972: 28). From his viewpoint, for a 'life free of racial exploitation, free of pollution in government, social institutions and environment, we only need to look within ourselves' (Armas, 1972: 28). Here our families are 'ourselves' and so are the values of *machismo*, *carnalismo* (brotherhood) and *compadrazgo* (a masculine rendition of co-parenting and extended family) and their attendant patriarchal structures.

Given this context, it is not surprising that, even though Armas' communitarian talk about the family and family values was itself being widely disputed within a bold-spirited socially engaged Chicana discourse at the time in which he published his famous interview, he makes no mention of this fact. Instead, he broaches the question of women's liberation with Octavio Paz in this way: 'And speaking of this aspect, (the traditional family) what do you think of the female movement that is known here as women's lib?' (Armas, 1975: 14).[22]

This is a loaded question given the fact that it comes after Armas explains to Paz that Anglo society is in a state of decomposition (we can suppose this is due primarily to a lack of strong Christian family values provoked by the 1960s counter-cultural revolt), and after he has already argued in favour of political familism. Although Paz acknowledges that the family itself has come under fire for being a centre of oppression and he reaffirms the importance of the family notwithstanding this fact, he does not endorse Armas' negative position on women's liberation. However, Armas does link Paz to his negative view in this summary of their conversation, which does target this social movement: 'We talked about the women's liberation movement being an extension to the white man's tentacles' (Armas, 1975: 10). We don't read this exchange in the transcription of the interview; however, there is enough in Paz's commentary on the family to suggest that women's liberation is not at all desirable for Chicanos or Chicanas. In Paz's moralistic rhetoric, which tempers Chicano nationalism with a universalist discourse, it is the *Chicana Mexicana mother* who provides the essential Mexican resemblance. In fact she is the one who is linked to a preservation of Chicano language, culture and traditional Mexican family values. Paz refers here to certain values that have been deposited in the family, values that have to do with good, bad, the attitude of youth in the face of sex (Armas, 1975: 12). Suffice it to say that Paz's representation of the Chicana offers an uncanny resemblance to those local nationalist representations of the family – the Chicano *holy* (patriarchal, heterosexist, Christian) family – featured in *De Colores* in which the Chicana is cast as the super Mexican virgin. It is no wonder that the Chicana Mexicana cannot meet her viewing public one-on-one in the graphic representations of *La familia de la raza*,[23] that she is intertwined with her man, and that she blends into a familial portrait which does privilege a Chicano male spectatorship through a frontal portrait of the Chicano father.

In this exchange women are symbolically 'left at home' while the men construct the intellectual and social legacy. There is not a hint of the fact that Chicanas and Mexicanas travel towards a different kind of individual or collective self-representation.[24] They are absented from the transnational male monologue that constructs a Chicana/o Mexicana/o tradition and they are silenced within a discursive exchange that is punctuated with a lingering (spoken or unspoken) command that has been identified with respect to a time-honoured authoritative male-centred Latin American essay: 'Do not interrupt me!'[25]

Chále/Heck, I'll interrupt you! Lessons in the Chicana analytical essay

Fortunately this masculine prerogative to reproduce this type of patriarchal connectivity at the discursive and political levels did not go uncontested. Without asking permission or making any apologies, many Chicanas boldly interrupted this monological stance. They took to the road intellectually, politically and sexually, exploring alternative social identities and practices, and speaking as '*pensadoras*' within what has been termed the 'analytical gender essay' (within the Latin American tradition) and within other analytical productions that theorized social dynamics.[26] From these locations they reimagined relations between Chicanas and Chicanos, Chicanas/os and Mexicanas/os, and the relations between Chicanas and Mexicanas and other people of colour. While they did not speak with one voice or move through one circuit or always bypass essentialism/culturalism, they responded to Paz and to the Chicanos who appropriated him, both directly and indirectly.

In contrast to the majority of critics who centred their critique on scrutinizing *The Labyrinth of Solitude* for its faulty representations of *pachuco* males, the majority of Chicana creative writers and critics who responded to this essay tended to scrutinize its psychosocial sexual interpretations of Mexican history;[27] masculinist heterosexist viewings of Chicana Mexicana bodies; and a failure to recognize the agency of Chicana and Mexican women throughout history.

One of the earliest responses to *The Labyrinth* was delivered by Dotti Hernández, who responded to Paz before the publication of Armas' interview and introduction. From the pages of a grass-roots production that breaks with time-honoured academic standards, she not only rejected the claim that Paz represents *our* culture and roots, but also the idea that his gender identity and existential philosophy could be universally enlisted in the service of everyone's liberation. Without any apologies, without regard for Paz's towering stature and without marking the differences between Mexican males, she forcefully tells us that 'I came to the realization that "the solitude of man" Octavio Paz is analyzing in his book, *The Labyrinth of Solitude*, is truly the solitude of the Mexican male species. . . . The solitude of woman is a unique dilemma not elaborated [on] here by Paz' (Hernández, 1973: 3). Hernández insinuates that Paz has not elaborated on the Mexican woman's predicament, he cannot be considered as a role model or an intellectual precursor; that because he subjects women to a man's reality and to the role that men give her, his patronage and traditions are oppressive and reinforce the historical legacies that configure men as earthly gods, here 'número uno' (Hernández, 1973: 3). Hernández proposes that another Mexican intellectual tradition needs to be consolidated which analyses women's 'thoughts and doubts' concerning the realities to which they are subjected (Hernández, 1973: 3). But here Hernández also suggests that Mexican and Chicana women need to go further: they need to shed the patriarchal mask and expose their personhood and uniquely feminine epistemologies.

Mexican men and those Chicano men who appropriate them are not let off the hook. Hernández proposes that they need to admit that Chicana Mexican women do have a philosophy of life – that these women are independent beings trapped by social roles that foment a dependency on men. Finally she makes it clear that when a repositioning of women in the social, symbolic and cultural order takes place, men will have to pay a price given that women will most likely become a 'competitive force in man's reality', a force which will cause men to become 'unsure of their [macho] identities' (Hernández, 1973: 3).

As a cultural production the grass-roots newspaper essay that features Hernández's reflection anticipates an alternative genealogy for Chicanas/Mexicanas and literally unmasks and 'introduces' them with a double-voiced representation that features the image of an armed and embodied Chicana brown beret, posed in a defiant position in the background of the essay. This visual representation of a Chicana Adelita does more than forecast a need for more equitable gender relations and a need to articulate a series of concerns outside of the 'numero uno' mentality that deprives women of a material reality of their own and suppresses their 'perpetual questioning' of their total assigned role. This visual is suggestive of a level of Chicana Mexicana militancy that is not present in the essay's yet incipient Chicana feminist reflection. For here (in this backgrounded visual representation) the Chicana Mexicana Adelita is not only a competitive force, she is also a combative force – a force that resists the time-honoured patriarchy (and the essayist and surrogate father Octavio Paz) through the hint of armed struggle as well as resisting the other forces of injustice that have propelled Mexican women (and men) into the public space of militancy and revolutionary activity throughout history.

Dotti Hernández was not the only one to launch a counter-discourse against transnationalist patriarchal formations. During the period – and shortly after – Armas published his *Familia de la Raza* (Armas, 1972) and his 'Entrevista con Octavio Paz' (Armas, 1975), many other Chicanas 'of the' Movement were encountering 'familism' head-on in their political speeches and writings, and exposing its ideological presuppositions and anti-feminist subtext. Anna Nieto-Gomez for instance identified familism/nationalism with a sexist philosophy that would have Chicanas support their men, and 'maintain traditional roles and preserve the culture' (Nieto-Gomez, 1976b: 99). To the accusation that the Chicanas were dividing the movement and engaging in a white woman's lib thing, her supporters retorted that feminism in the Chicano movement 'is in no way reactionary', 'not divisive', and 'it's definitely not a white trip' (Anonymous 1976a: 1).

Nieto-Gomez herself repeatedly used the term 'sexist racism' to counter those who would associate Chicana feminism with 'women's lib', explaining that '[u]nfortunately' Chicana feminists were discredited through an association with white feminism. Nieto-Gomez further explained that '[t]his sexist racism implies: 1) only white women can initiate and create change, and 2) all women who speak out against sexism have the same analysis as to the cause and resolution of the issue.' She concluded: '[i]t is clear that this ignorant criticism encourages a lack of support for Chicanas in their struggle for liberation' (Nieto-Gomez, 1976b: 99). But, Nieto-Gomez not only dug deep into the anti-feminist agenda that was more than at the doorstep of Chicano studies, she also interrogated and contested the very polarities that we see lingering behind the silence in Armas' interview with Paz, polarities which would require that Chicanas either be Chicanas (loyalists here) *or* Anglos (women's libbers). In a move that was sure to provoke the wrath of many, Nieto-Gomez courageously uttered: 'I am a Chicana feminist. I make that statement very proudly although there is a lot of intimidation in our community and in the society in general, against people that define themselves as Chicana feminists. . . . They say you can't stand on both sides – which is a bunch of bull' (Nieto-Gomez, 1976a: 53–4).

From another vantage point Francisca Flores en-countered the assumptions behind the culturalist/intellectual interpretations of familism (voiced by men and women), including the idea that a Chicana woman's place is in the home (and that her role is that of a mother with a large family) as well as the attendant proposition that this construction should be a 'tenet' of *la causa/raza* because it is the role of women and a part of our culture. With her now famous retort '*Our culture hell*', Flores de-linked Chicanas from their symbolic roles of 'reproductive mothers of la Raza' by citing the 'erroneous cultural and historical understanding' of what is meant here by 'our' cultural heritage as it relates to the family (Flores, 1971: 158) and further suggesting that the needs of women could not be 'filled with rhetorical abstracts' which, 'stripped of verb[i]age' (or intellectual romanticism), 'means the continued inequality and suppression of women' (Flores, 1971: 159).

From the conference route, Chicanas destabilized the idealistic constructions of *la familia* that we saw in the interview with Paz through point-by-point opinions that recorded the 'separation of' (not unity of) *la familia* and *el movimiento* and explained how '[t]he movimiento is an escape for el hombre (the man) who wants to get out of the house'; how *la familia* had to compete with the movement; the movement was making marriages break up; the '*casa chica*' (the practice of keeping a mistress) was being perpetuated through student–teacher relationships; and how '[i]n the *absence* of the man from la familia', the women had to 'make the decisions concerning the family' by themselves (Ugarte, 1971: 153–4).

However, it was their activism in the public sphere as organizers, workers, community workers, students, teachers, artists, and participants in movements for social and personal change that provided one of the strongest rebuttals to traditional familial representations in the intellectual and political sphere. And an important part of this activism was directed to altering the then emergent disciplinary representations of Chicano Studies. Rather than abdicating their intellectual agencies to patriarchal kinship arrangements of the type we saw earlier, the very women who were being erased from emerging traditions of Chicana/o studies expressed a 'great eagerness to learn about their heritage both as Chicanos and as mujeres'/women. However, as the editors of Encuentro Femenil explained afterwards, these women 'were very disappointed to discover that neither Chicano history, Mexican history, nor Chicano literature included any measurable material on la mujer.' They also explained that 'few [materials] dealt with the identity of la mujer in the family' (García, 1973: 114).

It is not surprising that, when confronted with this institutional context and the emerging patriarchal canons of Chicano Mexicano culture, many Chicana activists created alternative venues for intellectual and political expression (caucuses, talleres, newspapers, newsletters, magazines and revistas) that addressed these issues and lobbied for the establishment of a curriculum relevant to *la mujer*, even stipulating that the *mujer* course should be a requirement for graduation for *all* Chicano studies majors. As Anna Nieto-Gomez further explained in this postscript of a *mujer* workshop: 'This proposal *recognizes* the need to lift the veil of[f] the Virgin's face to show a real woman who is not exempt from the trials of life' (Nieto-Gomez, 1973: 131).

Lifting the veil not only meant uncovering alternative Chicana and Mexicana histories obfuscated within transnational masculinst traditions. This also meant reckoning with the very real consequences of those presuppositions that suggested that the Chicana 'has nothing to say and/or she does not care to participate in society' (García, 1973: 113), and that were, in fact, bolstered by the token representation of gender issues, the red-baiting of feminists of different ideological persuasions, the triple burden of Chicana oppression, and the precarious position of many Chicanas who taught these courses.[28] Let us not forget that, in the 1970s and 1980s, many of these women were subjected not only to a symbolic departure of the type we see in the exchange with Paz, but also to a very literal – painful and public – departure from Chicano studies programmes.

For Anna Nieto-Gomez, one of the most influential Chicana feminist intellectual-activists of the period, 'lifting the veil' meant engaging sexism in the movement and encountering 'the women's struggle' in one's own front yard and area studies – all the while insisting that Chicano studies had to present the histories of working-class Chicanas, attack the sexual stereotypes of men and women, and engage in a multidisciplinary multi-pronged social critique as well as social transformation of society (Anonymous, 1976a: 4). Lifting the veil also meant en-countering and naming the lacunae of the then dominant ideological framework – nationalism – the fact that '[i]n the case of Chicano nationalism racism is identified as the issue and cause of oppression' (Nieto-Gomez, 1976b: 99). Finally, lifting the veil meant endeavouring to formulate a theoretical construct which engaged other social registers and groupings, namely class and gender.

While her contributions may not have been fully accepted at the time in which they were having a transformative effect, Anna Nieto-Gomez's legacy resounded strongly in the words of her students and supporters (both female and male). They explained in *Women Struggle* that Anna Nieto-Gomez stands for this: '[i]f Class exploitation exists, then we must struggle to eradicate this exploitation'; '[i]f racism exists, then we must combat it'; '[i]f the exploitation of women exists, then we must also combat it. The point is, that the struggle against these three forms of exploitation must be comba[t]ed simultaneously, no [*sic*] "after the revolution." Wherever class, racial, and sexual exploitation occur, they must be combated' (Anonymous, 1976a: 1).

Given these dimensions of Anna Nieto-Gomez's contributions, it is not surprising that *La Gente,* a newspaper dedicated to the pueblos of the Americas, featured Anna Nieto-Gomez on the cover of an issue (Spring 1976) that celebrated International Women's Day. Her contributions and the contributions of those Chicana cultural practitioners with whom she collaborated are particularly relevant to the discussion at hand. In a period in which transnationalist intellectual formations were coining the 'tradition', these cultural practitioners facilitated Chicana 'feminist' encounters and conversations with Mexican women throughout history. They promoted alternative print venues such as 'Las Hijas de Cuauhtémoc', a production that remembered a Mexican woman's feminist press organization by the same name from the Revolution of 1910 and was devoted to informing 'the Chicana about herself through history', by reporting political activities and educating her about her socioeconomic condition. In addition to generating awareness about the Chicana's leadership potential, this pivotal newspaper 'reflected an unrecognized resource – Chicana *minds*, Chicana creativity, Chicana art, Chicana action, and Chicana obligations' (García, 1973: 114).

In an essay, the Chicana critic Rita Sánchez proposed that: 'There is, in her [the Chicana's] open expression and in the very act of opening up, a refusal to submit to a quality of silence that has been imposed on her for centuries. In the act of writing, the Chicana is saying, "No", and by doing so she becomes . . . a source of change' (Sánchez, 1977: 66). In their writings this generation of Chicana scholars suggested that for the word to be a source of change, it had to engage social differences and social transformations through practice. Their voices resonate in the works of well-known critical practitioners who have further nuanced earlier forms of Chicana feminist and Chicana/o critical analyses.

However, this is not to say that the lessons of this early generation of thinkers are needed by those contemporary pensadores who would side-step the keen insights of the 'Plan de Santa y Barbara' (Orozco, 1986: 267) in their

Figure 8 Cover, *La Gente*, artist Barbara Carrasco. Reproduced courtesy of Carrasco and *La Gente*

'contemporary' assessments of Chicana/o studies and would once again fault radical Chicana activists, lesbians and Chicana Chicano programmes for separating themselves from early notions of 'community' and for promoting the centrality of unorthodox family relations[29] – all in this period in which we, the children of divorce and separation, can no longer be ignored and will no longer be shamed, and in which there is an abundance of single-family households and people whose survival (social, economic and political) depends on side-stepping normative kinship structures.

But the culprits are not only to be found in this area of study. Twenty-three years after the publication of the famous interview with Octavio Paz (which does circulate within mainstream Latin American representations) and in the aftermath of Paz's untimely and unfortunate passing, memorials eulogized him as 'the father of Mexico' – 'nothing less' – (Weinberger, 1998) and as 'the unchallenged patriarch in his homeland' (Barnes, 1998). Without batting an eyelash, these critics reinscribed a familiar patriarchal connection, but without voicing the 'intruding' Chicano difference or homeland. To be sure, these eulogies lacked the tensions that we saw in the Armas interview, the ones which alerted us to the fact that it was easier to formulate an elite form of patriarchal connectivity at the discursive level than at the material level, to the fact that converging transnational formations of masculinity did not necessarily depart from the same social, political or cultural locations – notwithstanding their claims to *Mexicanidad* – and to the fact that there were specific local 'political' interests to be served in engaging in patriarchal connectivity across national borders.

Exiting the labyrinth: critical reflections on the future[30]

As we reflect on the legacy of this Chicano–Paz engagement, we need to continue to recover the broad range of critical responses that move us from an affirmative monologue to a critical dialogue with these patriarchal transnationalist constructions. We need to offer a more sustained analysis of the larger social and political currents and sexual positionings that promoted – and continue to promote – this particular intersection of *lo chicano/mexicano* as well as other more contemporary renditions of pan-ethnic nationalism that continue to make their way into our living-rooms and classrooms via the political and intellectual discourses of Mexicans and Latin Americans on *both* sides of the inter/national border.

In this article I have illuminated some of national, gender, ethnic, sexual and intellectual exclusions that accompanied the movement 'out of the labyrinth into the race' within specific cultural productions. It is important to 'connect these exclusions' and to reinforce the idea that they both implicated and implicate not only Chicanas and Mexicanas but also other women and people of colour. I would be remiss if I did not also address the fact that many times unearthing the foundational texts associated with the area studies in which we work and struggle means encountering a number of disturbing contradictions: many of those who took a leading role and actively promoted emergent Chicano productions with the audacious hope of cultivating 'alternative' geopolitical and intellectual relations from the margins of official Mexican and American cultures often wrote new stories into old frameworks, engaged militant (political) identities with mainstream (intellectual) ones, and wound up reproducing hegemonic forms of travel which are profoundly disturbing. However, the fact that these transnationalist constructions of identity and intellectual work are profoundly disturbing to many of us should not prevent us from re-en-countering their 'forbidden' languages of difference (the ones that are often complicitous with the social differences promoted in racist, patriarchal and capitalist formations).

At the very least this type of reflection on the movements of the past can provide us with an indication of how far many of our predecessors travelled in opposing these frameworks and with an indication of how far we must continue to travel as we attempt to practise a critical transnationalism that 'connects' the progressive social movements of Chicanas, Mexicanas, women of colour, Chicanos and Mexicanos, hemispheric Indígenas and other people of colour against oppression, exploitation and unequal access to social, political and cultural institutions and services. If we are to exit the labyrinth we need to form new intellectual and social partnerships and we need to engage innovative theories of social intersection that move us through other social, political, economic, sexual and geographical landscapes towards substantive social – not just discursive – change.[31] We need to militate against the theoretical signposts of dominant cultures that continue to read, 'No Mexicans allowed', 'No Chicanas Mexicanas here', 'No people of colour here', 'No unconventional families or sexualities here', 'No difference here', and we need to steer clear of the transnationalist bandwagon – and its dynamic of patriarchal connectivity – which is in vogue these days, notwithstanding the fact that it is profoundly dated.

Finally, we need to stop celebrating transnationalism just because it crosses borders. Celebrating transnational frameworks simply because they are Mexican or because they are mobile often encourages people to leave their critical arsenals at home or to fail to engage the home front, as if complex social arenas only exist on this side and not on that side, and as if we could will away the manner in which race, class, gender and sexuality intersect with one another within transnational global capitalism. This environment suggests that we cannot tackle intellectual work alone, that we have to develop new global networks and critical theoretical engagements if we are to produce a form of cultural studies that truly crosses social, international and state-sanctioned borders.

Notes

1   I dedicate this article to Anna Nieto-Gomez. I would like to thank my mother Angie and my sister Yolanda for providing inspirational lessons of womanhood; Ricardo for helping – not only me but also 'us' – to locate materials in important Chicana/o studies collections that need to be supported; Rafael and Myrtha for making Berkeley possible; and Zaré and Lisa for the continued support throughout this project.

2   I put the 'trans' before nationalist in order to reinforce the idea that Chicano nationalist formations do move across geopolitical, social and textual borders.

3   Juan Rodríguez, interview by Angie Chabram, May 1986. This is an abbreviated response. Rodríguez also referred to other writers in his insightful recollection, and spoke of the importance of cultivating our own Chicano theoreticians. I would like to thank him for reflecting on this and other trajectories.

4   I do not examine all the literature which promotes a connection to Paz. This literature counts with numerous interpretations and revisions which cannot be reduced to what is examined here. None the less, male-centred representations of *lo chicano* and *lo mexicano* abound although there are conflicting representations of Paz within these works which include: David Porath, 'Existentialism and Chicanos' (*De Colores*, 1: 2 (Spring 1972): 6–30); Eliu Carranza, *Pensamientos on los Chicanos: A Cultural Revolution* (Berkeley: California Books, 1969); Armando Rendon, *Chicano Manifesto* (New York: Collier, 1971). Works which refuted the historical basis of Paz's representation of Chicanismo but none the less incorporate some elements from *The Labyrinth* include: Arturo Madrid-Barela, 'In search of the authentic pachuco' (*Aztlán*, 4: 1 (1973): 31–60), and Octavio Romano-V, 'The anthropology and sociology of Mexican Americans: the distortion of history' (*El Grito*, 2 (Winter 1968): 13–26. Rudy Acuña also incorporates some aspects of Paz's representation of the *pachuco* while rejecting others; see *Occupied America* (San Francisco: Canfield Press, 1972), p. 200. For a more complete listing of these works, see Porath's bibliography.

5   Thus, it furnishes a mode of travel that we need to destabilize, an emergent canon formation that we need to debunk, and a social identity that we need to challenge.

6   I am inspired by Stuart Hall here who proposed: 'I want to suggest a different metaphor for theoretical work: the metaphor of struggle.' I give the metaphor of struggle a Chicana cultural studies connotation here. For his discussion see: 'Cultural studies and its theoretical legacies', in Lawrence Grossberg, Cary Nelson and Paula Treichler (eds) *Cultural Studies* (Routledge: New York, 1992), p. 280.

7   José Armas, 'Octavio Paz: on the journey to Octavio Paz', and 'Entrevista con Octavio Paz' (*De Colores*, 2: 2 (1975): 4–10 and 11–22, respectively). It is important to note that *De Colores* dedicated an issue to Chicanas entitled: 'La cosecha/The Harvest: The Chicana Experience' (4:3 (1978)). This issue carried an introduction which proposed that 'there is an immediate task for La Chicana and that is the self-definition of being a woman in a new era'. *De Colores* also published an issue entitled 'Literatura y La Mujer Chicana', edited by Linda Morales Armas and Sue Mocina (3:3 (1977)).

8   My translation. Because this summary incorporates a transnational patriarchal view of the family, which I discuss below, I cite it here as a Mexican representation of familism, although it is spoken within another context (as an example of the 'universal' ties that link Chicanos and Mexicanos historically) within the interview.

9   Octavio Paz propels this dynamic later on in a transcribed interview by tacitly
    accepting the idea that he is in fact a Chicano intellectual precursor (a role he
    flatly denies to the *pachuco*) and extending a paternal lineage of succession to
    his grandfather and father. José Armas actually states that '[t]he groping
    Chicano embraced Paz as their surrogate father who gave their identity some
    reassurance and offered some guidance from which to build their movement.'
    It is important to note that throughout the introduction to Octavio Paz, Armas
    reveals a deeply ambivalent and contradictory attitude towards Paz, at times
    claiming him as an early precursor and underscoring this notion of surrogacy,
    and at times lamenting Paz's failure to live up to his stature as a Chicano role
    model and figurehead. In this way, it is not surprising that although he under-
    scores Paz's intellectual surrogacy, he also makes it clear that the 'Chicano
    Movement is not the result of Paz' (Armas, 1975: 6).

10 This 'conversion' of Octavio Paz is not surprising since within early national-
    ist epistemologies it is the Mexican who marks the opposition to the Anglo.
    This representation of Chicanos and Mexicanos suggests that Mexicans are 'all
    the same among themselves' and that they are 'all different from the Anglo'.

11 José Armas incorporates a number of critiques of *The Labyrinth of Solitude* that
    centre on its representation of the *pachuco* and mythic dimensions. However,
    like many of his predecessors, he forgives Paz (see Armas, 1975: 7–8).

12 I drew from *The Random House Dictionary of the English Language*, College
    Edition (New York: 1968: 1362) for this explanation.

13 While Rendon admits that Chicanos 'owe a great debt to the black people of
    America for striking out against oppression', he also proposes that '[i]f it were
    not for color there would be little to distinguish black from white'. If this were
    not enough he identifies us with this perspective: 'We Chicanos see the Negro
    as a black Anglo.' Suffice it to say that this nationalist perspective and line of
    thinking is very offensive, but it does not reveal a 'general' opinion. Rendon's
    representation of the black Anglo bears a striking resemblance to the Chicana
    malinche who also figures in this work. For more on his construction of ethnic
    groups, see Rendon, 1971: 14–21.

14 For this discussion I am drawing from Mary Pratt's wonderful essay, 'Don't
    interrupt me: the gender essay as conversation and countercanon', in Dorris
    Meyer (ed.) *Reinterpreting the Spanish American Essay* (Austin: University of
    Texas Press, 1995): 10–26. The final section of my article incorporates Chi-
    canas into the counter-canon through Pratt's recovery of Victoria Ocampo's
    Testimonio. For more on this recovery, see Pratt, p. 13.

15 For this critique I have drawn from Ruth Frankenberg's discussion of social
    identity in *The Social Construction of Whiteness: White Women, Race Matters* (Min-
    neapolis: University of Minnesota Press, 1993): 236–8.

16 I am rephrasing Rendon to suit the purposes of my discussion.

17 I do not mean to homogenize Chicano revisions of *The Labyrinth* but to point
    to general trends that were apparent in culturalist-existentialist perspectives
    which interfaced with Chicano nationalism. An example which addresses the
    point at hand can be found in Eliu Carranza's *Pensamientos*. He quotes exten-
    sively from *The Labyrinth of Solitude* and punctuates Paz's text in this way: 'Such

a view may have been or may be true of the Mexican but it is no longer true of the Chicano. . . . For the Chicano has shown his face at last! He has shed the 'servant mentality' and denied the validity of the psychology of the master. He no longer shuts himself away from the stranger nor does he seek to disguise himself' (pp. 6–9).

18   My translation.

19   José Armas and Octavio Paz discuss a number of social, political and cultural dynamics that I have not incorporated here. All the statements made by Paz and Armas are taken from the interview, which is a 'construction' of their discursive exchanges and social identities. I am drawing from Judith Stacey's important work in the subtitle of this section.

20   My translation. Aida Hurtado's comments are instructive here; she points out that: 'la familia, which is patriarchal in nature, is considered a support group . . . a catalyst for political migration.' See *The Color of Privilege* (Ann Arbor: University of Michigan Press, 1996): 75. Armas' notion of the family is also a reaction to general ideological formations that faulted the Chicano family for the social woes of Chicanos.

21   Judith Stacey's contemporary critique of familism is instructive on this point. She proposes that '[d]espite the collectivist aspirations of communitarian ideology, the political effects of identifying family breakdown as the crucible of all social crises that have accompanied postindustrialization and the globalizaton of capitalism are privatistic and profoundly conservative' (1996: 74).

22   My translation.

23   The artwork for *La familia de la Raza* is credited to Walter Baca, although I have not been able to confirm whether the cover of this essay is also his production.

24   I have incorporated the phrase 'space travel' from Minrose Guin, 'Space travel: the connective politics of feminist reading' (*Signs*, 21: 4 (1996): 870–903), although I do not incorporate her perspectives as a way of defining Chicana travel. I am grateful to Inés Hernández-Avila for sharing this citation with me and for her insights about connective politics. She shared these insights in a presentation entitled 'Grounding and localizing narratives: Native American/Chicana connective politics', given at the conference, Coloring of the Humanities: (Inter)Disciplinary/Intertribal Discourses (UC Davis, 15 May 1997).

25   For more on this tradition, see Mary Pratt's recovery of Ocampo, p. 13.

26   I am incorporating Chicanas into the counter-canon tradition described by Mary Pratt with reference to the Latin American essay. For a review of these Chicana artistic and creative productions of the 1970s and 1980s, see my essays 'I throw punches for my race, but I don't want to be a man', in L. Grossberg, C. Nelson and P. Treichler (eds) *Cultural Studies* (New York: Routledge, 1992): 81–95, and '. . . And, yes the earth did part', in L. De La Torre and B. Pesquera (eds) *Building With Our Hands* (University of California Press, 1993): 34–56. For an example of the lesbian counterstance of the 1970s, see Veronica Cunningham's 'ever since' (1976, original, in *Capirotada*, Los Angeles). Reprinted in Tey Diana Rebolledo and Eliana S. Rivero (eds) *Infinite Divisons*

(Tucson: University of Arizona Press: 1993): 101. For an all important example of feminist contestations of the 1980s, see: Cherríe Moraga and Gloria Anzaldúa (eds) *This Bridge Called My Back: Writings by Radical Women of Color* (Kitchen Table: Women of Color Press, 1983) and Cherríe Moraga's *Loving in the War Years, lo que nunca pasó por sus labios* (Boston: South End Press, 1983). For more on Chicana feminism, see Alma García, 'The development of Chicana feminist discourse: 1970–1980', in Ellen Carol Dubois and Vicki L. Ruiz (eds) *Unequal Sisters* (Routledge: London, 1990): 418–31; Norma Alarcón, 'The theoretical subject(s) of this Bridge Called My Back and Anglo-American feminism', and Sonía Saldívar-Hull, 'Feminism on the border: from gender politics to geopolitics', both in Héctor Calderón and José David Saldí-var (eds) *Criticism in the Borderlands* (Durham: Duke University Press, 1991): 29–42 and 189–202 respectively, and Deena Gonzalez, 'Speaking secrets', in Carla Trujillo (ed.) *Living Chicana Theory* (Berkeley: Third Woman Press, 1998): 18–46.

27 For an early revision of Malintzín, see Adelaida del Castillo's 'Malinztín Tenépal: a preliminary look into a new perspective', in Rosaura Sánchez and Rosa Marínez Cruz (eds) *Essays on La mujer* (Los Angeles: Chicano Studies Research Center, 1977): 123–49. For a contemporary critique of Paz's cultural theory, see Emma Pérez, 'Speaking from the margin: uninvited discourse on sexuality and power', in *Building with Our Hands* (1993: 57–74), and Norma Alarcón, 'Traddutora, Traidora: a paradigmatic figure of Chicana feminism', in A. McClintock, A. Mufti and E. Shohat (eds) *Dangerous Liaisons* (Minneapolis: University of Minnesota Press, 1997): 278–97.

28 See Cynthia Orozco, 'Sexism in Chicano studies and the community', in *Chicana Feminism, the Basic Writings* (1986): 267.

29 See Ignacio M. García, 'Chicano studies since el Plan de Santa Bárbara', in David R. Maciel and Isidro D. Ortiz (eds) *Chicana/Chicanos at the Crossroads* (University of Arizona Press, 1996): 190–1 and 202, respectively.

30 While I propose to exit the labyrinth in a different way from that proposed by Lomnitz-Adler I would like to acknowledge the importance of his work in contributing to the semantic path of my symbolic departure.

31 I am responding to some of Teresa Ebert's concerns in 'Ludic feminism, the body, performance and labor: bringing materialism back into feminist cultural studies', *Cultural Critique*, 23 (1003): 5–50.

References

Aguilar Mora, Jorge (1978) *La Divina pareja: Historia y Mito en Octavio Paz*, México, DF: ERA.

Alarcón, Norma (1989) 'Traddutora, traitora: a paradigmatic figure of Chicana feminism', in McClintock *et al.* (eds) (1997) *Dangerous Liaisons*, Minneapolis: University of Minnesota Press.

Anonymous (1976a) Editorial, *Women Struggle*, Spring.

—— (1976b) 'Anna Nieto-Gomez Interview', *Women Struggle*, Spring.

Armas, José (1972) 'La Familia de la Raza', *De Colores*, 3(2) (1976): 1–55.

—— (1975) 'Octavio Paz: on the journey to reaching Paz', *De Colores*, 2(2): 4–10.

Baca Zinn, Maxine (1975) 'Political familism: toward sex role equality in Chicano families', *Aztlán*, 6(2): 13–26.

Barnes, Bart (1998) 'Mexican poet, essayist Paz dies at age 84', *Washington Post*, 21 April.

Bartra, Roger (1987) *La jaula de la melancholía: Identidad y metamorfosis del mexicano*, México, DF: Grijalbo.

Blanco-Aguinaga, Carlos (1973) 'El laberinto fabricado por Octavio Paz', *Aztlan*, 3(1): 1–12.

Calderón, Héctor and Saldívar, José David (eds) (1991) *Criticism in the Borderlands*, Durham: Duke University Press.

Carranza, Eliu (1969) *Pensamientos on los Chicanos: A Cultural Revolution*, Berkeley: California Books.

Chabram, Angie and Fregoso, Rosa Linda (eds) (1990) 'Chicana/o cultural representations: reframing alternative critical discourses', *Cultural Studies*, 4(3): 203–13.

Chabram-Dernersesian, Angie (1993) 'And, yes . . . the earth did part: on the splitting of Chicana/o subjectivity', in A. de la Torre and B. Pesquera (eds) *Building With Our Hands*, Berkeley: University of California Press.

Clifford, James (1989) 'Notes on theory and travel', *Inscriptions*, 5: 177–88.

Clifford, James and Dharsehwar, Vivek (1989) 'Preface', *Inscriptions*, 5: v–vii.

De Colores (1975) 'Entrevista con Octavio Paz: Paz on Chicano liberation, women's liberation, la familia, Marxism y más', *De Colores*, 2(2): 11–21.

Flores, Francisca (1971) 'Conference of Mexican women in Houston – Un Remolino', in Alma García (ed.) (1997) *Chicana Feminist Thought*, New York: Routledge.

García, Alma M. (1973) 'Introduction to Encuentro Femenil', in her (ed.) *Chicana Feminist Thought*, New York: Routledge.

—— (1990) 'The development of Chicana feminist discourse, 1970–1980', in E. DuBois and V. Ruiz (eds) *Unequal Sisters*, New York: Routledge, Chapman and Hall.

—— (ed.) (1997) *Chicana Feminist Thought*, New York: Routledge.

Guin, Minrose (1996) 'Space travel: The connective politics of feminist reading', *Signs*, 21 (4): 870–903.

Hall, Stuart (1987) 'New ethnicities', in H. Baker Jr. *et al.* (eds) (1996) *Black British Cultural Studies*, Chicago: University of Chicago Press.

Hernández, Dotti (1973) 'Número uno', Northridge, CA: *El Popo Femenil*, May.

Hurtado, Aída (1996) *The Color of Privilege: Three Blasphemies on Race and Feminism*, Ann Arbor: University of Michigan Press.

Joseph, Suad (1996) 'Relationality and ethnographic subjectivity: key informants and the construction of personhood in fieldwork', in D. Wolf and C. D. Derre (eds) *Feminist Dilemmas in Fieldwork*, Westview, CO: HarperCollins.

Leher, Jim (1998) 'The voice of Mexico', Transcript, 20 April.

Lomnitz-Adler, Claudio (1992) *Exits from the Labyrinth*, Berkeley: University of California Press.

Madrid Barela, Arturo (1973) 'In search of the authentic pachuco', *Aztlán*, 4(1): 31–60.

McLemee, Scott (1998) 'The labryinth of Paz', *Salon*, 28 April.

Nieto-Gomez, Anna (1973) 'The Chicana-perspectives for education', in Alma García (ed.) (1997) *Chicana Feminist Thought*, New York: Routledge.

—— (1974) 'La feminista', in Alma García (ed.) (1997) *Chicana Feminist Thought*, New York: Routledge.

—— (1976a) 'Chicana feminism', in Alma García (ed.) (1997) *Chicana Feminist Thought*, New York: Routledge.

—— (1976b) 'Sexism in the Movimiento', in Alma García (ed.) (1997) *Chicana Feminist Thought*, New York: Routledge.

Orozco, Cynthia (1986) 'Sexism in Chicano studies and the community', in Alma García (ed.) (1997) *Chicana Feminist Thought*, New York: Routledge.

Paz, Octavio (1961) *The Labyrinth of Solitude*, trans L. Kemp, New York: Grove Press.

Pérez, Emma (1993) 'Speaking from the margin: uninvited discourse on sexuality and power', in A. de la Torre and B. Pesquera (eds) *Building With Our Hands: New Directions in Chicana Studies*, Berkeley: University of California Press.

Porath, Don (1973) 'Existentialism and Chicanos', *De Colores*, 1(2): 6–30.

Pratt, Mary L. (1995) '"Don't interrupt me": the gender essay as conversation and countercanon', in D. Meyer (ed.) *Reinterpreting the Spanish American Essay: Women Writers of the 19th and 20th Centuries*, Austin: University of Texas Press.

Rendon, Armando B. (1971) *Chicano Manifesto: The History and Aspirations of the Second Largest Minority in America*, New York: Macmillan.

Rincon, Bernice (1973) 'La Chicana: her role in the past and her search for a new role in the future', in Alma García (ed.) (1997) *Chicana Feminist Thought*, New York: Routledge.

Sánchez, Rita (1977) 'Chicana writer breaking out of silence', in Alma García (ed.) (1997) *Chicana Feminist Thought*, New York: Routledge.

Stacey, Judith (1996) *In the Name of the Family*, Boston, MA: Beacon Press.

Ugarte, Sandra (1971) 'Chicana Regional Conference', in Alma García (ed.) (1997) *Chicana Feminist Thought*, New York: Routledge.

Vacio, Minerva and Buiz Esparza, Jorge (1998) 'Octavio Paz: Speaking the unspeakable', *Escala*, June: 70–5.

Weinberger, Elliot (1998) 'The voice of Mexico', in *The News Hour with Jim Lehrer* (transcript), 20 April.

Rosaura Sánchez and Beatrice Pita

MAPPING CULTURAL/POLITICAL DEBATES IN LATIN AMERICAN STUDIES[1]

> Y bien, ahora . . .
> ahora pensad lo que sería
> el mundo todo yanqui, todo
> Faubus . . .
> Pensad por un momento,
> imaginadlo un solo instante.
> (Nicolás Guillén)

Abstract

The theorization of postmodernism as the cultural logic of late capitalism has generated a number of debates among Latinos in the US and among Latin American critics in particular. This article examines a number of writings published between 1989 and 1994 by Latin American critics focusing on the viability of seeing Latin America as postmodern. We argue that in the rush to accept First World theoretical frameworks, there has been much confusion and a collapsing of economic, political and cultural categories. Conflating market growth and shifts with social change and the availability of a plurality of consumer goods with the distribution of goods and services, some critics have been quick to label cultural production in Latin America as 'postmodern'. What is needed is a delimitation of the categories used, an examination of the cultural debate in relation to other debates on development, social movements, democratization and alliance politics, as well as an examination of local intellectual debates within the global context of restructuring and transnational capital.

Keywords

postmodernism; new social movements; multinational corporations; late capitalism; cultural studies; culturalist analyses

TAKEN AS A WHOLE, the field of Latin American cultural studies, that is, the burgeoning body of analysis and theorization of cultural production and consumption in contemporary Latin America linked to a global schema of 'post-modernism', is a relatively recent phenomenon bringing together literary critics and theorists, anthropologists, political scientists and critics of popular culture. In the last decade in particular, these critics have focused their research on social movements, 'post-development' and the ubiquitous and much abused term, 'postmodernism', revealing not only the dominance of analyses of the margins from the centre but also, in some cases, a concern with engaging and interrogating dominant theoretical categories that shape their very analyses (for example, Yúdice, 1989).

Thus while there are critics who are all too ready to formulate analyses of the Third World[2] through the use of categories developed in the First World, there are increasingly also those who are wary or take issue or even reject out of hand the notion of reading the Third World as 'variations on a master narrative'; that is, from the perspective of preconceived categories (Chakrabarty, 1992: 1), especially within the fields of subaltern studies, postcolonial studies and cultural studies. What is particularly contested, in part or entirely, is the use of Euro-centric paradigms to refer to economic, political and cultural spheres in the peripheral world (Nelson Osorio, cited in Yúdice, 1989: 106). For other critics not only is the notion itself of 'centre/periphery' or even the category of 'Third World' taken to task, wholly or in part, but so too the very notion of 'development' (Escobar, 1992) or what Chakrabarty calls the 'transition narrative', used to explain the periphery in terms of an incomplete transition, a lack or an absence (Chakrabarty, 1992a: 4–5).[3] Although discrediting of the 'development' model is not unique to the periphery (see Touraine's critique in the 1981 translation), Third World theorists in particular reject discourses of modernity that have led to the representation of their continents as 'underdeveloped', stressing the need for new discourses and new forms of representation (Escobar, 1992: 48). Whether the posited alternative discourses challenge the foundations of capitalism or merely construct new local discourses that sustain the power of capital is, however, a key question.

The move away from totalizing paradigms and towards 'multiple responses/propositions' (Yúdice, 1992: 4), however fashionable today, suggests analyses framed in terms of the particular and the local, a microsocial approach that, while potentially in opposition to 'globalism', not only tends towards formulations in terms of 'the very fragmentation which a mobile capitalism and flexible accumulation can feed upon' (Harvey, 1989: 303) but also ignores the fact that particular 'master narratives' are strategically important for guiding particular social struggles (Fraser and Nicholson, 1990: 26), acknowledged or not.[4] Postmodern social theories posited to displace prior analytical categories must, in any case, take the nondiscursive into account; that is, the impact of globalization on a multi-tiered cultural sphere. Harvey, for example, suggests that the restructuring taking place in this period of late capitalism, with its multinational corporations, high-tech informatization, international working class, transition to flexible accumulation in the midst of a weakening to some extent of the autonomy and power of nation-states, has compressed time and space to the point where volatility and a growing homogenization are the rule and not the exception, within the centre as much as on the periphery (Harvey, 1989: 191). Thus envisioned, we are all within 'the culture of postmodernism' (Jameson, 1988: 111) and yet perhaps not all to the same degree.[5] Whether the apparent movement towards cultural homogeneity is likely to be sustainable, given evidence to the contrary even within First World societies themselves, is of course a question closely linked to the issue of economic and political alternatives.

Yet even as Eurocentric notions of universality are condemned and socialist paradigms are cynically rejected, new equally First World generated notions along the lines of postmodernism, 'new social movements', post-history, post-Marxism, post-ideology, post-colonialism, post-nation, post-development and liberal democracy gain currency with Third World intellectuals. In some cases these constructs are selectively taken up and reconstructed, like the term 'social movement' (Escobar, 1992: 36) or even 'postmodernism of resistance' (Beverley, 1993: 110). What is undeniably evident is a search among Latin American intellectuals for 'new' discourses and practices that stress cultural heterogeneity, difference, micropolitics, pluralism, democracy and popular culture, all of which suggests that the trashing of 'universals' or Eurocentric discourses is highly selective. It is as if there were a consumerist 'longing to be integrated into the world market' (Jameson, 1993b: 173) of ideas (a consenting, as it were, to hegemonic ideological discourses), even as the call for alternative theories is put out and the margins call attention to their own marginality, turning the tables, by de-centring the centre.

It goes without saying that the debate on 'postmodernism' is central to any analysis of the culturalist perspective (with its focus on 'representation') dominant today in Latin American studies; as Sánchez Vázquez states: 'es un hecho' (1990: 5). Yet at a practical level it is always important and in fact incumbent upon us to account for the proliferation of terms used to historicize, demarcate areas and specify the scope and application of terms employed, as suggested by West (1988: 272), for the term 'postmodernism' is used in so many different and divergent ways that it risks becoming meaningless (and in that alone, we suppose, quite 'postmodernist'), a floating signifier of sorts. As used by Jameson, for example, 'postmodernism' refers to a 'cultural dominant' (1991: 159), that is, 'cultural hegemony', but, to quote Jameson himself, the term is not restricted

to a 'specifically cultural category' but 'is designed to name a "mode of production" in which cultural production finds a specific functional place' (1991: 406).
Jameson's invocation of the term thus seeks to account for the interrelation of
the economic, political and cultural spheres within the social totality.

It is perhaps the collapsing of several categories under one catch-all rubric,
'postmodernism', that gives rise, even in the periphery, to reductive descriptions
of nearly everything as 'postmodernist', in the process failing to recall that
'hegemony' never precludes alternative forms, but rather builds itself on them,
as Jameson himself has noted (1991: 159):

> To describe (postmodernism) in terms of cultural hegemony is not to
> suggest some massive and uniform cultural homogeneity of the social field,
> but very precisely to imply its coexistence with other resistant and hetero-
> geneous forces which it has a vocation to subdue and incorporate.

That the goal of hegemony is the absorption and reconfiguration of dissent does
not imply that this is a *fait accompli* in Latin America today nor, we would hold,
does it imply that all Latin American cultural production or 'lived experience'
can be reductively classified as 'postmodernist'. Alongside an informal sector of
labour practices, there are coexisting modes of cultural production, subordinated
practices and counter-practices that need to be mapped out. It is in this regard
that most theoretical writing on newly developing countries is in effect caught
in a transcultural double-bind, constantly having to straddle the general and the
particular, the global and the local.

The concept of *postmodernism* is in fact a pre-eminent example of this engagement with categories that configure both consent and dissent and shape identity
and difference in Latin American theoretical writing, even as theorists endeavour
to create a sense of themselves as separate and distinct from the centre, albeit tied
to a global economic system. Tracing the emergence and proliferation of the terms
of these debates during the decade of the 1980s and early 1990s are a plethora of
publications, including several dealing specifically with Latin America.[6] At the
core of the problematic deployment of the term 'postmodernism', and its attendant corollaries, one finds, for the most part, a collapsing of differences between
the *postmodern* period of capitalism, *postmodernity,* and *postmodernism* and, secon-
darily, we would venture to say, in some cases at least, an eagerness to fit cultural
practices of Latin America within schemata born in and authorized by the First
World. The problem of inclusion and exclusion, as well as frame of reference, is
clearly central to any engagement with these theoretical categories.

To grapple with this complex and slippery set of notions, it would be useful
to attempt to disarticulate the term 'postmodernism', and stress that it variously,
and according to its users, means to encompass three different areas: (1) the world
system of late capitalism, that is, a postmodern global economy; (2) postmodernity as the general overall 'condition' and (following Jameson's comments on

modernity (1991: 310)), as what Raymond Williams calls a 'structure of feeling', that is, a particular 'lived experience' or logic of space and time (see Harvey, 1989: 39) that is political as much as cultural/ideological (West, 1988: 272), and (3) a cultural aesthetic, an artistic and intellectual dimension composed of different strands of postmodernism (*sans* quotation marks). Underpinning all three related categories, implicitly or explicitly, is of course the term 'modernization', the key notion implicitly being rejected but which, however imprecise and contradictory, best describes the globalization phenomenon presently underway in accelerated fashion in an ever more highly urbanized Latin America.

Thus whether one disagrees on matters of degree or substance and despite its many and serious shortcomings, this construct 'postmodernism' has to be dealt with. At worst it is a catch-all marketable, facile and fashionable term; at best it is symptomatic of the period and grapples with perceived shifts (however slight) in economic, political and cultural structures and practices. Once we are disposed to look at these three overlapping areas, we can examine contradictory assignments of the term 'postmodernist' to particular cultural products, like testimonials, using the genre as a test case around which to critically view the handling of the 'postmodernist' designation. Even critics questioning the adoption of the postmodernist paradigm, such as Larsen, insist on calling recent testimonials postmodernist (Larsen, 1990: 88). The testimonial can in fact serve as a useful way of considering different spheres encompassed by 'postmodernism' and of examining its position within literary spaces while at the same time noting its relation to the market and links to various social movements.

Contemporary Latin American testimonials, for example, are, at one level, indisputably commodities produced within this postmodern period; that is, within the transnational phase of capitalism, for a world market. This global restructuring of capitalist production (cultural and otherwise) is said to signal the triumph of modernization and the end of the modernist developmental or historical paradigm (Jameson, 1991: 324). But in fact, within the Third World, modernization is an ongoing project having a tremendous impact on the restructuring of Latin American economies, although not in the sense of 'emancipation from want' and full integration into a mass economic and political democracy, but rather of its penetration by massive foreign investment, multinationals, informational technology and hardware and its insertion within a global circuit of consumption, especially of cultural commodities. It goes without saying that whatever processes are at work at the cultural level, the postmodern period of capitalism has in fact meant increased capitalist penetration, indebtedness, balance-of-payment difficulties, inflation, rising unemployment and underemployment, the growth of an informal sector of the economy, the restructuring of local cultures, and of course, increased consumption, especially by local middle and upper classes, with access to videorecorders, radios, televisions and other cultural artefacts. Attendant to this widening consumer society, to which we will return below, is an intensification of uneven development itself, for the installation of growing numbers of assembly plants and manufacturing subsidiaries, especially from the US, motivated by local market penetration and the availability of cheap labour, has in good measure intensified marginality, poverty and, in some instances, illiteracy. We cannot ignore the fact that despite major changes in the global capitalist system since the end of the Second World War, two features of the Third World, and of Latin America in particular, have not changed: 'the chains of dependency binding the periphery to the center' and the ever-widening 'gap between the periphery and the center' (Sweezy and Magdoff, 1992: 11).

Given state policies in Latin America granting special advantages to local competitors (Sweezy and Magdoff, 1992: 13) and in the face of competition from Japanese, Korean and German multinationals, corporations in search of larger markets and greater investment opportunities have supported moves towards bloc trade agreements like that of the North American Free Trade Agreement (NAFTA), the first of what will undoubtedly be many more multilateral agreements in Latin America in the future (MacEwan, 1994: 25). The expansion of multinational investment will also bring not only a continuing shift of industries from the US to Latin America but the displacement, already evident in Mexico, of local Latin American industries unable to compete. The impact of the global economy on Latin American cultural industries may well be devastating too, as made clear by García Canclini in his assessment of the discernible patterns emerging even at this early stage of the process.

In his study of the effect of NAFTA on Mexican cultural production, García Canclini notes a crisis in the production and sale of books (1993a: 212), with a drop in sales and the bankruptcy of several national firms (1993a: 214). At a moment when only 30 per cent of the publishing houses represent Mexican capital and 10 per cent foreign capital (60 per cent are mixed capital) (1993a: 213), it would be important to note likewise that in the US several major publishing firms (McGraw-Hill, Prentice Hall, Penguin USA, Random House/Vintage Books, Doubleday and Dell/Delacorte Press) have begun publishing in Spanish, not only dictionaries and other educational materials, but literature as well (García Canclini, 1993a: 218; Colford, 1994: E8). García Canclini goes on to underscore that the only protected market in Mexico is that of the state in its publication of textbooks for public schools, but private firms, in need of the latest technology and high-quality paper, find that they cannot compete within an international market. NAFTA does not bode well for Mexican and other Latin American publishing industries as the volume of imported books will no doubt increase. Even at the level of audiovisual production, where privatization has facilitated the growth of monopolies like Televisa and the export of their programming to the United States and other Latin American countries, there are indications that competing industries on cable transmitting programmes produced in the US, such as Multivisión and Turner Network Television, will soon be making further inroads into the Mexican market to match that already evident in the sale and renting of videocassettes, primarily of dubbed or subtitled US films, as well as in the rise of sales of VCRs (García Canclini, 1993a: 228, 230).[7]

García Canclini's work is useful in any assessment made of postmodernity in Latin America. Primarily, he analyses the heterogeneous production and marketing of cultural artefacts within Latin American sectors (whether closely linked to a global or part of an informal economy), and their transcultural, hybrid nature (García Canclini, 1989a). In his essay 'El debate posmoderno en Iberoamérica', García Canclini is especially interested in examining the notion that with the advent of postmodernism divisions between popular and elite popular production have waned, commenting that these two spheres were never truly autonomous in Latin America, given its particular colonial and later political and economic development (García Canclini, 1989b: 80). This quasi-integration of elite, folkloric and mass culture within modernization, he notes, has in fact served ideologically to mask specific material differences between social classes and ethnic groups even while reproducing them (García Canclini, 1989b: 81).

Yet despite hybridization, Latin American folk art is said not to have disappeared; in fact García Canclini goes on to cite a growth in the number of artisans and in the volume of their production. What has changed however is not only the promotion of these products through mass media and state cultural agencies and their circulation within a world market (1989b: 85–6) but their very commodification; that is, their production for the market rather than as articles primarily for family or community use. The sale of Mexican pottery, Otavaleño ponchos and ruanas, Salasacan tapestries, other Indian belts, jewellery and art objects in major department stores within the US and their exhibition within museums and art galleries does not however mean that these products are all postmodernist. In fact, in most cases these crafts continue to be the product of labour-intensive cottage industries, although as García Canclini also indicates, some of these are 'hybrid products', hybrid like the economy itself, with artisans appropriating new technologies to modernize the production of their wares and at times incorporating new thematics, even while maintaining their own cultural practices in their daily lives (García Canclini, 1993b: 435). What is clear is the exploitation of the artisans as cheap manual labour, for the ones profiting from the sale of these items are the middlemen and stores rather than the producers.

The transcultural mix of orientations, both international and localized, is a good example of what Harvey terms 'coping with the phenomenon of time-space compression', intensified during this period of late capitalism but already initiated during the period of modernity (Harvey, 1989: 278). García Canclini's work is thus important in understanding the articulation of the global market with Latin American cultural production as a whole. The resulting 'hybridization', synthesis of both the global (centre) and local (periphery), as itself a postmodern phenomenon, is discussed at length in numerous essays.[8] Mixed economies are not of course unique to this period nor to the periphery, as Harvey explains in his analysis of the highly contradictory or hybrid situation that emerges with an increased flexibility in capital accumulation and geographical mobility. This flexibility allows for 'eclecticism in labor practices', even in advanced capitalist countries, with high-tech production intersecting with more traditional labour practices in the informal sector, especially in sweat shops and home industries (Harvey, 1989: 187). With these mixed forms of production, in the centre as well as on the periphery, come not only hybrid cultural practices and styles, what García Canclini calls 'cultural reconversions' (García Canclini, 1993b: 32), but a different positioning of culture itself within society[9] and a heightening of consumerism.

As is obvious to anyone who has been to Latin America recently, late capitalism has brought a marked intensification of 'modernization' in its consumerist version. The changes at the level of infrastructure, alongside a proliferation of military bases, are evident, for example, even in a small country like Ecuador. Otavaleño ponchos are now made with synthetic thread and Salasacan tapestries mix traditional themes with modern urban logos. Even homes in the smallest towns now have television reception, and Spanish language versions of *Murder She Wrote* are viewed in middle-class homes in Riobamba. The media is of course the single most important instrument of cultural/ideological and market penetration. But despite this consumption of imported mass culture, the poverty and misery remain in evidence, not only in the *sierra* but in large urban centres like Guayaquil; and more importantly, the exploitation and dispossession of the indigenous communities continues as well. Ecuador, like other Latin American countries, is marked by uneven development, experiencing conditions of both modernity and postmodernity. In fact, if we re-examine Jameson's descriptions of modernity and modernism, it becomes clear that the 'uneven moment of social development' or the 'simultaneity of the nonsimultaneous' and the 'synchronicity of the non-synchronous' are not limited to a modern moment but are in fact at the very heart of the 'postmodern' period as well (Jameson, 1991: 307).

This issue of 'simultaneity of the nonsimultaneous' is perhaps best addressed in Monsiváis' essay on Mexican culture on the eve of the signing of the North American Free Trade Agreement, in which he remarks at length upon the acceleration of modernization in Mexico, especially at the level of educational attainment, mass consumption of cultural goods, and greater access to information technology. What is striking is that these comments appear side by side with references to the high rates of functional illiteracy, poverty and limited access to information (Monsiváis, 1993: 194).[10] Thus despite assertions in studies looking to the mechanisms of the market for evidence of the end of boundaries between elite and popular culture and the end of rigid class divisions as far as 'taste' (García Canclini, 1989a: 81–2), class structures in Latin America continue in force and, cultural industries notwithstanding, access to information, education, literature and art is still determined by social location. Only now social class is disguised in terms of consumer potential and mass consumption is equated with the 'democratization' of culture. When unequal distribution and consumption are admitted, they are said to be of a different type: 'that inequality no longer has the same simple and polar form that we formerly attributed to it when we divided countries in terms of dominant/dominated or the world, in terms of empire/dependent nations' (García Canclini, 1989a: 93).[11] Postmodernist concern with discarding simplistic binary analyses serves in effect to conceal antagonistic relations, just as the 'flourishing of market rhetoric', as Jameson (1993a: 182) indicates, purposefully confuses consumer choice with freedom:

> the fundamental point to be made here is that the 'freedom of choice' of consumer goods (in any case overrated) is scarcely the same thing as the freedom of human beings to control their own destinies and to play an active part in shaping their collective life.

The continuing and widespread patterns of uneven or selective development resulting from late capitalism, what Amin, in speaking of the Third World, terms 'maldevelopment' (Amin, 1990), have undoubtedly produced uneven patterns of consumption in Latin America that need to be correlated with class and political relations.

Within this 'simultaneity of the nonsimultaneous', how then do we proceed to view any given cultural product from Latin America? Like other commodities, they may be produced for a global or local/regional market by either local individuals, cooperatives or companies, or transnational concerns, like book publishers. The fact that industries today target products for specific groups of consumers rather than simply for a mass market, what Callinicos calls the 'disaggregation of the mass market into segmented niches' (Callinicos, 1989: 134), is especially relevant in the area of literature and cultural products more generally; recent postmodernist fashions in the US and Europe have undoubtedly created a lucrative series of special markets for works dealing with 'marginality' and 'difference'. But does this mean that the texts produced in Latin America are inherently postmodernist? Here it would be useful to recall Larrain's point that the integration of colonial Latin America into the international market did not make it capitalist (Larrain, 1989: 202). In a similar way we could argue that the integration of Latin American cultural products into a global market does not automatically make them postmodernist, even if in their consumption patterns – in selected instances – they may well circulate as postmodernist commodities.

But let us return for a moment to the case of the widely known Menchú testimonial, which will serve as a good example. As a mediated/collaborative work produced, significantly, not in Guatemala but in France, the Menchú–Debray text has to be analysed both as a commodity packaged for a global market selling 'difference' and marginality and as a Latin American text narrated out of conditions of repression, exploitation and oppression; that is, from a geopolitical area with a long history of 'transculturation' (Yúdice, 1992b: 209). The space in which the Quiché live is unquestionably situated within the periphery and further marked by a history of repression, genocide, social inequity, insurgency/counter-insurgency and a guerrilla movement that addresses 'demands of ethnic identity as well as class' and places 'the concerns of the country's Indian majority at the center of the revolutionary struggle' (Jonas, 1990: 14). At one level the concern with Indian rights in Guatemala would appear to fit in with notions of 'alliance politics' or 'new social movements' posited in First World countries, except that here the alliances continue to be grounded in social class as much as ethnicity, as Menchú makes quite clear; hers, she says, is a revolutionary struggle (Menchú, 1984: 233). Social movements within Guatemala thus continue to include armed struggle, as well as militant action by peasants, workers, students and theology of liberation groups (Menchú, 1984: 232). Unlike social movements theorized by postmodernist intellectuals, who suggest that revolution has been superseded, those movements in Guatemala, as elsewhere in Latin America, arising in response to exploitation, state repression and dispossession, continue to be linked to macrosocial realities.

Postmodernity and postmodern politics

The issue of new social movements, central to any discussion of postmodernity in Latin America, is of course tied to the much discussed 'mode of experience of space and time' during this period of late capitalism (Harvey, 1989: 201). Harvey finds that the geographical mobility of capital and flexible accumulation in the First World is paralleled by an 'emphasis upon ephemerality, collage, fragmentation and dispersal in philosophical and social thought', a disorientation that ostensibly increasingly characterizes the experience of postmodernist life (Harvey, 1989: 302). It is striking to note none the less that this description is not far removed from that offered by Berman, for example, to refer to modernity (Berman, 1988: 15), except perhaps for the acceleration of turnover time in production and consumption that leads to 'quick-changing fashions' and 'cultural transformation' (Harvey, 1989: 151). In speaking of this phenomenon, Harvey, like other theorists of postmodernism, notes 'the search for personal or collective identity, the search for securing mooring in a shifting world' (Harvey, 1989: 302) in a world of uncertainty, traits that could describe as well cultural production at least since Romanticism, with its reaction to the consolidation of capitalism and the disappearance of older orders. Other critics however insist that what has changed is the very loss of the 'sense' that we are at a new place; memory itself is seen as a casualty of postmodern times (Jameson, 1991: 311, 366).

Jameson, of course, stresses the difference between modernity and post-modernity, noting that in the latter 'a fully "modernized" life-world can be experienced as well as imagined as a realized fact' (Jameson, 1993: 297). This difference between an experienced and an imagined 'fully "modernized" world' is what perhaps separates those in the unevenly developed periphery from those at the centre and what ultimately leads to different lived experiences, different 'structures of feeling'. In developing countries, 'modernization' is still a project to be realized rather than something taken for granted. The past, meaning not a pre-colonial past but the nineteenth and twentieth centuries, is not yet an 'object of nostalgia' in the Third World but rather still very much a part of today's reality; the resulting incongruities are of course jarring. For example, the adobe Indian huts of the Ecuadorian sierra, although now disappearing, are still visible to anyone driving on the now paved Pan American highway, from which, more-over, one can also glimpse an occasional satellite dish. To account for these jux-tapositions, one must realize, as Chakrabarty explains, that 'history exists in Third World societies precisely because it has not yet been devoured by con-sumerist social practices' (Chakrabarty, 1992a: 57). Something similar could perhaps likewise be said about the First World itself, where internal Third World and/or ethnic spaces lend credence to the idea that the death of history has been, to say the least, greatly exaggerated.

Proliferating notions of 'endism', like post-history, post-industrial, post-colonial, post-Marxism, post-development and postmodernism are very much a part of the latest economic/political and cultural phraseology. Aside from blatant grandstanding from the most reactionary quarters, these categories and this reconfiguring of explicatory frameworks are a response to an epistemological crisis closely linked to poststructuralism, to a rejection of metanarratives, in par-ticular of the Marxist paradigm, and to new formulations of political struggle within late capitalism (in what Touraine calls 'post-industrial' societies (Touraine, 1981: 6)) carried out by heterogeneous 'groupings' or social actors. The prolif-eration of works theorizing these new social movements during the 1980s in Latin America, as well as throughout the world, is a primary example of cultural pro-duction within postmodernity. Key to most if not all these writings is a 'retreat from class' as the fundamental division in society (Meiksins Wood, 1986). At bottom lies an assumption about the end of 'old polarities' (i.e. class antagonisms) and a 'new world order' and a call for new strategies substituting 'the political for the economic', replacing 'the question of capitalism with that of state power' (Jameson, 1993a: 174) and privileging cultural discourses and manifestations as the object of study. Modernization (i.e. 'consumer society'), democratization and popular culture thus become the new 'foundations' of 'pluralism'. What is lacking, ironically, in these presumably anti-foundationalist writings is a radical critique of liberalism, that is, of bourgeois democracy (Chakrabarty, 1992: 20).

Central to the body of literature on new social movements is the work of Laclau and Mouffe (1987), whose discursive model, like the sociology of action of Touraine (1981: 27, 139), focuses on constructs of identity, collectivity, democracy, historicity, as well as on social actors and alliance politics. Latin American theorists, like Escobar, interested in adapting these models for alterna-tive social projects, posit the struggle at the level of discourse. For Escobar, 'in

Latin America, social movements are economic, political and cultural struggles, that is, struggles over meanings, from the nature of national development to everyday practices' (Escobar, 1992: 41). For that reason, Escobar argues, the task for Latin American intellectuals is both to resist Eurocentric epistemologies and to construct 'collective imaginaries capable of orienting social and political action' (Escobar, 1992: 41); that is, new political discourses that allow for a re-definition of Latin America and which enable the mobilization of emerging new social actors. For this task Escobar signals three major discourses 'with the poten-tial to articulate . . . forms of struggle': the discourse of democracy, the dis-course of difference, and anti-development discourses (Escobar, 1992: 48), all, ironically, one would have to note, Eurocentric constructs as well.

The debate, for Escobar, who focuses on the need to dismantle the paradigm of development as a way of explaining the economic configuration of the Third World, is to be waged on the theoretical battlefield. Only the most intransigent theory bashers would take issue with the idea that a framework is necessary for analysis and particular discourses, for creating awareness as well as generating constructs of identity that can lead to collective action. Marxists have long recog-nized the value of a dynamic theoretical framework. Problems, however, arise with the notion of 'new social movements' and their almost exclusive focus on micropolitics, local struggles and everyday practices, all important for spon-taneous urban protests and alliances but analysable as what Harvey terms 'place politics' that put a heavy emphasis on 'the potential connection between place and social identity' (Harvey, 1989: 303), overlooking macrosocial relations. The clearest analysis of the underlying tenets of these social movement theorists is that offered by Meiksins Wood (1986: 76):

> the dissociation of politics from class; the establishment of the non-correspondence between the economic and the political; the dissolution of the social into discourse; the replacement of the working class by a 'dis-cursively constructed' plural subject; the subordination of socialist struggle to a plurality of democratic struggles in which 'democracy' is indetermi-nate, abstract, and loosely defined so as to conceptualize away the differ-ences and the antagonisms that separate socialism from capitalism.

One might venture so far as to say that there is a 'world' of difference between the strategies of articulation set in motion in Latin America and the 'broad democratic alliances' in the centre countries that revolve in good measure around 'status' (lifestyle, affinity groupings and patterns of consumption), occu-pation and income (Callinicos and Harman, 1989: 2–3). In Latin America, as Calderón and Jehlin indicate, these emerging new social movements are, for the most part, urban collectivities (organized around neighbourhood problems, housing and rent control, social services, access to food markets, and other kinds of local issues that affect one or several neighbourhoods), peasants, human rights groups, women's and feminist groups, youth organizations, and even guerrilla groups (Calderón and Jehlin, 1987: 28–37). Studies on these Latin American movements in large measure leave aside a consideration of what we can only refer to as relations of production. Thus attempts to separate exploitation from domination have led to a focus on 'power' and on different types of oppression, excising class relations from the social equation.

The work of Monsiváis, *Entrada libre*, provides a telling example. In it he proposes to focus on neglected everyday practices[12] which he finds framing dissent or providing alternative strategies for democratization. In view of the numerous acts of dissent and protest evident throughout Mexico in schools, the workplace, labour unions, the city and the region, his work clearly, at one level, seeks to counter constructs of Mexicans as passive and apathetic. The popular action dealt with by Monsiváis is primarily urban, as evident, for example, in his discussion of volunteer work efforts to rescue earthquake victims in 1985, and subsequent protests by organized groups of victims left without the necessary shelter, food and clothing, and tired of the same empty government promises (Monsiváis, 1992: 17–122). In the case of the victims of the San Juanico Pemex gas depot explosion in 1984 which left hundreds, perhaps thousands, dead and maimed, there was again a grass-roots mobilization for aid, donations of food, clothing and blood to assist the burned victims and those left homeless. In what was an accident simply waiting to happen due to the lack of safety measures, the victims were subsequently forced to organize to protest not only Pemex's dangerous operations in an urban area but also the government's failure to deliver goods and services, even after significant funds were provided by several foreign governments (Monsiváis, 1992: 141).

In these and other cases reported in *Entrada libre*, Monsiváis, perhaps Mexico's most insightful and incisive cultural critic, sees examples of popular action by 'la sociedad civil' (civil society), a Gramscian expression assuming the sense of a popular bloc and a political space of agency and opposition: 'Civil society is the communal effort of solidarity and action, a space, independent of the government, by definition, the space of antagonism.'[13] This action of solidarity is, as specified by Touraine (Touraine, 1981: 9, 142), collective, self-generated and free of intellectual constraints, to which Monsiváis adds: 'Each community, if it desires to be one, constructs in the process its own definitions, however much Marxist academics might condemn them.'[14] It becomes clear that these oppositional movements are confronting not merely the state but the Marxist paradigm, for Monsiváis, that is. For the population, necessity has led to decisive action, as it always has throughout history, be it that of students, electrical workers, railway workers, miners, women tobacco workers, teachers or *campesinos*. Only now, unlike in the past, with a quarter of the Mexican population residing in the greater metropolitan area of Mexico City, dissent and resistance are and will be primarily, although not exclusively, urban. (Chiapas immediately comes to mind.) These movements, however, arising as they do out of immediate crises, are shown to be sporadic, fragmented and frequently short-lived. Solidarity dissipates and 'normalcy', i.e. routine everyday practices and individualism, returns, all of which points to the fact that oppositional movements bound to a particular place, as Harvey insists, 'become a part of the very fragmentation which a mobile capitalism and flexible accumulation can feed upon' (Harvey, 1989: 303). This notwithstanding, Harvey goes on to note that these struggles for local autonomy offer valuable political experience and awareness of the power of mass action and thus may serve as:

> excellent bases for political action, but they cannot bear the burden of radical historical change alone. 'Think globally and act locally' was the revolutionary slogan of the 1960s. It bears repeating.

Equally important to note is that, for the most part, the mobilized victims that Monsiváis refers to in the San Juanico case are working-class people, for, as in the United States, refineries and gas deposits are much more likely to be found in areas surrounding working-class neighbourhoods, especially newly urbanized squatter sectors (Monsiváis, 1992: 136) than near more affluent communities. And after all, as Touraine remarks, 'the workers' movement was the first modern social movement,' and 'it still remains the most imposing so far of all the figures in the huge family of social movements' (Touraine, 1984: 293), especially in areas of the world still undergoing modernization, whatever immediate features the process may take, one could add.

Latin American social movements are thus as much working-class struggles as protests over domination and oppression encountered in everyday affairs. Theorists and cultural critics dealing with new social movements, on the other hand, often insist on delinking these oppositions and struggles from class, no doubt out of a strong resentment against particular leftist parties or perhaps because they envision the working-class struggle strictly in terms of institutionalized trade unions which they, following Touraine, see in decline throughout the world (Touraine, 1981: 11–13), forgetting that, in some labour areas, as with the service sectors and some ethnic groups, unionization is on the rise. The fashionable postmodernist stance to take is one that seeks to go beyond class, to present even clearly labour issue-centred movements in terms of 'alliance politics', of particular 'special interest groups', as is the case in superindustrialized societies. Even Touraine, to whom theorists of new social movements and alliance politics owe much, feels compelled to draw a clear distinction between social movements that arise in 'post-industrial' societies and 'socio-economic groups' that form in developing nations (Touraine, 1981: 9–10; 1989: 30). In Latin America, in view of the fact that the development model is still in place, what Touraine sees taking shape is a dialogue between various socioeconomic groups and the state in their struggle for representation as well as participation in the political arena (Touraine, 1989: 18, 30).

It would however misrepresent the case if one were to suggest that all new social movement theorists are of one mind in rejecting class issues. In the case of some Latin American theorists, for example, class is not totally dismissed or ignored; yet, given the operative notion of multiple subject positions, class location is not privileged, merely one of many positionalities considered (Calderón and Jehlin, 1987: 29), which may or may not be at the forefront at any given moment. Writing precisely against this pluralist politics of identification, Wright, for one, critiques this 'multiple oppressions' approach to understanding society, 'each rooted in a different mode of domination', for not positing 'any explanatory priority' of one over any other, and for ignoring the centrality of class for social and historical analysis (Wright, 1985: 57).

For a good many other Latin American political scientists, the struggle is political as much as intellectual and thus the theorizing is considered to be strategically important for a reassessment of the past and for the construction of new social movements themselves. With most of the Latin American nations coming out of a cycle of nationalist-popular models of government and a period of military dictatorships (with some exceptions, like Mexico, which has had its own 'peculiar institution'), and faced with a financial-economic crisis that includes the growth of an informal drug economy, theorists now perceive the beginning of a political change, at least in some countries (Touraine, 1989: 18, 35, 39). The political system, the state, is now being challenged by social actors which it previously controlled; intellectuals are no longer willing to defend the state or to support revolutionary nationalisms; having given up on these positions, they have in fact become '"professional" defenders of democratization' (Touraine, 1989: 40). For these intellectuals, micropolitical movements, the new social movements in their various manifestations, are a move back into the public sphere, posited as a radical political sphere that questions traditional political parties, seen as authoritarian, closed and not representative of the social heterogeneity, and that allows for a foregrounding of new issues, like those of women's rights, human rights, everyday concerns, democracy, popular religions, etc. (Touraine, 1989: 38–9). Beneath it all is a political concern with the emergence of new social actors and the construction of collective identity for collective action in a struggle for political power and hegemony (Calderón and Jehlin, 1987: 39–40), or with what Monsiváis terms 'grassroots democracy' (la 'democratización desde abajo'), which counters what Monsiváis calls the dual pitfalls of submissiveness and 'fatalisms of nation and class' (Monsiváis, 1992: 211).

Thus pluralism and democracy are keywords for these theorists of new social movements. Popular initiative, rather than that of parties and/or intellectuals is seen to be a critical issue in the formation of these movements (Touraine et al., 1983: 31). The thrust of these studies, consequently, is the analysis of new approaches towards democratization and the consolidation of both social and political democracy (Calderón and dos Santos, 1987: 11; Touraine et al., 1983:

49), distinguishing in this way between democratic participation and representation. The more urgent problem of distinguishing between political and economic liberalism (see Mouffe, 1988: 32) is not taken up, although in fact liberal democracy, i.e. bourgeois democracy, is more likely to be in the offing for these Latin American countries which are increasingly subject to decisions made at the global level by transnational corporations as much as by state policies. And yet, despite calls for non-violent action and new oppositional movements to attain democratization in Latin America, armed struggle continues to be seen as a viable course for triggering change and even dialogue, as the Chiapas Zapatistas have demonstrated.

At the level of political debate, it becomes increasingly clear that there is at times an intolerance and even impatience today among some Latin American intellectuals with the very notion of revolution and with those who would continue to assert the centrality of class location and who seek macrosocial transformations. This is evident in Monsiváis' recent article, translated and published in the *L.A. Times*, giving his reaction to the Chiapas Zapatista (EZLN) guerrillas, who rejected the government's first proposed peace plan. His comments reveal disappointment verging on exasperation with 'their unrealistic reasoning' (Monsiváis, 1994). Monsiváis does not support the Zapatistas' armed struggle nor does he see the need to continue it, despite admiring 'their sense of community' and sharing many of their grievances: 'the high-level corruption, the imperial presidency, the state party, the terrible abandonment of indigenous communities and the rejection of democracy.' As is clear, Monsiváis sees the problems of the indigenous populations in Chiapas in political terms and views the struggle in cultural terms. The political battle which he credits them with winning is the media war. We would have to agree that *sub-comandante* Marcos has made it a point to voice his demands in terms of more palatable discourses, such as subalternity (giving 'a voice to the voiceless, a face to the faceless', etc.); yet, what in effect the Indians claim is land, health benefits, education, work and political reform. The coinciding of the Chiapas revolt with the signing of NAFTA makes the point that the leaders explicitly meant to tie their grievances with the larger concerns of Mexican workers and citizens. Their call for democracy however leads Monsiváis to question their 'posing as national representatives' and their appropriation of the expression 'civil society', which he himself elsewhere used to describe non-state-linked urban movements (Monsiváis, 1992: 13), as if claims to 'civil society' were reserved to a select civilian sector and not to others.

It is perhaps an ironic and telling sign of the self-delusion of cultural and political critics that while some see armed struggle as passé, as a stage superseded by new social movements, 'U.S. policy makers envision more rather than less armed confrontation with Third World "enemies" (Marxist-Leninists, terrorists, drug-traffickers, religious fundamentalists, etc.)' (Jonas, 1990: 21). Reactions to social conditions themselves, which the United Nations Economic Commission for Latin America estimates leave 44 per cent of the region's population (183 million) living in poverty and 44 per cent of the workforce unemployed or under-employed, are a key issue. Latin American countries, following the neo-Liberal economic policies imposed by the IMF and the World Bank have in recent years imposed brutal austerity programmes reducing government expenditures, in effect instituting a process of pauperization for many (Petras and Vieux, 1992: 10–14). Thus fundamental questions of economic disparity and widespread con-ditions of human misery resulting from this drastic fiscal retrenchment could be said to contribute to continued popular mobilization and struggle, this (not sur-prisingly, perhaps) despite the defection of a number of leftist intellectuals to neo-Liberal policies. As Petras and Vieux indicate (1992: 19):

> As one generation of ex-leftists and guerrilla leaders joins neoliberal coali-tions, new leadership emerges: women in the neighborhood organizations of Santiago and the armed struggle of Peru, peasants blocking the highways of Colombia, striking railroad workers in Buenos Aires, metal workers battling police in Sao Paulo, students and slum dwellers confronting the army in Caracas.

For this reason, the uprising in Chiapas has led to new predictions, like that of Cooper, who, with a degree of sarcasm, suggests that:

> The shots fired in Chiapas on January 1 signal the End of the End of History. Rather than the final rattle on the snake of revolution, Chiapas is the first armed battle against the Global Market and simultaneously – in a way Americans cannot grasp – for Democracy.
>
> (Cooper, 1994: 2)

The outcome in Chiapas, as in Mexico, is yet to be played out, but again, clearly the 'rumours' of the death of armed resistance have been greatly exaggerated.

Neo-Liberal projects are also no doubt a response to the perceived failures of several revolutionary struggles, and the incapacity of Third World nations to survive as socialist states, given the crushing blockades, embargoes and destabil-izing counter-insurgency, backed overtly or covertly by the United States. The odds have been overwhelmingly against any small Third World nation seeking to delink itself from transnational corporate and US military domination, especially in the absence of regional alliances to provide support; the unviability of these efforts has led to a rethinking of social change and revolution among the Left. For this reason many have traded in socialism for neo-Liberal calls for redemoc-ratization and have grounded hopes for political action in the new social move-ments, forgetting that liberal democracy is the handmaiden of modernization; that is, the consolidation of bourgeois democracy, which tends, if anything, to preclude social transformation, much as has been historically the case in the United States, with its increasingly polarized class and racially divided society.

Support of efforts towards 'redemocratization' are mixed however. As Petras and Vieux point out, even when people have voted against the implementation of state fiscal policies, as was the case in the Mexican elections of 1988, fraud, deceit and coercion have enabled the governments of Mexico, as well as of Chile, Costa Rica, Venezuela, Peru, Argentina and Brazil, to impose 'free market shock policies' (Petras and Vieux, 1992: 15–16), despite popular opposition and rioting (1992: 16–17). Recent events in Mexico, with the assassination of the PRI candidate, Colosio, perhaps by the old guard in his own party, and the assassination as well of a Tijuana police chief, along with other murders and kidnappings of the last few years, point, at best, to a rocky transition to liberal democracy.

The emergence of these social movements and new social actors is thus said to mark the end of history, that is, in Touraine's sense, the end of the development model and the end of a revolutionary class struggle (Touraine, 1984: 290–1). New social movements are called upon to control their own historicity; that is, to construct their own history, identity, knowledge, cultural model and struggles (Touraine, 1981: 9). The dismissal of the cultural and political discourses manufactured by the state, by elites and by mass media as simulacra, especially the illusion of modernity, is thus considered to be the first step in constructing a new Latin American notion of economic and political modernization (García Canclini, 1989a: 20–5). Anti-foundationalist discourses that account for heterogeneity, both at an economic and cultural level, are thus ultimately posited as the answer to problems within capitalism. Each 'groupuscule', armed with its own discourses of 'difference', is to make its own fragmented 'history', engage in its own mini-collective struggle and fight against its own particular oppression. Aside from lacking a macrosocial analysis of the greater corporate and state domination and dealing with class and other social relations that make up Latin American society, what this emphasis on micropolitics suggests is not only a concerted effort to attack class politics and socialist discourses but a willingness among postmodernist intellectuals beyond the centre to consent to hegemonic ideologies and to appropriate 'trend-setting' discourses as their own new 'doxa' (Jameson, 1991: 277), disseminated by mass media and literature. Rather than countering them or disidentifying with these discourses, as Pecheux would suggest (Pecheux, 1975: 158), these intellectuals are using the latest theories on the market to build a consensus of their own that does not, in the last instance, necessarily address or threaten transnational capitalism.

Postmodernism as a cultural force

Postmodernity, whether in Latin America or elsewhere, operates under a kind of Heisenberg principle: uncertainty is at its core. Alongside the material insecurities produced by incomplete modernization and a global economy are those theoretical uncertainties arising out of what is considered to be the collapse of meaning, the triumph of simulation and an apparently endless slipping and sliding among ever-increasing numbers of vacuous signifiers. Given the cultural penetration of Latin America by information technologies, theoretical paradigms and mass media from the centre, it is not surprising that this postmodern 'structure of feeling' is in evidence in the work of Latin American literary critics as well.

What is purportedly a characteristic postmodernist feature, as previously indicated, is the tendency to see everything as fragmented, heterogeneous, ephemeral and contingent (Harvey, 1989: 285). Given the rejection of foundationalism and essentialism, there is a tendency to see everything as flat and to reject not only deep structures but the very notion of the subject. Little if any room is left for a notion of history, only 'nostalgia', pastiches of the past, expressed through representations of representations or, what is perhaps more the case, there is now an inability to distinguish simulacra from 'the real'. This is so since it is assumed that there are no longer any originals, only copies, endless replication in an image-producing society in which cultural production becomes central precisely because of its quality of self-consuming artefacts and its creation of a market eager to consume more and more products. The reification of the sign, the multiplicity or 'cannibalization' of styles, the loss of boundaries between the elite and popular, the notion of multiple identities or positionalities, the abstraction of space, all are described as postmodernist traits (Harvey, 1989: 284–307; Jameson, 1988a: 18), along with political notions of pluralism and radical democracy, that entail a longing for collectivity and 'groupuscules'. These are all cast together ahistorically by privileged fractions, who fancy, for example, that inclusion of minority or Third World literature within their literary canon is a great equalizer, and that insertion of Third World cultural products within their markets makes them postmodernist.

Of all of these features, only a select few could be said to characterize Latin American cultural production, for there undeniably remains today in Latin America a modernist 'structure of feeling'. This stage of modernity produced by 'incomplete modernization', with all its incongruities and ruptures, accounts for Latin America's still modernist (and not *modernista*) literature with an emphasis on the divided self, an anguished subject, a fragmented structure marked by ambiguity and complexity, simultaneous time spaces, an elitist concept of art (despite allegations to the contrary), all qualities present in modernism that have all too often also been linked to postmodernism (Harvey, 1989: 273; Jameson, 1991: 6–66; Perloff, 1992: 158). Postmodernism cannot, as a result, be seen to be anything other than a fuzzy concept; at best it is an ideological field marked by overlapping and slippages of meaning. Perhaps for this reason and citing 'the heterogeneous local forms produced within and sometimes against its logic', Colás, for example, takes issue with postmodernism and finds it 'an unsatisfactorily homogenizing term' (Colás, 1992: 267). It is, as we have previously indicated, and as even a cursory glance at the literature will demonstrate, a lax term, used at times to describe anything and everything.

The utilization of the label 'postmodernism' is furthermore increasingly unsettling as one sees minority literature in the US and Third World literature in general grasped and inserted within the network of cultural commodity circulation and classified as postmodernist examples of 'difference'. In a time–space dimension where it is 'the thing' to be 'ethnic' and 'different', First World critics sometimes 'forget' to examine the Third World cultural work within a peripheral context, eviscerating the text in the process. Menchú's testimonial again serves as a good example in this regard, although equally as good, although less in vogue, perhaps because her class interests are less palatable (to proponents of new social movements, for example) is that of Domitila Barrios de Chungara (*Let Me Speak!*) (1978). Yet if we further examine the Menchú text, we are struck not only by its mediated format, its arrangement according to the anthropologist's questions and scheme, but also by its historicity, its call upon collective memory, its discourses of resistance and social transformation, its concern with the survival of Quiché culture, its denunciation of the exploitation of both indigenous *and Ladino* farm workers and the dispossession of the Indians. Clearly there is no crisis of historicity here and no absence of revolutionary discourses. The way Menchú and her people feel about themselves and their world has little to do with 'identity politics' in the First World or with the consciousness of middle-class consumers in the United States – or elsewhere – within this period of postmodernity. Much as critics may attempt to force the work into new representational models and into a framework of pluralism and difference, it clearly results in an uncomfortable fit. The dimension of class and political/economic disparity is still paramount in Menchú's testimonial, and the alliances that Menchú sees developing with labour unions, students, peasants and a variety of Indian groups are not modelled after the 'alliance politics' theorized in 'advanced countries' but are instead a continuation of alliances forged within and as a result of both colonial and capitalist development.[15]

If place politics, that is, 'links between place and the social sense of personal and communal identity', are modernist (Harvey, 1989: 273, 302), then perhaps that is where we can situate Menchú's construction of the Quiché's collective identity. Identity may be multiple (Quiché, Catholic, working class, political activist, woman) but it is not constructed as variable; in fact Menchú sees herself always and foremost as a Quiché Indian. As Yúdice indicates, for the subaltern, 'identity is a major weapon in the struggles of the oppressed' (Yúdice, 1988: 221). In circumstances of exploitation and oppression, one cannot afford to abdicate any means of struggle or any discourses useful to the struggle of the collectivity.

We have suggested above that Menchú's work may have in fact entered into postmodern market circulation but is itself not postmodernist by any stretch of the imagination. Yet a number of critics have described this text, as well as a good many others ranging from the *crónicas* of the conquest to Latin American 'Boom' or 'post-Boom' literature[16] as postmodernist. Thankfully there are also sceptics. Ruffinelli, for example, is not totally convinced. Either 'postmodernism' is the displacement of modernity ('el desplazamiento definitivo de la modernidad'), he says, or the crisis of that modernity ('una crisis de esa modernidad incompleta') (Ruffinelli, 1990: 38). It is to the cultural decentring and the focus on marginality, popular culture, feminism and testimonials found in the Latin American literature of the 1980s that he finally concedes a postmodernist logic. Like other critics he too posits a specific Latin American postmodernity – and consequently postmodernist cultural production – arising as part of an incomplete modernity (Ruffinelli, 1990: 41).

Its seeming ubiquity has led some on the Left to look at the emergence and proliferation of postmodernist discourses from the perspective of what can be 'salvageable' or 'usable'. Thus, while Ruffinelli's focus is on micropolitics and popular culture, Larsen's take is more directed at the philosophical and political. Larsen is particularly concerned with the vehemently anti-Marxist and post-structuralist bent of the proponents of new social movements, along the lines of Mouffe and Laclau, and, for example, their misappropriation of the term 'hegemony' (Larsen, 1990: 77–82). In his critique Larsen makes a case for a Leftist postmodernism concerned with marginal groups and anti-imperialist struggles, although he fears that even a Leftist postmodernist movement cannot avoid being tinged with a degree of Rightist apologetics (Larsen, 1990: 83, 84). Arguing however that no historical period is exempt from manifestations of resistance, Larsen acknowledges that some strands of postmodernism will undoubtedly exhibit contestatory discourses. Jameson too notes that post-modernism 'includes a space for various forms of oppositional culture, those of radically distinct residual or emergent cultural languages', those of the Third World within the First World. Although the implication is that these oppositional forms are alternatives to hegemonic, i.e. postmodernist, discourses, Jameson, like Larsen, also finds cultural products that, despite the paradigm, are 'clearly postmodern and equally clearly political and oppositional' (Jameson, 1991: 159).

Contestatory culture need not, however, be revolutionary in all instances; that is, committed to structural change. Larsen grants a discrete terrain to specific types of texts and in effect considers, along with Yúdice, positing a Latin American paradigm of postmodernism (what Yúdice calls a 'postmodernism of resistance' (Beverley, 1993: 110)) linked to social movements and concerned with the subaltern; encompassed in this field would be, among others, the work of Menchú, Poniatowska, Galeano and Argueta, in opposition to what might be termed 'reactionary-orthodox' postmodernism (Larsen, 1990: 88). Larsen further holds that the work of these Latin American writers focuses on the marginal, to a degree delinked from national and regional identity, à la 'new social movements',[17] but we would argue that for Menchú and Argueta at least, national liberation is still very much closely tied to notions of class and ethnic liberation.

With the new recognition of social actors, the question of identity has become collective, not in the old sense of class, nation and race but in the newer senses of gender, sexuality, ethnicity, occupation, age, neighbourhood, etc. But in the new postmodernist representational models, identity also undergoes fragmentation and is subject to change according to position within different social spaces. This assessment of contingency not only allows heretofore marginalized positions to take their turn on the discursive stage but, as previously indicated, tends to treat class identity as merely one more among others. The recognition of identity as a construction, rather than a given or an essence, is however one of the major gains of postmodernism. In the case of national identity, despite the globalization of the economy and the intensification of modernization in Latin America, discourses of nationalism, while not threatened at a cultural level, are beginning to be scrutinized and to undergo reconstruction. Proponents of new social movements are especially keen to reject those discourses of nationalism manipulated by an authoritarian nation-state aiming to accelerate its process of modernization, in the end, in great measure indifferent to the political and economic needs of the population and to the latter's strategies of assimilation of the new without discarding the traditional (Monsiváis, 1992: 12). It is here, in the theorization of the construction of new social actors, that postmodernist models are particularly evident; for though linked to the local and to particular interests, these groups are seen to be self-constructed in terms of particular oppressions and social relations.

What is at stake in the game Bartra plays in his kaleidoscopic, hybrid text, *La jaula de la melancolía*, is the historical construction of a multiplicity of Mexican identities, from colonial times to the present period of modernization, in terms of ethnicity, region, class, gender, and in terms of a variety of myths as constructed by Europeans, the Mexican state, Mexican intellectuals, everyday mini-narratives (jokes, games, puns, etc.), Mexican literature, mass culture, and even zoologists. Like García Canclini, Bartra captures the heterogeneity of the Mexican nation and its 'uneven development' or incomplete modernization through a variety of narrative styles and the recurring image and multivalent rendering of an axolotl salamander as a truncated metamorphosis that leaves the amphibian in what is seemingly a larval state of suspended transformation but in reality is a new species. Thus the axolotl, like the Mexican nation, although constructed as 'underdeveloped' by some, is in actuality an entirely different organism with its own features, thwarting conventional classification (Bartra, 1987: 189). In the end, however, even in Bartra's deconstructive project, social antagonisms are recognized as powerful agents that provoke a dispersion and fragmentation of national culture, giving rise to a recognition that ideological discourses, however outdated, serve to maintain the sociopolitical system and to position Mexicans as melancholy, violent, submissive, deserving of their dominated status, etc. New images, new identities are therefore called for since they are neither larval forms nor axolotls. Like the theorists of social movements, Bartra argues for new constructions, perhaps along the lines of non-national collectivities.

Positing multiple identities and the incorporation of the previously marginal as an additional positionality has not however eliminated the oppressed's feeling of powerlessness or increased people's sense of agency, either within the centre or on the periphery. This is perhaps especially clear in the case of Latin American women, although as Calderón and Jelin report, they too are increasingly involved in a number of social movements organized around a variety of social/political needs as well as for women's rights more generally (Calderón and Jelin, 1987: 33–4). These 'new social movements' as well as discourses on 'difference' and 'marginality' have spurred new writing by women, as Franco (1992a: 69), who takes an ambivalent stance *vis-à-vis* the postmodernist valorization of feminist voices, notes:

> it is no coincidence that women's writing and new social movements have emerged at a time when the nation has ceased to be the necessary framework either of political action or of writing and when a dominant ideology of pluralism seems to undermine oppositional stances that rest on marginality.

Demonstrating a measure of scepticism as to not only the depoliticized implications of 'pluralism' but as to the ultimate contestatory function that these voices entail, Franco raises issues which point to the tendency among postmodernists to eliminate significant social distinctions. Thus, levelling 'marginality' and 'difference', as if they were synonymous, much like attempts to obviate distinctions between exploitation and oppression or relations of production and consumption, can clearly be put into service by the Right as strategies 'to undermine oppositional stances'. It goes without saying that for those who come together as marginalized social actors, marginality continues to have social significance, one that can be erased only through collective action. Where marginality is taken to be so extensive as to be rendered meaningless, there is an obvious breakdown in the capacity to gauge social relations.

What is undeniable, however, is that the fact that postmodern 'pluralism' and 'diversity' are in fashion has made gender politics and its discourses marketable (Franco, 1992a: 69), opening up significant representational spaces for women. In her article, Franco again hints at contradictions between theorists/intellectuals and popular classes and 'the gulf between different class positions on sexuality', all of which are made evident in literary strategies used in Latin American women's literature dealing with these issues (Franco, 1992: 69). Disarticulation of these specific formal and ideological elements can thus serve to unmask the underlying – and unresolved – social contradictions that continue to separate women along class lines and can also be useful in unmasking in many cases the absence of contestation of dominant values in many of these texts (see Beverley, 1993: 107).

In all of this, it bears repeating, the global, the national and the local are overlapping but distinct social spaces. Culturally these spaces are often in collision, with one 'global cultural space' often threatening to appropriate the space of the others; only in the slippages is there evidence of negotiation and new aggregates. To what extent the 'cultural logic' or 'structure of feeling' of postmodernity overlaps with Latin America modernity is difficult to determine and, as Franco points out, would have to be examined at every level, for 'the global is inflected differently in every locality' (Franco, 1992b: 39). None the less, given Latin America's uneven development and incomplete modernization, it is more than likely that these notions have reached only the upper classes and intellectuals, especially theorists and critics, all of them avid consumers of postmodern cultural commodities and discourses. Assumptions about homogeneity may in fact simply overstate the reality and denote a lack of fully considering or misreading local heterogeneity. A cautionary note is, we think, in order: Latin American theorists are perhaps at times too caught up with heterogeneity, fragmentation, the articulation of difference, the fragmented subject, pluralism, popular culture, etc. to see what West calls 'the ragged edges of the Real, of Necessity' (West, 1988: 277), but those living in urban misery, the unemployed and underemployed, the low-wage workers, the workers who head north, are very much in touch with it. For them, the world around them is rapidly being modernized and they find themselves brutalized by their unmitigated marginality, dislocated and often lumpenized.

Survival for many, in both the First World and the Third, is still an issue and not a matter of lifestyle or subcultural group allegiance or identification alone. Those left out of the consumerist loop can ill afford to relinquish social change for the 'carnival of choices' that the postmodernist vision presages. Postmodernity for many, let us not forget, also means conditions of homelessness, drug addiction, violence and despair and a continuation of exploitation in the First World as well as the Third.

Perhaps what needs to be done is what West suggests and what this article has attempted to outline: a closer periodization and demarcation of cultural practices (West, 1988: 272). The last two decades have brought new approaches to the analysis of cultural practices: the very notion of cultural products as constituted by practices and discourses, the very notion of knowledge and cultural know-how as cultural capital, the reworking of notions of identity and agency, the idea of an active construction of our knowledge of reality through discourses, the analysis of social space, the distrust of all foundational discourses and rejection of essentialist descriptions, the analysis of capitalism in terms of a third phase of flexible accumulation, multinationals and informational technology. These and many more insights have gained currency within and outside academia. Some have served the Right as well as the Left. The Right, in rejecting all truth-seeking discourses, renouncing all ideas of social transformation and proposing a pragmatist acceptance of 'consensus beliefs', that is, the status quo as determined by the liberal-democratic polity, takes as an implicit foregone conclusion the bankruptcy of claims calling for any and all alternatives to the capitalist mode and the market (Jameson, 1993a: 182; Norris, 1993: 278–84).

Assuming a critical standpoint today in fact means rethinking the advisability of notions assimilable to hegemony, theorizing the local in conjunction with the global, not merely staying in step with the latest theoretical trends but remaining committed to mapping class consciousness, and creating models that provide for critical analysis and substantive material, not solely discursive, change. Without fundamental social and economic structural change, the working class, growing and changing, not only in Latin America but everywhere, will have left to it only a plurality of choices in the market place without the means to consume most of them and, more importantly, still remain enmeshed in exploitative relations of production. In this climate of acquiescence to hegemonic discourses, the abdication of teleology and the utopian impulse implies a retreat not only from class but from global struggles against exploitation and oppression and a ceding of the terrain to forces with vested interests in the status quo.

Notes

1   This article was written in 1994. Since then a number of articles, even journals, on Latin American cultural studies have appeared, readings not considered here but addressing many of the same issues dealt with in this study. Our only addition is note 4.

2   The category 'Third World' is still a serviceable term as it continues to recognize an economic and military difference between the superpowers and a good portion of the rest of the world subject to its pressures and domination.

3   It is crucial, according to Escobar, to question these constructs or discourses, for they are not only used to 'make' and 'know' the Third World but also underpin all planning within the peripheral areas (Escobar, 1992: 24–5).

4   In their anthology *Global/Local. Cultural Production and the Transnational Imaginary* (1996), the editors Rob Wilson and Wimal Dissanayake note the importance of theorizing a 'global/local nexus', and linking 'local struggles with global support' (1996: 3).

5   Callinicos does not find that this latest phase of capitalism represents a real break (Callinicos, 1989: 132). Harvey also suggests it may be merely an intensification of monopoly capitalism (Harvey, 1989: vii).

6   These include *Nuevo Texto Crítico* (Año III, no. 6, 1990; Año IV, no. 7, 1991), *Cuadernos hispanoamericanos* (no. 463, 1989), *Revista de Crítica Literaria Latinoamericana* (Año XV, No. 29, 1989), *The South Atlantic Quarterly* (92: 3, summer 1993), and *Boundary* (2 (20): 3 1993), *On Edge* (University of Minnesota Press, 1992), Beverley's *Against Literature* (University of Minnesota Press, 1993), and the *Journal of Latin American Cultural Studies*, among others.

7   Were one interested in focusing on the concomitant development of 'industries' undermining this market, one could of course point to high-tech copying services that have also made reproduction easy, whether of music tapes, videos or the work of García Márquez, whose *Del amor y otros demonios* (*Of Love and*

Other Demons) saw numerous bootleg editions in Colombia (NACLA, 1994: 45), but the issue remains whether these 'underground' economies do in fact threaten or merely reinforce and widen the market they intercept.

8   In several essays there is at issue Paz's ahistoricizing notion that Latin America was postmodern *avant la lettre* and his elitist eagerness to dissolve the distinction between centre and periphery (Beverley, 1993: 110; Yúdice, 1992b: 6). These discursive sublations, like that of popular/elite or marginal/centre, are games in which intellectuals engage, both within the periphery and at the centre, more often than not leaving social relations out of the picture.

9   Jameson acknowledges this crucial point: 'even if all the constitutive features of postmodernism were identical with and continuous to those of an older modernism . . . the two phenomena would still remain utterly distinct in their meaning and social function, owing to the very different positioning of postmodernism in the economic system of late capitalism and, beyond that, to the transformation of the very sphere of culture in contemporary society' (Jameson, 1991: 5).

10   In Monsiváis' words, 'se vive bajo definiciones miserables de "modernización"' (Monsiváis, 1993: 194).

11   In his words: 'Sigue habiendo desigualdad en la apropiación de los bienes simbólicos y en el acceso a la innovación cultural, pero esa desigualdad ya no tiene la forma simple y polar que creímos encontrarle cuando dividíamos cada país en dominantes y dominados, o el mundo en imperios y naciones dependientes' (García Canclini, 1989a: 93). Our English translation appears in the main body of the text.

12   In Monsiváis' words: 'lo cotidiano, negado o ignorado por muchísimo tiempo' (Monsiváis, 1992: 14).

13   In his words: 'sociedad civil es el esfuerzo comunitario de autogestión y solidaridad, el espacio independiente del gobierno, en rigor la zona del antagonismo' (Monsiváis, 1992: 79).

14   'Cada comunidad, si quiere serlo, construye sobre la marcha sus propias definiciones, así la academia marxista las condene' (Monsiváis, 1992: 79).

15   Even if they are dead, Westernizing and male, it bears remembering that as early as 1904 González Prada was warning of the critical need to consider ethnicity or 'social race' for social change in Peru and by the 1930s Mariátegui was pressing for an articulation of ethnicity and class in Peru as well. In the US too, throughout the nineteenth century, ethnicity and class were inseparable in workers' movements, as they were, especially from the 1920s onward, in the US Southwest in particular.

16   The phenomenon of the so-called Latin American literary 'Boom' of the 1960s and 1970s has already been shown to have been in good measure orchestrated by publishing houses (see Mario Benedetti, 'Las prioridades del escritor' (1971)).

17   Larsen, however, subsequently retreats in part from his dual assessment of postmodernism to avoid essentializing the marginal as inherently revolutionary, and focuses instead on the implications of a total abandonment of Marxist

political strategies and the culturalist orientation of the Latin American Left (Larsen, 1990: 90–1). The shifts and reconsiderations in Larsen point to the contradictory and influx state of the theoretical debate on 'postmodernism' in Latin America.

References

Amin, Samir (1990) *Maldevelopment*, London: Zed Books.

Barrios de Chungara, Domitila (1978) *Let Me Speak! Testimony of Domitila, a Woman of the Bolivian Mines. With Moema Viezzer*, trans. Victoria Ortiz, New York: Monthly Review.

Bartra, Roger (1987) *La jaula de la melancolía: Identidad y metamorfosis del mexicano*, Mexico: Grijalbo, SA.

Benedetti, Mario (1977) 'Las prioridades del escritor', in *El Escritor Latinoamericano y la Revolución Posible*, Mexico: Editorial Nueva Imagen.

Berman, Marshall (1988) *All That Is Solid Melts Into Air*, New York: Viking Penguin Inc.

Beverley, John (1993) *Against Literature*, Minneapolis: University of Minnesota Press.

Calderón, Fernando and dos Santos, Mario (1987) 'Movimientos sociales y democracia', in G. Calderón and M. R. dos Santos (eds) (1987) *Los conflictos por la constitución de un nuevo orden*, Buenos Aires, Argentina: CLASCO.

Calderón, Fernando and Jelin, Elizabeth (1987) *Clases y movimientos sociales en América Latina: perspectivas y realidades*, Buenos Aires, Argentina: CEDES.

Callinicos, Alex (1989) *Against Postmodernism. A Marxist Critique*, New York: St Martin's Press.

Callinicos, Alex and Harman, Chris (1989) *The Changing Working Class*, London: Bookmark.

Chakrabarty, Dipesh (1992a) 'Postcoloniality and the artifice of history: who speaks for "Indian" pasts?', *Representations*, 37: 1–28.

—— (1992b) 'The death of history? Historical consciousness and the culture of late capitalism', *Public Culture*, 4(2): 47–65.

Colás, Santiago (1992) 'The Third World in Jameson's postmodernism or the cultural logic of late capitalism', *Social Text*, 31/32: 258–70.

Colford, Paul D. (1994) 'Publishers catch on to Spanish-language titles', *Los Angeles Times*, 8 July.

Cooper, Marc (1994) *The Zapatistas*, Open Magazine Pamphlet Series 30.

Escobar, Arturo (1992) 'Imagining a post-development era? Critical thought, development and social movements', *Social Text*, 31/32: 20–56.

Franco, Jean (1992a) 'Going public: reinhabiting the private', in G. Yúdice, J. Franco and J. Flores (eds) *On Edge. The Crisis of Contemporary Latin American Culture*, Minneapolis: University of Minnesota Press.

—— (1992b) 'Remapping culture', *Latin American Literary Review*, XX (40): 38–40.

Fraser, Nancy and Nicholson, Linda J. (1990) 'Social criticism without philosophy: an encounter between feminism and postmodernism', in Nicholson (ed.) *Feminism/Postmodernism*, New York: Routledge.

García Canclini, Néstor (1989a) *Culturas híbridas*, Mexico: Grijalbo.

—— (1989b) 'El debate posmoderno en Iberoamérica', *Cuadernos hispanoamericanos*, 463: 79–92.

—— (1993a) 'Las industrias culturales', in Guevara Niebla and García Canclini (eds) *La educación y la cultura ante el TLC*, Mexico: Nueva Imagen/Nexos.

—— (1993b) 'Memory and innovation in the theory of art', *The South Atlantic Quarterly*, 92(3): 423–43.

—— (1993c) 'Cultural reconversion', in G. Yúdice, J. Franco and J. Flores (eds) (1992) *On Edge. The Crisis of Contemporary Latin American Culture*, Minneapolis: University of Minnesota Press.

Harvey, David (1989) *The Condition of Postmodernity*, Cambridge, MA: Blackwell.

Jameson, Fredric (1988a) 'The politics of theory: ideological positions in the postmodernism debate', in Jameson, *The Ideologies of Theory. Essays 1971–1986*, Volume 2 *Syntax of History*, Minneapolis: University of Minnesota Press.

—— (1988b) Regarding postmodernism – a conversation with Anders Stephanson', in A. Ross (ed.) *Universal Abandon. The Politics of Postmodernism*, Minneapolis: University of Minnesota Press.

—— (1991) *Postmodernism or The Cultural Logic of Late Capitalism*, Durham, NC: Duke University Press.

—— (1993a) 'In the mirror of alternate modernities: Introduction to Kōjin's *The Origins of Japanese Literature*, *South Atlantic Quarterly*, 92(2): 295–310.

—— (1993b) 'Actually existing Marxism', *Polygraph*, 6/7: 170–95.

Jonas, Susanne (1990) 'Central America in the balance: prospects for the 1990s', *Monthly Review*, 42(2): 11–24.

Laclau, Ernesto and Mouffe, Chantal (1987) *Hegemony and Socialist Strategy. Towards a Radical Democratic Politics*, London: Verso.

Larrain, Jorge (1989) *Theories of Development. Capitalism, Colonialism and Dependency*, Cambridge: Polity Press.

Larsen, Neil (1990) 'Posmodernismo e imperialismo: teoría y política en Latinoamérica', *Nuevo Texto Crítico*, III (6): 77–93.

MacEwan, Arthur (1994) 'Notes on U.S. foreign investment and Latin America', *Monthly Review*, 45(8): 15–26.

Meiksins Wood, Ellen (1986) *The Retreat from Class. A New 'True' Socialism*, London: Verso.

Menchú, Rigoberta (1984) *I . . . Rigoberta Menchú. An Indian Woman in Guatemala* (with Elisabeth Burgos-Debray), trans. Ann Wright, London: Verso.

Monsiváis, Carlos (1992) *Entrada libre. Crónicas de la sociedad que se organiza*, Mexico: Biblioteca Era.

—— (1993) 'De la cultura mexicana en vísperas del Tratado de Libre Comercio', in Guevara Niebla and García Canclini (eds) *La educación y la cultura ante el Tratado de Libre Comercio*, Mexico: Nueva Imagen/Nexos.

—— (1994) 'The Zapatistas have gone too far in rejecting plan', *L.A. Times*, 19 June.

Mouffe, Chantal (1988) 'Radical democracy: modern or postmodern?', in A. Ross (ed.) *Universal Abandon. The Politics of Postmodernism*, Minneapolis: University of Minnesota Press.

NACLA (1994) 'New García Márquez novel', *NACLA*, XXVII (6) (May/June): 45.

Norris, Christopher (1993) *The Truth about Postmodernism*, Cambridge, MA: Blackwell.

Pecheux, Michel (1975) *Language, Semantics and Ideology*, New York: St Martin's Press.

Perloff, Marjorie (1992) 'Modernist Studies', in S. Greenblatt and G. Gunn (eds) *Redrawing the Boundaries*, New York: MLA of America.

Petras, James and Vieux, Steve (1992) 'Myths and realities: Latin America's free markets', *Monthly Review*, 44(1): 9–20.

Ruffinelli, Jorge (1990) 'Los 80: ¿Ingreso a la posmodernidad?', *Nuevo Texto Crítico*, III (6): 31–42.

Sánchez Vázquez, Adolfo (1990) 'Radiografía del posmodernismo', *Nuevo Texto Crítico*, III (6): 5–15.

Stephanson, Anders (1988) 'Interview with Cornel West', in A. Ross (ed.) *Universal Abandon? The Politics of Postmodernism*, Minneapolis: University of Minnesota Press.

Sweezy, Paul M. and Magdoff, Harry (1992) 'Globalization – to what end', Part I and Part II, *Monthly Review*, 43(9) and 43(10) (February and March).

Touraine, Alain (1981) *The Voice and the Eye. An Analysis of Social Movements*, Cambridge: Cambridge University Press.

—— (1984) *The Workers' Movement*, Cambridge: Cambridge University Press.

—— (1989) 'La crisis y las transformaciones del sistema político en América Latina', in F. Calderón (ed.) *Socialismo, autoritarismo y democracia*, Lima, Peru: IRP ediciones.

Touraine, Alain, Dubet, François, Wieviorka, Michel and Strzelecki, Jan (1983) *Solidarity: The Analysis of a Social Movement, Poland 1980–1981*, trans. David Denby, New York: Cambridge University Press.

West, Cornel (1988) 'Interview with Cornel West by Anders Stephanson', in A. Ross (ed.) *Universal Abandon. The Politics of Postmodernism*, Minneapolis: University of Minnesota Press.

Wilson, Rob and Dissanayake, Wimal (1996) 'Introduction: tracking the global', in their (eds) *Global/Local. Cultural Production and the Transnational Imaginary*, Durham: Duke University Press.

Wright, Erik Olin (1985) *Classes*, London: Verso.

Yúdice, George (1988) 'Marginality and the ethics of survival', in A. Ross (ed.) *Universal Abandon. The Politics of Postmodernism*, Minneapolis: University of Minnesota Press.

—— (1989) '¿Puede hablarse de postmodernidad en América Latina?', *Revista de crítica literaria latinoamericana*, XV (29): 105–28.

—— (1992a) 'Postmodernity and transnational capitalism in Latin America', in G. Yúdice, J. Franco and J. Flores (eds) *On Edge. The Crisis of Contemporary Latin American Culture*, Minneapolis: University of Minnesota Press.

—— (1992b) 'We are not the world', *Social Text*, 31/32: 202–16.

María Angelina Soldatenko

MADE IN THE USA: LATINAS/OS?, GARMENT WORK AND ETHNIC CONFLICT IN LOS ANGELES' SWEAT SHOPS[1]

Abstract

In the 1990s Latino identity is increasingly constructed as a 'universal', 'classless' and genderless pan-ethnicity. In this article I problematize this construct through an ethnographic study of Latina workers in the Los Angeles garment industry whose jobs are not only gender and ethnic specific but also immigrant specific. These women are located at the bottom of a complex organizational structure of an industry that promotes Third World conditions in the US in addition to promoting inter-ethnic and intra-ethnic conflict among workers. The voiced testimonies of these Latina garment workers provide a vivid record of contractor abuse, the unrelenting demands and difficulties of garment work, and the exploitative conditions and ethnic rivalries that make it difficult for Latinas to forge an effective culture of resistance. I argue that the survival of Latina garment workers rests on their ability to negotiate collaborative relations based on their unique struggles and experiences within the garment industry as women, immigrants, racialized workers and specific types of Latina Americanas. Finally, I highlight the importance of recording the insights of those women who not only experience the contemporary conditions of global capitalism, but also endeavour to speak rather than silence these conditions.

Keywords

Latino identity; Latino pan-ethnicity; ethnic conflict; Latina garment workers; Los Angeles apparel industry; sweat shops

Introduction

IT IS NOT UNCOMMON for scholars in Latino and Latin American studies to argue that (Latino) pan-ethnicity can serve as a rallying point for organizing. The assumption here is that Latinos can unite 'for a common end' on the basis of an originary 'tie' that exists between people from Latin America and the Caribbean who now reside in the United States.[2] This study of 'Latina' workers in the Los Angeles garment industry counters these facile assumptions by demonstrating how Latina/o identities are 'disarticulated' and 'differentiated' within a capitalist workplace, organized by complex hierarchical structures, competitive labour practices and co-ethnic relations that promote inter-ethnic and intra-ethnic conflict and racist perceptions which foment tensions and divisions among garment workers instead of uniting them.[3]

This study also parts with research on the Los Angeles garment industry that focuses primarily on its structural aspects. Here workers of colour are often presented as pawns in the processes of global production (Blumenberg, 1994; Bonacich, 1991; Bonacich *et al.*, 1994; Scott, 1984). Thus, little or no attention is devoted to recording the complex social positionings, identities and agencies of 'Latina' immigrant women whose work relationships are shaped not only by the economic dictates of the global economy and the requirements of labour within the garment industry, but also by racial and ethnic perceptions and relations that are 'made in the USA'.

In view of these disturbing trends, I have opted for an ethnographic study of 'Latina' garment workers which records their testimonies of contractor abuse, lived experiences of Third World working conditions, ethnic conflicts with co-workers and bosses, and most importantly, their unique agencies as racialized women, garment workers, and as heterogeneous 'Latina' Americanas.[4] I introduce this analysis with a general description of the place of 'Latina'[5] garment workers within the complex organizational structure of the Los Angeles garment industry.

'Latinas' in the garment industry

No reliable estimates exist regarding the total number of workers in the garment industry in Los Angeles. Available figures refer mainly to the manufacturing firms and licensed contracting shops. The underground sector of the industry remains difficult if not impossible to document. This sector is comprised of sweat shops and homeworkers that exist in total violation of the law, but which go unreported and operate freely. With this caveat, the International Ladies' Garment Workers' Union (ILGWU) estimated that about 120,000 of these workers were in Los Angeles at the time of the study.

Due to present economic conditions, 'Latina' workers and other immigrant women of colour are concentrated at the bottom of the stratified labour market in the United States (Phizacklea, 1986; Sassen-Koob, 1984; Westwood and Bhachu, 1988). Their jobs are not only gender and ethnic specific (Ruiz, 1987), but also immigrant specific (Hossfeld, 1994).[6] For many years, the Los Angeles garment industry's lowest paid workers (sewing machine operators, trimmers and homeworkers) have been Mexicanas and 'Latinas' (Duron, 1984; Laslett and Tyler, 1989; Monroy, 1980; Pesotta, 1987).[7] These 'Latinas' labour at all the different types of shops (manufacturers, jobbers, contractors and homeworkers) and perform a variety of jobs, from the 'skilled' sample makers to the 'unskilled' trimmers.[8] Some 'Latinas' who work in established manufacturing firms receive hourly wages and some benefits. Others work for licensed contractors where labour conditions and wages are not as good as in large firms.[9] A large percentage of 'Latinas', however, can be found in sweat shops (small investment operations that work outside of the industry's structure of regulations) and doing homework.

At the sweat shops, apparel workers labour for piece rates, contractors pay them less than the minimum wage, cheat them of their wages, and pressure them to work odd and long hours. Moreover the working conditions are terrible. Health and fire hazards are a constant danger (Dawsey, 1990; Newman and Lee, 1989). These women lack health coverage, social security and retirement benefits. The 'unskilled' workers who endure these conditions are 'Latina' and Asian immigrants, although Mexicanas form the majority of workers. Before the Second World War, white and African American women worked together with Chicanas and Mexicanas in the industry. With the increase in 'Latina' immigration in the 1960s (Carnoy et al., 1993; Peñaloza, 1986), the industry witnessed a transformation of its ethnic composition. Though Mexicanas remained in the majority, non-Mexican 'Latinas' began to enter the industry in larger numbers (Laslett and Tyler, 1989). Interestingly enough this migration coincided with the proliferation of contracting shops (Bymers, 1958).

Third World conditions of work

The situation of 'Latinas' who are concentrated in contracting shops and doing homework in the United States is similar to that of women who work in Third World countries (Fernandez-Kelly, 1983; Petersen, 1992). Some 'Latinas' work piece rate for more than forty hours a week without receiving overtime pay. In addition, there is constant pressure from the owners to increase production. As María, a 'Latina'-Mexicana trimmer who worked for a Korean contractor, explains:

> 'Me gusta mi trabajo pero no me gusta la presión. . . . I enjoy doing my work, but I do not like the pressure that exists at the shop. When they start putting pressure on me I do not feel comfortable. I get a feeling in my stomach, I get upset, I become nervous . . . I feel humiliated. . . . They tell me . . . [apurate] hurry up! hurry up! Hurry up!'

Lourdes, a garment worker from Mexico who had been in Los Angeles for a year at the time of the interview, also recorded how this pressure to produce results in inhumane conditions of work and generates ethnic conflicts between workers and owners from different ethnic groups:

> 'Nunca me dan un descanso. . . . They never give me a break. We only have an hour for lunch. We work from eight to five. I cannot even run to the rest-room . . . the other day I had to go and the owner followed me all the way to the rest-room. She told me "Mexicans are too lazy" . . . and I answered that Mexicans work too hard and Chinese ["Chinos"] pay too little.'

According to Alicia (a retired worker from Costa Rica):

> 'La costura es muy difícil y nos tratan muy mal. . . . Garment work is too hard and they treat us like dirt . . . as if they do not care for us at all. When we go to lunch they want us to eat fast, we have to stand up and run to the sewing machine. I suffered a lot because I stayed at the shop for ten years, and they never gave me any holiday or vacation. I finally quit. I told my husband that I could not take it anymore . . . now I have high blood pressure and I need lots of rest.'

Some workers spoke of deductions that were taken from their wages – purportedly for social security – that were never reported to the agency. As a retired Mexican garment worker explained:

> 'Me quitaban [deducciones] de mi cheque. . . . They made deductions from my check, but they never reported it to the social security office. . . . Once the owner took some money from all of us because he said he had to send money to her mother in Korea.'

Another worker from Mexico, who never gave her social security number to her boss but nevertheless had social security deductions taken from her cheque, explained that:

> 'Siempre me pagaba con cheque. . . . He always paid me with a cheque, and made deductions, but never wanted to take my social security number. So I asked to whom that money was going . . . all he said was that it was going to another social security number, not mine.'

In some cases, employers force workers to take work home on top of working forty hours in the shop. The workers who refuse are asked to resign, as occurred in the case of Lucy, a Mexican worker who recently retired. She reported:

I refused to take work home because . . . you know . . . it is illegal. The boss then asked me to leave the shop which I gladly did because I felt it was time for me to retire. The rest of the girls have to do it. They have families to support.

Employers pay 'Latinas' piece rate if they are moderately skilled; if they are good at what they do, they receive the minimum wage. Employers set the piece rates very low; for example, at one shop the pay is ten cents for hemming blouses, thirty cents for stitching a collar. One would have to sew one hundred blouses to get the equivalent of ten dollars. In order to make thirty dollars, it would be necessary to stitch one hundred collars. When one becomes acquainted with the different operations and the concentration and skill that these operations require, this type of labour is even more challenging.

The power machine requires coordination of hand, eye, knee and foot. The speed with which the machine can be operated is amazing. However, the demands of this work do not stop there; these women must continuously develop new skills in order to work with different materials and different styles. Everyone develops tricks to complete a given operation faster and to work more efficiently. The conceptualization of tasks is different every time a new bundle arrives. These women constantly re-create the whole labour process. The only way of making some money is by developing skills and speed in a particular operation. When styles constantly change it is almost impossible to become skilled at one operation.

In addition, working conditions in the sweat shops are unhealthy. In some shops there is no ventilation; in others there are draughts. Many of the shops are infested with rats and cockroaches. Rest-rooms are filthy and a health hazard; garbage is not adequately disposed of. Workers are exposed to all types of dyes and materials which may cause allergic reactions.[10] When accidents happen these shops are not even prepared for emergencies. Lita, a Costa Rican worker, showed me her thumb with a small fraction of a needle embedded in it and explained:

'Se me enteró la aguja en el dedo gordo. . . . The needle went through my thumb in and out, but then it stayed there. I was screaming, the boss got a pair of pliers and took it out, but only part of it came out. This happened years ago, I have to go to the doctor . . . but I am afraid.'

These conditions are aggravated by the fact that these workers lack the opportunity to complain and receive no health benefits, added to which the public health system is in trouble. One need only visit one of the Los Angeles county hospitals to witness the disarray and overcrowded conditions which await these workers who have been injured.

For those doing 'homework' the situation is worse. They are paid piece rates, sometimes lower than those offered at the sweat shop. These women care for their children while working at the sewing machine. They rent their own machines and pay for the electricity and the maintenance of the equipment they use. Many work overnight in order to comply with their deadlines. Children are usually involved in the labour process; they are given tasks such as trimming and sometimes sewing in violation of child labour laws (Efron, 1989b). The whole family is exposed to all the health and industrial hazards of a factory. These women labour under conditions that compare to the putting out system of seventeenth- or eighteenth-century England or nineteenth-century United States (Boris and Daniels, 1989).[11] However, a description of these working conditions is not complete without taking into account how labour relations are mediated by co-ethnic relations within the garment industry in Los Angeles.

Intra-ethnic and inter-ethnic conflict in the garment industry

Historical research on the garment industry in the United States suggests that ethnic relations are an integral part of the development and structure of this industry. At the turn of the century co-ethnics worked in the garment industry on the East Coast.[12] These arrangements sometimes helped to mobilize workers towards forming labour unions; sometimes they stunted their efforts to gain labour demands. Today, paternalistic relationships enacted between co-ethnics in the garment industry continue to occur among Dominican and Chinese shops in New York (Waldinger, 1984) or among Cuban shops in Miami (Fernandez-Kelly and García, 1985).

These relationships among co-ethnics point to a system of loyalty and trust between workers and employers. Co-ethnic owners benefit enormously from this liaison; paternalistic relations of obligation towards supervisors and owners are further strengthened by cultural traditions specific to different groups. Some co-ethnic workers seem to benefit as well from this relationship; however, upon closer examination all workers suffer from this arrangement. Divisions among workers who are loyal and those who are not work to the detriment of workers' unity.

In the Los Angeles garment industry co-ethnic paternalistic relationships exist among both Asian and Latinos(as). Again, supervisors or owners who are from the same ethnic group as their workers demand more work, overtime and homework from their workers who comply out of a sense of duty. Co-ethnic workers benefit from this relationship in several ways: they might be assigned the most desirable work, receive the easier materials to work with, benefit from more work, retain employment when there is not enough to go around, or land a sewing machine that is in good working condition. Thus an ethnic division is created at the workplace, which intensifies competition and mistrust among workers from different ethnic backgrounds.

'Latinas' working for Latino supervisors may benefit from these types of paternalistic relationships as well, depending on the national origin of the supervisor. Because the garment industry has been predominantly Mexican, Mexican origin 'Latinas' have the upper hand. This formation of 'Latinaness' is contested and problematized when non-Mexican 'Latina' ('Latina'-Salvadorean, 'Latina'-Costa Rican, 'Latina'-Guatemalan) workers interrogate and resist the dominant position of Mexican workers. 'Latinaness' also gets broken down into finer subdivisions in terms of national origin and seniority when 'Latina' workers describe not only their country of origin but their locality in an attempt to differentiate themselves.

Probably as a result of the fierce competition in the industry, the position which Mexican workers occupy, and the negative stereotypes of Mexicans in the United States, 'Latinas' who are not Mexican are often offended when they are labelled 'Mexicans'.[13] Even when non-Mexican 'Latinas' try to separate themselves from Mexicans and negative stereotypes, their supervisors generally refuse to distinguish between people of Mexico, Central and South America. According to them (and a popular widespread popular belief), everyone who is from South of the border must be Mexican.

There also exists intra-ethnic conflict among 'Latinas' themselves, especially because they compete for the same low paying jobs. Every time a new immigrant comes into the shop, there exists the possibility that this person will take someone else's job. Owners create this type of competition among workers by forcing new workers to take the lowest wage and throwing out those who have demanded more in the past. For this reason the fear of losing one's job to someone else is not unfounded. As Rita, a 'Latina'-Mexicana trimmer, describes:

> 'Cuando llegó estaba dispuesta. . . . When she [a Salvadoran woman] arrived she was willing to take twenty cents less per piece. I had to leave the shop.'

This scenario is repeated among women of different 'Latina' Americana origins. For example, Ester, from El Salvador, experienced this same type of displacement. Although she made up a whole wedding dress for the price of $40.00 (in 1987), she was forced to leave her job and do homework because another 'Latina' from South America was hired who was prepared to work for less. She explains: 'An Argentinean woman came in and she said she would do the whole dress for half the price of what I asked. I was asked to do the same or leave.'

Labour relations in the garment industry are so intense and exploitative that it is difficult for these women to create an effective culture of resistance (Lamphere, 1987; Ruiz, 1987; Sacks, 1984; Soldatenko, 1991; Zavella, 1987).[14] They do not stay in the same shop long enough to create the types of networks that might allow them to organize and, in addition, anyone who walks into the shop looking for work can easily replace them. Added to this difficult scenario is the fact that Mexican women, including Chicanas, have been in the industry since the 1920s (Laslett and Tyler, 1989; Pesotta, 1987) and they have been able to work themselves into more secure and privileged positions. By contrast, most recently immigrated 'Latinas' begin at the bottom and have the most unstable jobs.

Favouritism also exacerbates these tensions and divisions, particularly when a co-ethnic relationship that is not Latina/o determines the distribution of work. In this case those who are co-ethnics get better bundles and make more money than the rest of the workers.[15] However, differential treatment of these workers is evident at other levels as well. There are contractors who favour their own ethnic group by paying them higher wages for doing the same work that workers from other ethnic groups do for a lower wage.[16] Through this dual system of wages they promote a hierarchical and artificial division of workers based on ethnicity. These divisions are further exacerbated by the terrible working conditions, the low wages forced on the workers by the bosses, and the high turnover rate.[17]

To summarize, intra-ethnic and inter-ethnic conflict arises in the labour process where different ethnic groups compete for meagre opportunities (Hossfeld, 1994) in a context in which few opportunities exist for immigrant women and minorities. The stage is set for this type of competitive environment by ethnic entrepreneurs who also compete for limited opportunities to survive within the garment industry by hiring ethnic workers at very low wages (Hess, 1990). These immigrant entrepreneurs, who arrive in Los Angeles with some capital or pool resources, typically enter the garment industry as contractors and subcontractors. In some cases they organize by national origin, as is the case of the Korean Contractor's Association, yet they do not necessarily hire from their own ethnic group.[18] In fact, contractors may hire from their own ethnic group as well as from other groups. Whichever the case, they are important actors in a labour process that not only promotes inequality and exploitation but also 'differentiates' 'Latina' women (on the basis of race, ethnicity and social class) and nationality.

'Latinas'' racial perceptions of their bosses

In addition to co-ethnic relations, Euro and American racist perceptions that circulate within a US-Latin American context also mediate labour relations in the garment industry. These perceptions resonate not only among bosses but also among 'Latina' workers who themselves have been targets of prejudice and who are embroiled in unequal power relations. In the interviews I conducted with them they regularly 'marked' the ethnicity of their managers and owners. For instance, when the managers were Asian there was a tendency among 'Latinas' to refer to them as 'Chinos', which literally means Chinese. Those 'Latinas' who used this term were aware of the fact that their bosses were from different Asian countries, not only from China. Within this context, the use of the term 'Chinos' denoted not only a homogenization of Asians but also disrespect (Horton, 1995).

Clearly, these perceptions were fuelled by the resentment which these workers felt as a result of the exploitative nature of their work relationship with their bosses and by stereotypical representations that circulate in a Latin American-US context. 'Latinas' tended to downplay the fact that Asian and Latino contractors are squeezed by retailers and large manufacturers who have the last word in setting prices. To these workers, it was their immediate boss or owner (generally 'Asian') who abused and exploited them and demanded extra work from them.[19]

This is not to say that 'Latinas' did not blame Latino contractors as well for abuses and engaging in cruel and humiliating forms of one-upmanship based on class and patriarchal privilege. As a 'Latina'-Costa Rican worker told me:

> 'Mi patrón se reía de mi. . . . My (Latino) boss used to laugh at me when I threatened to leave. He used to say you always come back because everywhere it is the same and you need this job.'

However, it was evident to me that a qualitative difference existed when these workers expressed disgust about an Asian boss. The reflections of this 'Latina' Costa-Rican confirm how these differences were marked:

> 'Hay con esos "Chinos" nunca. . . . The Chinese no way! [waving her hands and laughing]. . . . And the Koreans my God to work with them is so terrible that I will rather beg in the streets.'

It is important to note that these kinds of racial and ethnic differences were themselves subject to change, depending on circumstances. This same respondent, who insinuated that she might work for a boss who was not Asian, backed away when I pressed a point she had made about an abusive Latino boss. She looked thoughtful, and made it clear that *all* bosses are bad, thus stressing their similarities:

> Todos son iguales. . . . All of them are the same when it comes to pay and work; they are all the same; they all have made my life impossible. The ones that gain out of all this are the ones above, but the contractors abuse us.

Racial perceptions, actions and misunderstandings work both ways, from employer to worker and from worker to employer. According to accounts by 'Latinas', contractors regard workers who are from a different ethnic group as uncultured, worthless and lazy. The workers perceive and also stereotype their bosses and view them as uncultured. These exchanges are based on unequal relations of power; employers can always set prices and fire workers but workers have to keep quiet or risk losing their jobs. In most cases, employers enjoy class and gender privileges that these workers lack. In this way, these employers can act on their sexist and racialized views in ways that 'Latina' workers cannot.

These unequal relationships work to the detriment of women of colour who are the lowest paid in the garment industry. They work to the benefit of manufacturers and retailers who can distance themselves from the labour process and pressure contractors and workers without taking major risks. The ultimate beneficiaries of this system are the large manufacturers and retailers who contract out, and who are neither Latinos nor Asians.[20]

Manufacturers and retailers, by exercising their capital and power, have created a system of production that rests on a specific hierarchy of gender, immigrant and ethnic divisions, and privileges. They stay in Los Angeles knowing that immigrant contractors are willing to take risks and that immigrant 'Latinas' and Asians must take these jobs because they lack other options. On occasion, some manufacturers express a concern for the reputation of this industry in Los Angeles and demand that guilty contractors be punished. But they do not acknowledge that if it were not for these illegal contractors many manufacturers and retailers would be out of business or relocating to Asia or Latin America.

Conclusion

By squeezing contractors, retailers and manufacturers set in motion a whole chain of exploitative relationships that end in the sweat shops and the homes of these immigrant women. For a select group of large capitalists, the profitable success of the Los Angeles garment industry rests on the gender, ethnic and immigrant divisions in its midst. These divisions have created a Third World industry in the United States. Unless workers are treated with fairness at all levels of the industry and homework and sweat shops are eradicated for good, the garment industry in Los Angeles will continue its abuses.

The survival of 'Latina' garment workers in the garment industry rests on their ability to negotiate collaborative relations based on their unique struggles and experiences within the garment industry as women, immigrants, racialized workers and as specific types of socially constituted 'Latina' Americanas. Some of the garment workers I interviewed acknowledged that survival in the US depended on the formation of another type of transnational identity, which we could provisionally characterize as a materially situated 'emergent' pan-ethnic identity. This identity describes the experience of immigrant women who are denied protection due to their immigrant status and the policies of the state and who none the less courageously fight for survival in an extremely exploitative industry. This emergent identity refutes homogenizing and absolute ethnic, 'genderless' terms of the universal Latino. In order to realize its oppositional potential such an identity would need to attend to the way ethnicity and gender are rearticulated in the capitalist workplace and to negotiate – not erase or down-play – specific ethnic and national differences.

As the ethnographic testimonies of the women who offered the 'glimpses' of this yet emergent identity confirm, there is much to be learned from incorporating the agencies, voices and contestations of those at the bottom of the organizational hierarchy into studies of the garment industry. While these workers were not always aware of the structural or systemic dimensions of this workplace and lacked the necessary organizational networks from which to launch an effective resistance, they offered invaluable insights into the way in which some workers experience the contemporary conditions of global capitalism and endeavour to 'speak' rather than silence these conditions. I submit that those of us who work in cultural studies and sociology would benefit enormously by drawing from their insights and courage.

Notes

1   Thanks to Angie Chabram-Dernersesian and Michael Soldatenko for their valuable comments and support.
2   See Hayes-Bautista *et al.*, 1988; Oboler, 1995. Padilla (1994) presents a different perspective by calling attention to the need to contextualize identity.
3   In order to avoid the pitfalls of pan-ethnic constructions, I see 'Latina' as an identity formation that is situational and fluctuates as nationality, race, class, gender and immigration status get articulated and rearticulated in the workplace.
4   My study is based on twenty extensive interviews with 'Latina' garment workers as well as informal interviews with contractors, manufacturers and union leaders from 1989 to 1993. I also engaged in a form of participant observation at the ILGWU, a sewing school and a sweat shop.
5   The women who I refer to as 'Latinas' in this study are from different countries and regions and have been in the United States for different periods of time. Mexican women are the oldest and most established group of garment workers whereas Salvadoran women are the newcomers. Their immigration patterns are related to recent civil wars in the region, which date back to the late 1960s and 1970s (Peñaloza, 1986). To avoid essentializing the heterogeneous group of workers I place quotation marks around 'Latinas' and I specify my use of 'Latina' by marking specific national affiliations, for example, 'Latina'-Mexicana, or 'Latina'-Salvadoreña.
6   By immigrant specific I call attention to the undocumented status of most 'Latina' garment workers. For a further discussion of this issue see Soldatenko (1991).
7   From the 1960s to the present, a significant number of Asian immigrant women have also appeared. Chinese garment shops were initially concentrated in the area of Chinatown (Li and Wong, 1974; Nee and Nee, 1972; Wong,

1979). They soon expanded throughout Los Angeles and Orange County. More recently, other Asian groups, such as Korean, Thai, Vietnamese and Cambodian, have come to work in the garment industry. We need more studies that focus on these groups in Los Angeles.

8   In order to contextualize where these 'Latinas' fit in the garment industry in the United States, we have to look at sewing as a historically gender, ethnic and immigrant specific occupation (Furio, 1979; Glenn, 1983).

Early studies have demonstrated how certain occupations have been reserved for women (Bradley, 1989; Foner, 1982; Walby, 1986). At the turn of the century, the East Coast garment industry employed both East European men and women. Immigrant men and women toiled long hours at the sewing machine; they worked in sweat shops and took in homework. These two systems have been well documented (Furio, 1979; Glenn, 1983; Waldinger, 1984). With the development of the industry and unionization drives, men were able to secure 'skilled' positions as cutters, tailors and pressers. This is the period when the artificial division between 'skilled' and 'unskilled' positions appears. The split between men's and women's work corresponds to the division between 'skilled' and 'unskilled'. Though immigrant women gained from unionization efforts as well, they were kept outside of the more desirable and better paid positions, even when they had the necessary skills before arriving in the United States. Women remained sewing machine operators and were considered 'unskilled' workers (Glenn, 1983). When the industry shifted away from the East Coast this new separation continued (NACLA, 1982).

9   The garment industry is divided into four types of shops: manufacturers, jobbers, contractors and homeworkers. The established manufacturers can accomplish all levels of production such as designing, purchasing, cutting, sewing and selling the garment under one roof. In some cases manufacturers may contract out different parts of the operation. The jobbers usually design, buy fabric and sell the garments, but they do not manufacture them. Jobbers contract out the sewing and finishing. Contractors operate in licensed and unlicensed shops. The licensed contracting shops work for retailers, manufacturers and jobbers; they possess their own well-established organizations. Most of the research done on contracting has been about this group (NACLA, 1982; Scott, 1984; Waldinger, 1984). The unlicensed contractors run the sweat shops. They work for everyone: retailers, manufactures, jobbers and licensed contractors. These sweat shops are small investment operations that work outside the industry's structure of regulations. They move from one location to another and can appear and disappear overnight.

Contractors and subcontractors form the crux of the garment industry in Los Angeles. Both work for manufacturers and retailers who set very low prices. When contractors go out of business, new immigrant entrepreneurs are usually ready to replace them quickly. Contractors and subcontractors are the risk takers of the industry. They must finish orders on time and they depend on a constant flow of orders to survive. Much competition exists among contractors and subcontractors; they must compete for the best orders just to keep afloat. Retailers, manufacturers and jobbers set prices at an extremely low level because there is always the possibility that someone else can complete an order for a lower price. As the manufacturers pressure contractors the workers in turn are squeezed. Contractors push workers to the limit and pay them the lowest possible wage. The system lends itself to the worst type of exploitation.

10 It has been reported how cotton dust produces damage to the lungs (Schlien, 1982).

11 Since 1986 the labour department tried to lift the ban on homework. It was partially successful in 1988 when the ban was lifted for jewellery and embroidery only. Homework in the manufacture of garments is regarded as a misdemeanour in California; however, it is widespread in Los Angeles and vicinity.

12 In particular, the Russian, Italian and Irish worked for co-ethnic contractors (Furio, 1979; Glenn, 1983; Pesotta, 1987).

13 At the time of this study Chicanas were older retired workers. Little conflict was reported between Chicanas and Mexicanas at the shops as had been previously observed by some researchers (Fernandez-Kelly and García, 1985).

14 In the works of Lamphere (1987), Ruiz (1987), Sacks (1984) and Zavella (1987), networks and work culture play an important role. I did not find these networks at the sweat shops. Exploitation, competition and mistrust run high. The work culture at the sweat shops is not one of camaraderie and friendship to humanize the workplace (Soldatenko, 1991).

15 This type of differential treatment was reported by 'Latinas' who worked for Asian supervisors and told horror stories about what it was like to work for an Asian boss. Elia, for example, reflected on the abusive practices of her boss while instructing me on the challenges of her work, as this excerpt which chronicles how I was introduced to garment work demonstrates: 'E. is teaching me to do straight sewing in an industrial sewing machine installed in her room. I tried to stitch as she has demonstrated, I keep messing up and cutting long lines of wasted thread. E. jokingly reminds me that I have to be thrifty with the thread, specially if I hope to work for "Chinos" who according to her will measure every bit of thread I waste and charge me for it.'

16 The dual system of wages existed before to differentiate white workers from workers of colour in some industries (Barrera, 1979).

17 'Latina' workers know how the system is maintained in order to keep them dependent on supervisors for constant work and possible favours.

18 This is very different from New York City where Chinese and Latino contractors try to work with their own ethnic groups (Waldinger, 1984). In Los Angeles, contractors and workers are not typically from the same ethnic group.

19 This type of ethnic re-representation is not new. Retired Chicana workers often compared Asians to Jewish owners.

20 See the recent scandal on slave Thai garment workers at Los Angeles, Mervyns and Montgomery Wards being investigated in this case. See also the case of J.C. Penney and Chinese workers in 1990 (Baker, 1990).

References

Baker, Bob (1990) 'Alleged sweatshop with 100 Thai workers closed by state', *Los Angeles Times*, 19 July: B3.

Barrera, Mario (1979) *Race and Class in the Southwest*, Notre Dame: University of Notre Dame Press.

Blumenberg, Evelyn and Ong, P. (1994) 'Labor squeeze and ethnic/racial recomposition in the U.S. apparel industry', in E. Bonacich *et al.* (eds) *Global Production: The Apparel Industry in the Pacific Rim*, Philadelphia, PA: Temple University Press.

Bonacich, Edna (1990) 'Asian and Latino immigrants in Los Angeles garment industry: an exploration of the relationship between capitalism and racial oppression', unpublished presentation.

Bonacich, Edna, Cheng, Lucie, Chinchilla, Norma and Ong, Paul (1994) 'The garment industry in the restructuring global economy', in her (ed.) *Global Production: The Apparel Industry in the Pacific Rim*, Philadelphia, PA: Temple University Press.

Boris, Eileen and Daniels, Cynthia R. (eds) (1989) *Homework: Historical and Contemporary Perspectives on Paid Labor at Home*, Urbana: University of Illinois Press.

Bradley, Harriet (1989) *Men's Work, Women's Work: A Sociological History of the Sexual Division of Labor in Employment*, Minneapolis: University of Minnesota Press.

Bymers, Gwendolyn June (1958) 'A study of employment in women's and misses' outerwear manufacturing Los Angeles metropolitan area 1946–1954', unpublished dissertation in sociology, University of California, Los Angeles.

Carnoy, Martin, Dalcy, Hugh M. and Ojeda, Raul Hinojosa (1993) 'The changing economic position of Latinos in the U.S. labor market since 1939', in R. Morales and F. Bonilla (eds) *Latinos in a Changing U.S. Economy: Comparative Perspectives on Growing Inequality*, Sage Series on Race and Ethnic Relations, Vol. 7.

Dawsey, Darrel (1990) '16 hurt as 100 flee fire in garment district building', *Los Angeles Times*, 3 October: B3.

Duron, Clementina (1984) 'Mexican women and labor conflict in Los Angeles: the ILGWU dressmakers' strike of 1933', *Aztlan*, 15 (winter): 145–61.

Efron, Sonni (1989a) '"Hot goods" law revived as anti-sweatshop tool', *Los Angeles Times*, 26 November: A1.

—— (1989b) 'Mother's plight turns a home into sweatshop', *Los Angeles Times*, 28 November: A1.

Fernandez-Kelly, M. Patricia (1983) *For We Are Sold I and My People: Women and Industry in Mexico's Frontier*, Albany: State University of New York Press.

Fernandez-Kelly, M. Patricia and García, Anna M. (1985) 'The making of the underground economy: Hispanic women, homework, and the advanced capitalist state', The Institute for the Study of Man.

Foner, Philip S. (1982) *Women and the American Labor Movement: From the First Trade Unions to the Present*, New York: Free Press.

Furio, Colombia Marie (1979) 'Immigrant women and industry: a case study of the Italian immigrant women and the garment industry 1880–1950', unpublished Ph.D. dissertation, New York University.

Glenn, Susan Anita (1983) 'The working life of immigrants: women in the American garment industry 1880–1950', unpublished Ph.D. dissertation, University of California Berkeley.

Hayes-Bautista, David E., Schink, Werner O. and Chapa, Jorge (1988) *The Burden of Support: Young Latinos in an Aging Society*, Stanford, CA: Stanford University Press.

Hess, Darrel E. (1990) 'Korean immigrant entrepreneurs in the Los Angeles garment industry', unpublished MA thesis, University of California, Los Angeles.

Horton, John (1995) *The Politics of Diversity: Immigration, Resistance and Change in Monterey Park, California*, Philadelphia, PA: Temple University Press.

Hossfeld, Karen (1994) 'Hiring immigrant women: Silicon Valley's "Simple Formula",' in Maxine Baca Zinn and Bonnie Thornton Dill (eds) *Women of Color in U.S. Society*, Philadelphia, PA: Temple University Press.

Lamphere, Louise (1987) *From Working Daughters to Working Mothers: Immigrant Women Workers in a New England Industrial Community*, Ithaca, NY: Cornell University.

Laslett, John and Tyler, Mary (1989) *The ILGWU in Los Angeles, 1907–1988*, Inglewood: Ten Star Press.

Li, Peggy and Wong, Buck (1974) 'Garment industry in Los Angeles Chinatown, 1973–74', Working Papers, Los Angeles: Asian American Studies Center.

McCreesh, Carolyn Daniel (1985) *Women in the Campaign to Organize Garment Workers*, New York: Garland Publishing.

Monroy, Douglas (1982) 'La Costura en Los Angeles, 1933–1939: the ILGWU and the politics of domination', in M. Mora and A. del Castillo (eds) *Mexican Women in the United States: Struggles Past and Present*, Los Angeles: Chicano Studies Research Center.

NACLA Report of the Americas (1982) 'Capital's flight: the apparel industry moves South', in M. Mora and A. del Castillo (eds) *Mexican Women in the United States: Struggles Past and Present*, Los Angeles, CA: Chicano Studies Research Center.

Nee, Victor and Nee, Brett de Barry (1972) *Longtime, Californ': A Documentary Study of an American Chinatown*, New York: Random House.

Newman, Maria and Lee, John H. (1989) 'Garment district blaze fans safety fears', *Los Angeles Times*, 7 December: B1.

Oboler, Suzanne (1995) *Ethnic Labels, Latino Lives*, Minneapolis: University of Minnesota Press.

Padilla, Felix M. (1994) 'On Hispanic identity', in his (ed.) *Handbook of Hispanic Culture, In the United States: Sociology*, Houston, TX: Arte Publico Press.

Peñaloza, Fernando (1984) *Central Americans in Los Angeles*, Spanish Speaking Mental Health Research Center.

Pesotta, Rose (1987) *Bread Upon the Waters*, New York: Cornell University Press.

Petersen, Kurt (1992) *The Maquiladora Revolution in Guatemala*, Occasional Papers Series, 2 Orville H. Schell, Jr. Center for International Human Rights at Yale Law School.

Phizacklea, Annie (1988a) 'Entrepreneurship, ethnicity and gender', in S. Westwood and P. Bhachu (eds) *Enterprising Women: Ethnicity, Economy and Gender Relations*, London: Routledge.

—— (1988b) 'Gender, racism and occupational segregation', in Sylvia Walby (ed.) *Gender Segregation at Work*, Philadelphia, PA: Open University Press.

—— (1990) *Unpacking the Fashion Industry: Gender, Racism and Class in Production*. London: Routledge.

Ruiz, Vicky L. (1987) *Cannery Women, Cannery Lives: Mexican Women, Unionization, and the California Food Processing Industry, 1930–1950*, Albuquerque: University of New Mexico Press.

Sacks, Karen (1984) 'Computers, ward secretaries, and a walkout in a southern hospital', in her and Dorothy Remy (eds) *My Troubles are Going to Have Troubles with Me: Everyday Trials and Triumphs of Women Workers*, New Brunswick: Rutgers University Press.

Sassen-Koob, Saskia (1984) 'From household to workplace: theories and survey research on migrant women in the labor market', *International Migration Review: Special Issue of Women and Immigration*, XVIII (4) (winter): 1144–67.

Schlein, Lisa (1982) 'Los Angeles garment industry sews a cloak of shame', in M. Mora and A. del Castillo (eds) *Mexican Women in the United States: Struggles Past and Present*, Los Angeles: Chicano Studies Research Center.

Scott, A.J. (1984) 'Industrial organization and the logic of intrametropolitan location, III: a case study of the women's dress industry in the Greater Los Angeles region', *Economic Geography*, 60(1): 3–27.

Soldatenko, Maria A. (1991) 'Organizing Latina garment workers in L.A', in V. Ruiz (ed.) *Aztlan: Special Issue on Las Obreras*, 20 (1 and 2) (spring and autumn): 73–96.

Walby, Sylvia (1986) *Patriarchy at Work: Patriarchal and Capitalist Relations in Employment*, Cambridge: Polity Press.

Waldinger, Roger (1984) 'Immigrant enterprise in the New York garment industry', *Social Problems*, 32(1) (October): 60–74.

—— (1989) *Through the Eye of the Needle: Immigrants and Enterprise in New York's Garment Trades*, New York: New York University Press.

Westwood, Sally and Bhachu, Parminder (eds) (1988) *Enterprising Women: Ethnicity, Economy and Gender Relations*, London: Routledge.

Wong, Charles Choy (1979) 'Ethnicity work and community: the case of Chinese in Los Angeles', unpublished Ph.D. dissertation, University of California, Los Angeles.

Zavella, Patricia (1987) *Women's Work and Chicano Families: Cannery Workers of the Santa Clara Valley*, Ithaca, NY: Cornell University Press.

Yvonne Yarbro-Bejarano

SEXUALITY AND CHICANA/O STUDIES: TOWARD A THEORETICAL PARADIGM FOR THE TWENTY-FIRST CENTURY[1]

Abstract

In this article I propose that we make the study of sexuality central to Chicana/o studies, using it to rethink the whole field rather than just 'adding it in', which would continue its current marginalization. In addition to examining the stakes of this type of theoretical expansion for gays and lesbians of colour, I examine the profound difficulties of expanding analytic categories in such a way as to give expression to the lived experience of the ways race, class, gender and sexuality converge (Childers, hooks). Finally I suggest that Chicana/o studies can be an ideal site for contesting rather than reproducing hegemonic scripts such as male or white supremacy, upper-class superiority or compulsory heterosexuality. Within this context, I argue that our task for what remains of the 1990s and into the twenty-first century is to retain the contestatory critique of US state domination and of our narratives of exclusion, and to examine how and why those area studies which concern 'identities' (ethnic studies and women's studies, gay and lesbian studies) are being subjected to such intense scrutiny at this point in time within educational and political settings.

Keywords

Chicana/o studies; gay and lesbian studies; sexuality; community; relational theories; queer theory

T HE PROTESTS AND HUNGER STRIKES of 1994 at Stanford, UCLA and UC Santa Barbara remind us that the university is not a friendly place for

Chicana/o studies. Everything we achieve has to be struggled for, and if we stop pushing in order to further our academic project within the university, to simply go about the business of being students, staff and faculty, the hard-won ground we have gained begins to erode from beneath our feet. We face harsh realities as academics, such as the fact that the numbers of faculty, students and staff, especially staff in high-ranking positions, and particularly the number of Latinas in those high positions, have not significantly increased from their levels of twenty years ago.

These realities oblige us to reconsider the popular conception in Chicana/o studies of the breach between the university and the 'community' we were created to serve (Chabram, 1990). This division can lead to an exclusive definition of the subject of Chicana/o studies as the most disadvantaged, marginalized, usually male and heterosexual subject. The positioning of the academic as somehow 'outside' of the community reveals a lingering reluctance to theorize and deploy a political agency from our own socioeconomic location. We are now beginning to reconceptualize the populations of Chicana/o faculty, students and staff in the universities as a kind of embattled community in itself, and to undertake what Angie Chabram calls 'a critical analysis of the lived experiences of Chicano/Chicana intellectuals in their multiple sites' (Chabram, 1990: 243).

At the same time, recent setbacks, ever present obstacles to progress, and the need for militant action to establish and protect minimal academic programmes for our discipline validate the founding ideologies of Chicana/o studies, under the auspices of a nationalism understood to be a contestatory ground for a critique of and resistance to social, economic and racial domination under the US state, of which the university is a part. In its multiply besieged positionality, Chicana/o studies contributes to our repertory of images and narratives about our identity, shared values and interests, producing and reconstructing histories that mythologize or demystify the past, the present situation, and the collective desire for a better future.

In her talk at Stanford University in spring 1994, Wahneema Lubiano offered an insightful critical agenda for ethnic studies in thinking about nationalism. For Lubiano, at the heart of black nationalism's project is a critique of the US state's prescriptions of what the social formation is and ought to be. It is within these dominant notions of social formation and ideal social subject that Chicanas and Chicanos have been racialized, exploited and excluded in the US. But nationalism can simultaneously reinscribe the functions of the state within its own narratives of resistance, by prescribing its own ideas of the ideal social formation and the ideal subject and setting the parameters for acceptable forms and images of national identity. This internal repression often occurs in narratives of the family, in which our self-imaginings are cast in patriarchal and heterosexist moulds that restrict the possible gamut of roles for women *and* men. Our task for what remains of the 1990s and into the twenty-first century, then, is to retain the contestatory critique of US state domination, while exercising increased vigilance over the ways our own narratives can dominate and exclude.

Even as we regroup under certain nationalist narratives in response to outside pressures, increasing internal debate poses 'being Chicano' as an open-ended identity. The response to this critique, developed by many Chicana and Chicano thinkers, may be to fall back on the 'family' as a trope for recentring an idealized notion of culture or community (Gilroy, 1991). As internal diversity becomes more visible and audible, alternatives to this narrative of homogeneity compete with the desire to forget our differences in the image of the 'race-as-family', which reproduces itself ethnically and culturally through women (Gilroy, 1991: 307).

The impulse to police the political correctness of Chicano cultural representations *vis-à-vis* the dominant culture relates to a binary concept of Chicano identity: 'us' (the race-as-family) versus 'them'. Separatist ideologies, expressed in certain nationalist rhetoric, support other borders which must not be crossed: self/other, straight/queer, male/female. As Gloria Anzaldúa points out in *Borderlands*, the feeling of safety in the 'home' of the separate group demands an exclusion. The 'positive image' of identity will always entail repressing the 'others' *within* the culture. In attempts to maintain certain cultural borders defining racial and sexual identity, the term 'Chicano' can be monopolized to exclude 'non-ideal' others who identify as part of that community: women, queers and the racially diverse (Julien, 1991).

This examination of the sources of exclusion both outside and inside our communities encourages dialogue over the cultural construction of gender roles and the recognition of diverse racial and sexual identities. Our social identification as a 'community' (which we may call nationalism) manifests itself in Chicana/o studies. The term 'cultural nationalism' stresses the importance of culture as a medium of domination and resistance, stereotyping and self-affirmation, given the lack of economic resources, land, or full political participation of Chicanas/os as a social group or 'nation'. One of our ongoing discussions as Chicana/o intellectuals is and has been this prominence of the cultural. The crux of the 'cultural' in 'nationalism' is to avoid the potential eclipse of economic factors and class relations or the possibility of a more radical restructuring of society, in the understanding of the crucial role of cultural representation in an individual's or a community's self-image and sense of agency.

Without undermining the importance of the cultural, it is good to remind ourselves of the nature of this field of representation, whether in popular culture, literature, visual art or film. Rather than presenting the 'truth' of 'who we really are', for Stuart Hall, 'popular culture is where we discover and play with the identifications of ourselves, where we are imagined, where we are represented' (Hall, 1991: 32). Chicano cultural practices provide the opportunity for us to identify with stories and images of our lives so woefully 'under-represented' in mainstream culture. Of course, the ways we imagine our lives together are not homogeneous. For example, both Luis Valdez's play *The Shrunken Head of Pancho Villa* (1964) and lesbian playwright Cherrie Moraga's *Heroes and Saints* (1992) put on stage a character who is only a head. The two plays share an esthetic and a visual/verbal vocabulary, but galvanize them to strikingly different ends and effects.

As consumers of these images we may or may not accept the invitation to identify with them, but we are no longer innocent about the politics of these representations (Hall, 1988). The fantasy and love of 'Chicano' can exclude many who would be part of the collective. As bell hooks suggests, the emerging critical consciousness of diversity within ethnic communities, exemplified in many texts and images by Chicanas, will surely change the nature of the pleasure some are used to taking in our cultural representations, but it may enable us to have even greater pleasure in less exclusive imaginings of community.

As a 'bi-racial', middle-class, Chicana-identified lesbian academic, to name but a few of my subject positions, I am particularly interested in how Chicana/o studies participates in imagining 'us' as a social group in ways that limit the participation of women and define 'authentic' belonging in terms of a normative racial, class and sexual identity. Ethnic studies, women's studies and queer theory have taught us valuable lessons about the power of the unmarked category. Just as whiteness constructs itself as the centre and the norm in its very invisibility, an uninterrogated heterosexuality (defined coercively along the axes of monogamous marriage and procreative sex) stands as the universal of human sexuality, positioning homosexuality as the abject but necessary 'outside' to a normative heterosexuality which seems to flow unproblematically from a binary notion of gender as active masculinity and passive femininity. Only by subjecting the categories of whiteness, masculinity and normative heterosexuality to constant scrutiny can the fiction of their monolithic power be decentred and fragmented: no longer the one and the same that defines itself in terms of its other but another among others.

The possibility of transforming the research agenda of Chicana/o studies for the twenty-first century means combating a kind of ghetthoization within the discipline. The men continue to do pretty much what they always did, the women do gender analyses and the lesbians and (to a lesser extent) the gay men critique homophobia and heterosexism. What would Chicana/o studies look like if everybody did gender along with race and class, and if everybody took sexuality seriously as impacted by and impacting the way we experience ourselves as Chicana or Chicano? What would it be like if we all interrogated our own dominant discourses on race: mestizaje, contemporary interracial relationships and the 'coyote' offspring of white and Mexican unions? What if Chicano scholars routinely considered the role of gender in shaping the experience of immigration or labour? What if cultural critics, instead of tagging only homosexual identity, spoke of the textual construction of heterosexuality as well?

I propose to make the study of sexuality central to Chicana/o studies, using it to rethink the whole field rather than just 'adding it in', which would continue its marginalization. This proposal, that the analysis of sexuality can make us look at things differently, meets with various kinds of resistance, not the least of which is the thundering silence around issues of desire and sexuality in Chicana/o culture, particularly women's silence. While I feel that we have much to learn about ourselves by examining the cultural representation of what moves us sexually, the analysis of sexuality is not limited to who does what to whom in bed, but encompasses the analysis of desire as what moves us, period. By studying the sexual yearnings and practices expressed in our collective imaginings, we also learn about the links between sexual longing for the other and the ongoing search for and commitment to 'community' that underlies the very construction of Chicana/o studies. In the study of culture, why do we not ask where and how we take our pleasure? The reluctance to speak of pleasure in what we do relates to a dual legacy of puritanical Marxist and Indian Catholic legacies. Yet the realities we face as academics – the workaholism, the stress-related illnesses, the vicious circle that keeps the few doing the teaching, mentoring and committee work that should be done by a faculty of colour twice or three times our size – make it more important than ever to construct what we do in the university as pleasure and passion.

In her keynote address 'Technologies of Desire', presented to the 1995 National Association of Chicano Studies (NACS) conference plenary session, Emma Pérez spoke of desire as the prime mover of social change, with the power to disrupt repressive social machines as well as to transform us. For Pérez, we can hope to redress the negative results of repression within our political movements in the recognition of desire as an 'open passion system' that empowers rather than seeks power over. Pérez poses key questions for our academic project: how is our desire for Chicana/o studies wrung out of us in the university, with the rationality of its 'academic standards', and what happens to the passion that stems from our activism as scholars? It is no coincidence that Chicana lesbians have been at the forefront of this reclaiming of the revolutionary potential of desire in all its personal, collective and political ramifications.

The stakes in the theoretical expansion of Chicana/o studies as an academic discipline are particularly high for lesbians and gays of colour, given the exclusionary politics of domination that have characterized the histories of both women's studies and American ethnic studies.[2] Even today within this branch of ethnic studies, for example, debates have emerged concerning gender, but lesbian and gay issues continue to be marginalized. From other quarters, ongoing critiques (see, for example, the 1990 anthology *Making Face, Making Soul/ Haciendo Caras*) expose the ways discourses on difference have been appropriated by white feminists, addressing new forms of racism, and calling attention to the 'inclusion without influence' of women of colour in women's studies programmes and research (Uttal, 1990).

There are, of course, changes that merit our attention. In the last five years we have witnessed within our professional organization a shift away from the heterosexual male dominance of earlier times: namely, the increasing female and lesbian presence within NACCS brought about by the refusal of Chicana lesbians and feminists to remain silent and invisible.[3] Yet even with these developments often heterosexual women of colour, including Chicanas, can see clearly their multiple marginalization in terms of race, gender and class origins, yet can remain unconscious of their heterosexual privilege. Heterosexual males of colour, including Chicanos, often privilege race and class over gender and sex, thus obscuring heterosexual male dominance and sexual privilege.

The need for an analysis of multiple oppressions and multiple privileges in racial/ethnic identity is greater than ever, in order to help channel the energies of cultural nationalism along paths that diverge from invisibility, misogyny and homophobia. But one of the problems we face in developing the theoretical paradigm for Chicana/o studies I have been outlining is overcoming the very academic training that taught us to focus on one or two issues as if they exist separately from the others, whether it be gender, race, class or sexuality. As I have pointed out elsewhere, the rigid separation of these categories in our analyses reveals a general resistance to acknowledging the ways one experiences racial and cultural identity inseparably from gender and sexual constructions of the self (Yarbro-Bejarano, 1995: 127).

The solution to this problem is not one of inclusion 'after the fact'.[4] The 'additive' model of 'including' previously excluded categories maintains power in the hands of those who constitute the 'norm', 'graciously inviting the different in', and inhibits an understanding of the relations among the elements of identity and the effect each has on the others (Spelman, 1988: 115; Uttal, 1990; Yarbro-Bejarano, 1995: 127). The critique of the additive model has been accompanied by an awareness of the necessity of producing a *relational* theory of difference, examining the formation of identity in the dynamic interpenetration of gender, race, sexuality, class and nation (Alarcón, 1990; Mohanty, 1991: 2). The theory is also relational within each binary set, for example, a man lives his masculinity through his cultural, sexual and class identifications, but also in relation to a certain construction of femininity which for the man is essential to his manhood.

Critics who endeavour to replace ways of thinking with new ones are faced with a profound 'conceptual and theoretical difficulty' (Gordon, 1991: 101–2). What is needed is a new paradigm in Chicana/o studies that permits the expansion of analytic categories in such a way as to give 'expression to the lived experience of the ways race, class, sexuality and gender converge' (Childers and hooks, 1990; Yarbro-Bejarano, 1995: 128).

Given current intellectual developments, it would be regressive to consider the experiences of lesbians and gays of colour as 'different' or to merely include them under the auspices of this area of studies: '[t]he fluidity and heterogeneity of forms of sexual identity (exemplified in the emergence of the category of queerness) speak for possibilities of analysis far beyond a mere gay/straight dichotomy.'[5] In a similar way, new conceptions of ethnicity in cultural studies incorporate a 'recognition of the extraordinary diversity of subject positions, social experiences and cultural identities' which comprise the categories Chicana/o, black and people of colour (Hall, 1988).[6] One result of this shift in thinking about identity is 'the blurring of boundaries' among formerly rigid and separated analytic categories. This permits us to perceive what Katie King calls the 'race of sex' and the 'sex of race, for example'.

A recently articulated position against the relational paradigm is that 'everything cannot be done at the same time and fitted into a single, comprehensive theory' (de Lauretis, 1991: 270), or even that such projects suggest an 'epistemological imperialism' (Butler, 1993: 18), arrogant in its dilettantish claim to such expansive authority in so many areas. This objection raises important questions about the production of Chicana/o studies theory, and theory in general. What assumptions underlie the perception that the introduction of some issues somehow interrupts or defers the discussion of others? By choosing to focus on one or two elements, usually relegating the others to a footnote with the appropriate bibliography, do we provisionally and tactically privilege one or two categories in the hopes that the analysis thus produced would be useful to others' own projects involving other categories? Does the relegation of the pursuit of a particular power vector, such as race or gender, to those for whom it is the 'central focus of one's work' reinforce the artificial boundaries among analytic categories? Should the analysis of sexuality or gender, for example, be confined to those texts or practices that foreground them in particular ways? These questions and the very linguistic difficulties involved in trying to articulate the terminology of the relational paradigm demonstrate the limitations of our current theories for broaching the interdefining of multiple structures of domination in cultural identities, or even for formulating certain kinds of questions and not others.

While the critiques of people of colour are crucial in this project of theoretical expansion, 'everyone's sex has a race and vice versa, just as everyone's gender identity is constructed in the interplay among race, class, sexuality and nation' (Yarbro-Bejarano, 1995: 130). No one becomes who they are in relation to only one social category (Alarcon, 1990), and no representation of sexuality or desire is free of racialization (even in the absence of people of colour) (Yarbro-Bejarano, 1995).

I suggest that the writing and theory of many Chicanas have laid the ground for a new paradigm of multiple and shifting identities, consciousness and political agency that can form the theoretical framework of Chicana/o studies for the future.[7] Chicana/o studies can be an ideal site for contesting rather than reproducing hegemonic scripts such as male or white supremacy, upper-class superiority or compulsory heterosexuality. We can produce counter-hegemonic guidelines for scholarship and activism by problematizing the construction of a single, linear development of either Chicana/o identity or Chicana/o political movement. An important piece of this project is recognizing and interrogating the heterogeneity of racial and sexual identities. For the 1990s, and into the twenty-first century, we could work with the terms 'Chicana' or 'Chicano' as dynamic processes rather than a fixed and homogeneous identity.

There is reason to be hopeful that the recent history of debate around exclusionary practices will reorient the research agendas of Chicana/o studies in the awareness of the ways both our social formation and ourselves as subjects are structured in and through the overlapping experience of race, class, sexuality, culture and gender. Yet in spite of our best efforts, the outcome will be affected by institutional constraints that determine the availability of resources and radically restrict the possibility of training, hiring and retaining Chicana/o studies scholars whose work involves such analysis. This returns me to the point where I began.

As we move into the twenty-first century, Chicana/o studies must retain an allegiance to contestation and resistance against all forms of domination in the US, while working with the terms 'Chicana' and 'Chicano' as constantly producing identities (rather than as fixed and immutable categories) and as engaging productive tensions that are vital to continued projects of theoretical expansion. No doubt there are those who would question the fact that these sites of social, political and cultural struggle continue to be important from the point of view of intellectual or political practice. Unfortunately, even within the progressive sector we find scholars who are not able to discern new complex movements and identity formations and theoretical positionings within institutionally marginalized disciplines that 'speak' embattled social identities.

Those of us who work in cultural studies and seek to interrogate power relations need to further engage the issue of why these disciplines continue to be invalidated and dismissed within institutions of higher education. We also need to examine how these institutions generate political subtexts and implicate particular social and political subjects in the process. Recent events have provided us with a case worth mentioning.

Last week, UC Regent Ward Connerly, who was behind the regents' 1995 vote to ban race-based admissions and hiring as well as the passage of Proposition 209, which effectively abolished affirmative action in the State of California, also announced his plans to review ethnic studies programmes. This regent specifically 'questioned the legitimacy of women's studies, along with gay and lesbian studies or any discipline that probes issues of identity' (Chao, 1998).[8] Significantly, Connerly also proposed a ban on separate graduation ceremonies, adding this justification for his position: 'All of the infrastructure [of these programmes] created back in the 1970s and the 80s as a result of the black nationalism and the black power movement, I think we need to re-examine it [the infrastructure] now' (Lempinen, 1998). As with the arguments in favour of Propositions 187, 209 and 227, Connerly offers a disconcerting example of how these area studies are demonized, essentialized and balkanized, and ultimately ill served by reductionist interpretations that ignore their specificity and critical internal engagements and developments. Given the way certain area studies continue to be imbricated in the social and political predicaments of a population which has not shed its marginal status, and given the recent policies of a state (California) that has reversed the clock of progress on multiple fronts, it is important that we not only encourage but also practise a different disciplinary representation and evaluation. Now more than ever the stakes in doing so are very high.

Notes

1   This is a slightly revised version of my presentation at the plenary session of the 1994 regional NACCS Conference in Santa Cruz.

2   I have made this point and the subsequent point in reference to another related context in my essay, 'Expanding the categories of race and sexuality in lesbian and gay studies', in *Professions of Desire*, eds George E. Haggerty and Bonnie Zimmerman (New York: The Modern Language Association of America, 1995). There I elaborate: 'Many lesbians and gays of color remained on the fringe of 60s and 70s feminist and civil rights struggles or paid the high price of alienation, ostracization and closeting for doing political work which demanded the privileging of race, gender or class over sexual identity' (Saalfield and Navarro, 1991: 353–4). While sexual identity prohibited feeling completely 'at home' in racially based social movements, the cultural and class experiences of lesbians of colour led to a far-reaching critique of categories such as 'women' that universalized white middle-class women's experience (p. 124).

   This information, along with some of the quotes from the same 1995 essay concerning the difficulties associated with the production of a theory of relational difference, has been reprinted by permission of the Modern Language Association, although it is reframed and often re-elaborated within a Chicana/o context here.

3   I have also pointed out that Chicanas have had to fight for women-only spaces within the institutional structure of NACCS, yet by the 1992 Conference in March, the schedule included a lesbian caucus meeting, a lesbian round table and a lesbian panel. Gay Chicanos, who had been less vocal over the past two decades compared to Chicana lesbians, formed the National Association of Latino Gay Academics (NALGA) during the 1992 Conference. See Yarbro-Bejarano (1995: 125).

4   Some of the referenced and quoted information that appears on this page and the following is from my essay, 'Expanding the categories of race and sexuality in lesbian and gay studies' (1995: 127–8).

5   Yarbro-Bejarano, 1995: 128. In spite of the dangers of exclusionary definitions of queerness, as in Queer Nation that imagined itself primarily as white and male, the term points to an awareness of plural and shifting identities as an alternative to monolithic binary oppositions.

6   This debate has moved us from an us/them dichotomy underpinning a unitary

notion of identity and experience to a recognition of the constructed, political character of terms such as 'Chicano', and 'black' or 'people of colour'. For a more in-depth discussion of queer identities, see *Professions of Desire*, pp. 126–7.

7   See my discussion of the works of Chela Sandoval and Gloria Anzaldúa, p. 132.
8   Connerly also questioned the 'educational value' of these programmes and, in addition, he proposed that 'many courses and departments in African American, Latino and Asian studies may promote racial divisions rather than racial integration' (see Lempinen, 1998).

References

Alarcón, Norma (1990) 'The theoretical subject(s) of *This Bridge Called My Back* and Anglo-American feminism', in Gloria Anzaldúa (ed.) *Making Face, Making Soul/Haciendo Caras*, San Francisco, CA: Aunt Lute, 356–69.

Anzaldúa, Gloria (ed.) (1990) *Making Face, Making Soul/Haciendo Caras*, San Francisco, CA: Aunt Lute.

Butler, Judith (1993) *Bodies That Matter: On the Discursive Limits of 'Sex'*, New York: Routledge.

Chabram, Angie (1990) 'Chicana/o studies as oppositional ethnography', *Cultural Studies*, 4(3): 228–47.

Chao, Julie (1998) 'Ethnic studies professors mount defense', *The San Francisco Examiner*, 18 June.

Childers, Mary and hooks, bell (1990) 'A conversation about race and class', in Marianne Hirsch and Evelyn Fox Keller (eds) *Conflicts in Feminism*, New York: Routledge.

de Lauretis, Teresa (1991) 'Film and the visible', in Gina Dent (ed.) *How Do I Look? Queer Film and Video*, Seattle: Bay Press, 223–76.

Dent, Gina (ed.) (1992) *Black Popular Culture*, Seattle: Bay Press.

Gilroy, Paul (1991) 'It's a family affair', in Gina Dent (ed.) *How Do I Look? Queer Film and Video*, Seattle: Bay Press, 303–16.

Gordon, Linda (1991) 'On difference', *Genders*, 10 (spring): 91–111.

Hall, Stuart (1988) 'New ethnicities', in Kobena Mercer (ed.) *Black Film/British Cinema*, London: ICA, Document 7.

Hall, Stuart (1991) 'What is this "Black" in black popular culture?', in Gina Dent (ed.) *How Do I Look? Queer Film and Video*, Seattle: Bay Press, 21–36.

Julien, Isaac (1991) 'Black is, black ain't: notes on de-essentializing black identities', in Gina Dent (ed.) *How Do I Look? Queer Film and Video*, Seattle: Bay Press, 255–63.

King, Katie (1990) 'Producing sex, theory, and culture: gay/straight remappings in contemporary feminism', in Marianne Hirsch and Evelyn Fox Keller (eds) *Conflicts in Feminism*, New York: Routledge, 82–101.

Lempinen, Edward W. (1998) 'Connerly calls for review of UC ethnic studies', *San Francisco Chronicle*, 17 June: A17.

Mohanty, Chandra Talpede (1991) 'Introduction: cartographies of struggle', in C. T.

Mohanty *et al.* (eds) *Third World Women and the Politics of Feminism*, Bloomington: Indiana University Press, 1–47.

Saalfield, Catherine and Navarro, Ray (1991) 'Shocking pink praxis: race and gender
on the ACT UP frontlines' (Inside/Out: Lesbian Theories), in Diana Fuss (ed.)
Gay Theories, New York: Routledge, 341–69.

Spelman, Elizabeth V. (1988) *Inessential Woman: Problems of Exclusion in Feminist
Thought*, Boston, MA: Beacon Press.

Uttal, Lynet (1990) 'Inclusion without influence: the continuing tokenism of women
of color', in Gloria Anzaldúa (ed.) *Making Face, Making Soul/Haciendo Caras*,
San Francisco, CA: Aunt Lute, 42–5.

Yarbro-Bejarano, Yvonne (1995) 'Expanding the categories of race and sexuality in
lesbian and gay studies', in George E. Haggerty and Bonnie Zimmerman (eds)
Professions of Desire, New York: The Modern Language Association, 124–35.

Tamara R. Dukes

BEYOND THE BINARY OF CUBAN IDENTITY: REVIEW ESSAY OF *BRIDGES TO CUBA/PUENTES A CUBA*

Abstract

The aftermath of the 1959 Cuban Revolution produced not only a trans-formation of the political landscape, but also a painful and problematic bifurcation of Cuban identity and nationhood. It is against this backdrop that I review *Bridges to Cuba/Puentes a Cuba*, a literary anthology whose unifying axis is found in the 'Cuban' experience of its contributors. Rather than investing one experience of 'Cubanness' with authenticity at the expense of the rest, the richness of this collection lies in the complexities and hybridities of Cuban identity and nationhood which the contributors to this volume explore. Edited by Ruth Behar, their diverse voices and literary genres are testimony to the existence of 'border subjects' that inhabit various worlds, cultures and languages simultaneously, albeit unequally. While pointing to the inadequacy of essentialist notions of identity, the objective of this anthology is far from academic. As its title suggests, it hopes to bridge the ideological chasm (and heal the wounds) by forging a more inclusive, complex and heterogeneous vision of what it means to be and to belong to the Cuban nation.

Keywords

Cuban identity; nationhood; culture; revolution; hybridity; border subjects

*B*RIDGES TO CUBA/PUENTES A CUBA, which first appeared in slightly altered form as a special double issue of the journal *Michigan Quarterly Review* (Behar, 1994: 639–43),[1] is a collection of essays, interviews, poetry and prose whose unifying axis is 'Cuban' experience as differently and differentially experienced and expressed by those who in some way lay claim to 'Cubanness' as a result of historical, political and social/cultural factors. As such, this book is an ambitious project seeking to both reclaim and problematize the very meaning of Cuban identity and culture that has been so hotly contested since the revolution of 1959. The challenge it proffers becomes further highlighted when we consider that its impetus and objectives clearly originate on the US side of the great ideological divide that since 1959 has separated the Cuban nation-state from the United States (and, to a lesser extent, from the rest of the capitalist West).[2] Both the form and content of this anthology constitute a formidable attempt to bridge a chasm that seems even more difficult to navigate than the ninety-mile stretch from Cuba to the tip of Florida in which so many *balseros* have lost their lives. Speaking to this problem in her introduction, editor Ruth Behar writes that 'there [has been] little room for a more nuanced and complex vision of how Cubans on the island and in the diaspora give meaning to their lives, their identity, and their culture in the aftermath of a battle that has split the nation at the root' (Behar, 1995a: 2).

The diversity of the contributors as well as the wide-ranging nature of their contributions to this anthology are, in and of themselves, a testimony to the absurdity or futility of investing *one* experience of 'Cubanness' with authority or authenticity at the expense of the rest. Isleños (those living in Cuba), first- and second-generation Cuban Americans, and Cuban immigrants or exiles living in other countries alike populate these pages, and the genres they choose as literary vehicles range from autobiographical essays to historical investigations to interviews, from the *poesía intimista* of Dulce María Loynaz (Pablo Armando Fernández) to the photographic narrative of Eduardo Aparicio. The content of their narratives is itinerant as well, from instantiations of Cuban Jewish experience in the diaspora (Ruth Behar, Ester Rebeca Shapiro Rok) to the reflections of a gay Cuban-American's 'queerness' in both Cuba and the US (Flavio Risech), while the geographic evocations include Miami, La Havana and the US/Mexican border, among others. Cuban poet Nancy Morejón aptly summarizes what could be considered the *lema* of this collection when she says 'I can't, and no one can say "Cubanness goes this far and no further"' (Behar and Suárez, 1995: 137).

Much as Gloria Anzaldúa's *Borderlands/La Frontera* (Anzaldúa, 1987) presents a hybrid identity that inhabits the hyphen,[3] this collection is equally an invitation to explore and itself an exploration of the densely inhabited and yet often unacknowledged space which exists between the bifurcation of Cuban identity and nationhood post-1959. If it seems impossible to occupy the space *between* a bifurcation because its nature only allows for two, mutually exclusive possibilities, then the reader has grasped the very crux of the challenge that this book poses. *Bridges to Cuba/Puentes a Cuba* calls into question essentialist notions of identity and nationhood through its examination of multiple constructions of Cuban identity and nationhood in the wake of a revolution that was both cause and consequence of a struggle to reclaim Cuban identity.[4] 'Walls can be turned on their side so they become bridges' (Behar, 1995a: 5), writes Ruth Behar in a brilliant metaphor that succinctly and eloquently expresses the *raison d'être* of this collection. The bridges traversed by the contributors are, however, multiply located and unevenly placed, such that no two experiences of border or bridge crossing are the same. This nuanced and at times contradictory poliphony of voices and discourses on Cuba, unmediated by an authorial or authorative voice,[5] attests to the inadequacy of absolute, impermeable dividing lines which deny the existence or possibility of 'border subjects' that inhabit various worlds, cultures, languages, etc. simultaneously.

María de los Angeles Torres, for example, speaks of her own multiple crossings and rejection of binary formulas:

> Every time I return across time and space, between cultures and economic systems, I am more convinced that I do not want or need to accept the either/or definition of my identity which demands that you choose sides. My identity is far more complex than this. . . . I am 'white' when I wake up in Havana, but I am 'other' because of my migratory experience. I am again 'other' when I journey the thirty minutes through airspace to Miami because I am no longer 'white', and because my commitment to return to Cuba and have a normal relationship with my home country makes me politically 'other' among Miami Cubans. . . . I now understand that I do not have to accept categories which split who I am. Instead I must construct new categories, new political and emotional spaces in which my multiple identities can be joined.
>
> (Torres, 1995: 36)

Although this condition of being 'border subject'[6] may seem rather obvious in the above cited case, or for Lourdes Casal, who describes herself as 'too *habanera* to be *newyorkina*, too *newyorkina* to be — even to become again — anything else' (Casal, 1995: 22), many other 'border subjects' are revealed and discussed in this book as well: María de los Angeles Torres' already split identities as a Cuban American were further intersected by her involvement in Raza Unida and the Chicano movement (Torres, 1995: 28); Flavio Risech recounts his experiences as a gay Cuban American who feels 'queer' in one way in the conservative, homophobic atmosphere of Miami and yet differently 'queer' in the more politically liberal Anglo Northeast; Ester Rebeca Shapiro Rok confesses that '[f]or many unexamined years I considered my Cuban identity an exotic appendage to my true Jewish American self' (Risech, 1995: 87); Eliana S. Rivero writes of her experience in academia that

> I was a token Latina in an academic environment, 'too white' to really represent a minority group; too upper middle class to suit the taste of several Latino colleagues. I had the wrong color, the wrong ethnic origin in this part of the country [Arizona], and even exhibited traces of a radicalized 'other gender' persuasion.
>
> (Rivero, 1995: 342)

Patricia Boero, a Cuban-Uruguayan-Australian, tells how she would imagine a world 'free of rigid categories like *comunista* and *capitalista*' (Boero, 1995: 194) while living in Cuba from 1985–90; the list goes on and on once we understand that there are ideological, racial, generational, gender(ed), class and countless other borders that criss-cross us all. I am reminded of a statement frequently heard these days in California in response to the infamous Proposition 187: 'We don't cross the borders, the borders cross us.' While this observation has been made in the specific context of geographical demarcations, it serves to highlight the importance of recognizing these and other borders as similarly constructed and as sites of possible contestation and change. Furthermore, we don't need to move or travel to cross borders because the borders are within us and travel with us wherever we go (and even if we stay put). Thus does María de los Angeles Torres write of her experience of racism and hatred as a young girl in the United States:

> The incident I remember most clearly occurred the day after Kennedy was assassinated. By this time, my two first cousins had come to live with us. Every morning we would walk about two blocks to catch the school bus. The kids on the block started following us and yelling at us that we had killed Kennedy. . . . 'You dirty Cubans, You killed our President.' I screamed back that we were not those kind of Cubans, that we had fled the island. But the geographical and political boundaries which had restructured our entire lives and redefined our identities meant little to those who only saw 'dirty Cubans.' The next day, we found our bicycles smashed.
>
> (Torres, 1995: 27)

This quote is especially telling, for it forcefully illustrates the way in which the Cuban ideological binary of 'us' and 'them' underwent erasure in the face of a more powerful US racializing discourse that (symbolically) reunited the Cuban national body as irretrievably alien.

   Other contributors shift the focus away from building bridges across the rift of identity, nationhood and culture produced in the aftermath of the Cuban Revolution in order to examine perhaps less apparent but equally important borders and bridges within and among Cuban identities and cultures. Moving away from singular or essentialized notions of what it means to be 'Cuban', their writings explore in greater depth the complex hybridities of Cuban culture. Ruth Behar writes that 'Rather than starting with the assumption of Cubanness as a given, the aim is to unpack the layers of meaning which are crammed into that bulging suitcase' (Behar, 1994: 640). These layers of meaning, however, once again do not reveal themselves as discrete, easily identifiable and bounded items, for each person's identity suitcase has been packed differently depending on the circumstances surrounding it.[7] Collectively, Cubanness is not any one thing or even an amalgamation of *things* but a complex web of sources and influences. What do reflections on Cubans and airports (Teofilo Ruiz), the legacy of slavery and colonialism that led to an African presence in Cuba (Miguel Barnet), Cuban painters in France (Lourdes Gil), the strange sycretism of Miami (Elías Miguel Muñoz), commercial translations in Miami rendered incomprehensible in both Spanish and English (Gustavo Pérez Firmat), the 'bridges of the heart' in the poetry of Emily Dickinson and Dulce María Loynaz (Pablo Armando Fernández) and a portfolio of recent Cuban visual art have in common? Taken together, they articulate a refusal to put 'Cubanness/la cubanidad' into a box (or suitcase) and hermetically seal its boundaries.

A further achievement of this collection is its insistence on reinscribing Cuban identities within geographical and ideological cartographies that are simultaneously situated and yet displaced. In other words, its form and content propose that 'la cubanía' is neither monolithic nor geographically anchored. Rather, Cuban identity and culture are multiple, fluid and fragmented experiences or processes that transgress artificially constructed, although practically operative and normative, boundaries of place and space. This polifacetic 'Cubanness' persists despite the existence of a dominant, hegemonic discourse (if not originating then most strongly vociferated in Miami) that would erase Cuba from the map and illegitimate it not just politically but historically and culturally as well, and despite a counter-discourse, in its opposition equally essentialist, that claims that the only 'true' Cubans are those who remained in Cuba after the revolution. In a statement that could be considered characteristic of the tone of this collection in its refusal to endorse a monolithic, two-dimensional reality, Alan West writes:

> [t]he revolution is the literacy campaign, defeating the invasion at Playa Girón (Bay of Pigs), the Second Declaration of Havana, the elimination of hunger as it is known in the rest of Latin America (although since 1990 there have been severe food shortages), the defense of Angola against South Africa, and the sending of doctors to Mozambique. The Revolution is also the backing of the invasion of Czechoslovakia, censorship, the UMAP (internment camps in the mid-'60s), Mariel, and the Ochoa trial and execution.
>
> (West, 1995: 382)

At the same time, however, the above quote is an indication of the book's recognition that these discourses emerge in a historical context. In this way, 'la cubanía', while deterritorialized, is not presented as decontextualized or dehistoricized – it is not the totalizing 'voice from nowhere' claiming universality and objectivity so characteristic of Western social science.[8] Thus, while both the US/capitalist discourse and the Cuban/socialist discourse appear to be equally essentializing and hegemonizing *qua* discourse, they are *not* equally positioned because of the significant power differential between the US and Cuba. While the US can erase Cuba from the map (both literally and figuratively),[9] Cuba's experience of colonialism and neocolonialism, as well as its current experience of the US trade embargo, does not allow Cuba to ever erase the US from its map.[10] In this light, it is perhaps even more significant that a journal published and circulated in the United States is not only bent on restoring Cuba to the US map, but suggests its restoration need not and should not align itself with traditional demarcations of geographical and political boundaries.

The creative, liberating power of articulation for redrawing these maps of self, nation and culture is undeniable after a reading of these diverse texts, given that writing, and by extension any form of cultural creation, is not just a discursive tool devoid of material implications but rather an important component in any struggle in the domain of knowledge and its political correlatives. A vivid example of the dynamic interplay between these two forces is Ruth Behar's account and analysis of the video released by an unidentified member of the Cuban government which showed Miami attorney Magda Montiel kissing Fidel Castro at the end of a conference (organized by the Cuban government and highly attended by Cuban Americans) to discuss Cuba's relation to its diaspora (Behar, 1995b: 409–15). The conference was seen as an attempt to dialogue, to normalize travel and cultural exchanges in both directions, and yet this video was shown in Miami 'over and over . . . until [it] became a maddening litany, unleashing hatred and rancor in the exile community against those who'd gone to the conference' (Behar, 1995b: 413). Behar's analysis of this incident in which the creation of a dialogic space was subverted and destroyed by both poles is also, paradoxically, a reclaiming of this space. Her nuanced insights into the role of women within the heterosexist patriarchy of both communities constitute a critique that reverts the example to focus and, by deconstructing its silences, rewrites the road map of Cuban and human relations.[11] If her conclusion – that this incident's motivation and consequence was to make it more difficult for women, and especially Cuban American women, to be taken seriously in any effort to inscribe themselves into the narratives of Cuban identity – is disheartening, her self-reflective presence in this collection, along with that of many other Cuban and Cuban American women in these pages, undoubtedly points to women's crucial role in this process.[12]

There is a pervasive acknowledgment of silence in this collection, whether it be the silence of being between capitalism and communism (Behar, 1995a: 2–3, 194), the silence which accompanies diaspora by eternalizing emotions and interrupting all conversation (Behar, 1995a: 180), the silences in the Cuban film *Strawberry and Chocolate* with respect to race and lesbianism, etc. (Behar, 1995a: 398), or the silences of the sixteenth-century Spaniard Quevedo's poetry that Marilyn Bobes uses to create new meanings.[13] Invoked by a polyphony of authorial voices, the presence of the absence is at once a step towards bridging or lessening that silence. Nevertheless there are other silences, such as the exclusion of two excellent essays on Afro-Cuban music and on African-American/Afro-Cuban relations that were present in the original double issue, which go unnoted and, as such, serve to reinforce hegemonic and falsely de-racialized visions of *la cubanía*.[14]

As befits this discursive/cultural production, it should come as no surprise that a fairly constant theme reiterated by the contributors to this collection is the power of culture and cultural creation not only to transform reality through rewriting history but also to heal by creating dialogues to serve as bridges that traverse, and, more importantly, populate and affirm the space between the binary of seemingly incommensurate positions. These notions are applicable insofar as culture is understood as a complex set of symbol-forming and subject-constituting interpellative practices[15] and not as some supplementary, dispensable luxury produced by and accessible to a privileged few. It is clearly this conception of culture that Nancy Morejón refers to when she says: 'That's why I maintain that without Cuban culture there is nothing, no Cuban identity, no Cuban history' (Behar and Suárez, 1995: 134). Calling on the Cuban poet José Martí who wrote that 'Los libros sirven para cerrar las heridas que las armas abren', Ruth Behar affirms that '[s]uch is the hope of *Bridges to Cuba* – that this book will help to close the wounds that weapons have opened' (Behar, 1995a: 18).

The extent to which this book can help close wounds, however, also depends on the impact and circulation of its readership, and I am left wondering how many Cubans or Cuban Americans will have access to this anthology, especially in its English edition. Cultural production/creation most certainly has political consequences, but it would seem that reception must also be taken into account as an equally critical phase of cultural activity. Neil Larson suggests a possible solution in '"consumptive production" whereby the metropolitan cultural import, rather than simply being recodified and reinserted into the same, exclusive network of cultural distribution, undergoes an even more radical subversion by being directly appropriated as . . . a motif of mass culture' (Larson, 1991: xiii) and indeed, there are cultural workers doing 'border art' in an attempt to reach larger segments of the population in this way.[16] In this vein, I recently saw a television programme entitled *Miami/Havana* that reminded me of this book in its inclusion of many voices from both Miami and Havana, in its focus on the simultaneous closeness and distance between the two cities, and in its appeal for dialogue and reconciliation. In short, it was (and continues to be each time it is shown) an attempt to bridge the gap between what the two cities stand for, an attempt to inhabit and validate the border. It was also completely bilingual, and, as a forty-five-minute production aired by TV Latina, it presumably had a significant and diverse audience. For me, it evoked many of the same feelings as *Bridges to Cuba/Puentes a Cuba* and made me reflect on how to 'construct' bridges/*Bridges* to reach more people.

My only other criticism regarding this collection is at once testimony to the breadth and inclusivity of its vision. In her essay 'Performative identities: scenes between two Cubas', Lillian Manzor-Coats maintains that there is no space in Cuba in which a *queen* can perform, as evidenced, according to her, by the name Cuban Spanish gives to them – *locas* (the crazy ones) (Manzor-Coats, 1995: 263). Not only is this reading of the word 'loca' too narrow by disallowing its positive, gender and norm-breaking connotations as reclaimed by the community itself, but it also happens to be inaccurate. An American friend of mine who lives and works in Cuba and is very active in the queer community there reports that drag shows are not only happening in La Habana despite a scarcity of resources, but are public performances at times supported by local institutions, and the documentary film *Gay Cuba* (de Vries, 1995) bears witness to this reality as well.[17] The opening of this public space is, however, a fairly recent one, and so perhaps at the time of writing the essay Manzor-Coats' assertion was, in fact, true.

In any case, minor quibbles about the perspective of any one author do not indicate a fundamental flaw in this collection but rather speak to its strength. As mentioned above, its poliphonous, nuanced nature allows for many voices and experiences for writer and reader alike, and thus for differing opinions or interpretations. Perhaps Eliana S. Rivero's assertion that '[f]ortunately, we [Cuban Americans] seem to be able to claim a collective identity, both existential and public, that can benefit from our hybridism, and not be narrowly framed by limitations of how we are perceived by society at large or other subgroups (Rivero, 1995: 343) is overly optimistic, and yet it certainly resonates with the call being put out not only for Cubans and *la cubanía* in this anthology, but within Latina/o communities (and others similarly forged in opposition and resistance to dominant/repressive discourses and realities), for a more inclusive, complex and heterogeneous vision of what it means to *be* and to *belong*. To the extent that this collection achieves that goal, I would agree with editor Ruth Behar in her assessment of this anthology as a ground-breaking event, and as a space for possible reconciliation and renewal.

Notes

1   The changes made are as follows: First, whereas the original double issue was co-edited by Ruth Behar and Juan Leon, the book is edited by Ruth Behar alone. Second, in the double issue, Ruth Behar wrote an introduction at the beginning of each volume; here she condenses those two introductions into one. Third, whereas the double issue is thematically divided into two, the book reorders the contributions through a tripartate presentation. Finally, several essays have been added and deleted, and two excellent pieces on Afro-Cuban music and on African-American/Afro-Cuban relations – Chrisman (1994) and West (1994) – published in *Michigan Quarterly Review* are unfortunately absent from the book.

2   In her introduction to the book, Ruth Behar discusses both the genesis and goals of this anthology that originated as a special double issue on Cuba (Behar, 1995a: 1–18).

3   See Norma Alarcón (1990) and Lavie and Swedenburg (1996) for their analyses of the implications of Anzaldúa's work for the contestation/creation of political and personal identities. Alarcón writes of Chicana/o identity and identification

in response to the 'Mexican-American' hyphen as follows: 'The apparently well documented terrains of the dyad Mexico–United States were repositioned and reconfigured through the inclusion of the excluded in the very interiority of culture, knowledge and the political economy' (Alarcón, 1990: 248).

Lavie and Swedenburg (1996) draw on and expand Bhabha's (1990) notion of a third time-space in order to stake out and explore a terrain 'old in experience and memory but new in theory'(Lavie and Swedenburg, 1996: 165). Identifying it as a creative response to the binary oppositions of the Euro-centre, they explain both the necessity and difficulty of inhabiting hyphens and borders. As mobile territories 'where the Third World grates against the First and bleeds' they are not just 'places of imaginative interminglings and happy hybridities' but also zones of loss, alienation, pain and death (Anzaldúa, 1987: 2–3, 167). Cuban identities obviously occupy similarly rocky terrains.

4   See Louis A. Pérez, Jr.'s article in this anthology for an analysis of the displacement and dispossession of Cuban identity through its 'Americanization'.

5   I draw on Bakhtin's notion of *poliphony* in the novel in which 'a "culture"' is 'an open-ended, creative dialogue of subcultures, of insiders and outsiders, of diverse factions' (Clifford, 1988: 47) and *dialogism* whereby 'a word, discourse, language or culture becomes relativized, de-privileged, aware of competing definitions for the same things' (Bakhtin, 1981: 427). While Clifford astutely notes that, even in a collaborate effort of multiple authorship and voices, '[t]he authoritative stance of "giving voice" to the other is not fully transcended by the anthropologist [or alternately the novelist] who in the end assumes an executive, editorial position' (Clifford, 1988: 51) by deciding what to include or exclude, I would still emphasize the importance of a relatively decentred, de-privileged and multiply positioned text such as this one for displacing any one source as complete and definitive.

6   Emily Hicks writes that 'the border crosser "subject" emerges from double strings of signifiers of two sets of referential codes . . . and therefore experiences double vision thanks to perceiving reality through two different interference patterns' (Hicks, 1991: xxvi, xxix).

7   See Frankenberg and Mani (1993) for a discussion of identity formation. They describe subject formation and identity as 'a tangle of images and practices' (p. 298) along differential and historically specific axes of domination and resistance; these axes are 'moments, social formations, subject positions and practices which arise out of an unfolding axis of colonization/decolonization, interwoven with the unfolding of other axes in uneven, unequal relations with one another' (p. 307).

8   See Chatterjee (1993), Chicago Cultural Studies Group (1992) and Said (1978, 1986), for further discussions about the totalizing nature of Western Enlightenment discourse.

9   Whereas, as Ruth Behar notes, in the nineteenth century and up until 1959 Cuba was so commonplace in the American imagination that it was included in maps of Florida (Behar, 1995a: 1), after 1959 the US 'erased' Cuba from its map of the world. In 'Fragments from Cuban narratives: a portfolio by

Eduardo Aparicio' Pamela María Smorkaloff writes: 'My grandmother used National Geographic books to teach me where Cuba was, because after the revolution it was not shown in the weather forecasts; it had been erased' (Smorkaloff, 1995: 146).

10   Ruth Behar observes that 'Cuba and its diaspora are always defined within a U.S. framework, on the right and the left' (Behar, 1995a: 2). Similarly, Louis A. Pérez, Jr. writes of the Cuba–US relationship that 'The revolution changed the terms of that relationship in dramatic terms, driving one portion of the population into the United States with the other against the United States. Cubans all, they continued to define their world as a function of their relationship with the North' (Pérez, 1995: 179). Said also comments on this asymmetry/erasure as follows: 'They the colonials, must always take us, the European conquerors, into account; for us, however, they are an episode we experienced before we went on to other things' (Said, 1986: 58).

11   Ruth Behar writes: '[s]adly, tragically, the absent daughter of Cuban patriarchy was reinserted into this heterosexual version of *Fresa y Chocolate* and cruelly manipulated by the Miami media in collusion with the most hard-line elements of the Cuban power structure' (Behar, 1995b: 414).

12   Noting that many of the initiatives to build cultural and emotional bridges across this separation have come from women, and that conversely, most writing on exile has been done by men, Behar asks whether this is because women don't have a country to lose, and are therefore in a unique position to lead and promote a healing process. She writes: 'Perhaps the bridge to Cuba, like Independence, is best imagined in the shape of a woman' (Behar, 1995a: 13).

13   Poet Marilyn Bobes takes poetry by Quevedo and erases words from the originals in order to create new poems called 'Quevedianos'; the one presented here is called 'Dangers of Speaking and Staying Quiet. Language of Silence' (Bobes, 1995: 197).

14   See A. M. Alonso (1994) and Brackette Williams (1993) for their discussions of how unmarked, normative national identities are constituted through and in opposition to racially, ethnically, gendered and sexual categories marked as 'other'. Margaret Randall (1992) suggests that the post-revolutionary Cuban national identity is normatively male, and Marvin Leiner (1994) identifies it as heterosexual; I would propose that it is light-skinned as well.

15   See Homi Bhabha (1990: 210).

16   See Coco Fusco (1989).

17   Directed by Sonja de Vries, this documentary contains footage of a well-attended drag show performed outside, in one of La Habana's barrios, as part of the barrio's '26 de julio' celebration.

References

Alarcón, Norma (1990) 'Chicana feminism: in the tracks of "the" native woman', *Cultural Studies*, 4(3): 249–56.

Alcalay, Ammiel (1993) *After Jews and Arabs: Remaking Levantine Culture*, Minneapolis: University of Minnesota Press.

Alonso, A.M. (1994) 'The politics of space, time and substance: state formation, nationalism, and ethnicity', *Annual Review of Anthropology*, 20: 379–405.

Anzaldúa, Gloria (1987) *Borderlands/La Frontera: The New Mestiza*, San Francisco, CA: Spinsters/Aunt Lute.

Aparicio, Eduardo (1995) 'Fragments from Cuban narratives', in R. Behar (ed.) *Bridges to Cuba/Puentes a Cuba*.

Bakhtin, Mikhail (1981) *The Dialogic Imagination*, trans. Caryl Emerson and Michael Holquist, Austin: University of Texas Press.

Barnet, Miguel (1995) 'Pilgrims of the dawn', in R. Behar (ed.) *Bridges to Cuba/Puentes a Cuba*.

Behar, Ruth (1994) 'Introduction', *Michigan Quarterly Review*, 33(4): 639–43.

Behar, Ruth (ed.) (1995a) *Bridges to Cuba/Puentes a Cuba*, Ann Arbor: University of Michigan Press.

—— (1995b) 'Queer times in Cuba', in her (ed.) *Bridges to Cuba/Puentes a Cuba*.

Behar, Ruth and Leon, Juan (1994) *Michigan Quarterly Review*, 33 (3 and 4).

Behar, Ruth and Suárez, Lucía (1995) 'Two conversations with Nancy Morejón', in R. Behar (ed.) *Bridges to Cuba/Puentes a Cuba*.

Bhabha, Homi (1990) 'The third space: interview with Homi Bhabha', in J. Rutherford (ed.) *Identity: Community, Culture, Difference*, London: Lawrence and Wishart.

Bobes, Marilyn (1995) 'Dangers of speaking and staying quiet. Language of silence', in R. Behar (ed.) *Bridges to Cuba/Puentes a Cuba*.

Boero, Patricia (1995) 'Cubans inside and outside: dialogue among the deaf', in R. Behar (ed.) *Bridges to Cuba/Puentes a Cuba*.

Bravo, Estela (dir.) (1992) *Miami/Havana*, TV Latina.

Casal, Lourdes (1995) 'For Ana Velford', in R. Behar (ed.) *Bridges to Cuba/Puentes a Cuba*.

Chatterjee, Partha (1993) *Nationalist Thought and the Colonial World: A Derivative Discourse?*, Minneapolis: University of Minnesota Press.

Chicago Cultural Studies Group (1992) 'Critical multiculturalism', *Critical Inquiry*, 18: 549–50.

Chrisman, Robert (1994) 'Nicolás Guillén, Langston Hughes, and the Black American/Afro-Cuban connection', *Michigan Quarterly Review*, 33(4): 807–20.

Clifford, James (1988) *The Predicament of Culture: Twentieth-Century Ethnography, Literature, and Art*, Cambridge: Harvard University Press.

de Vries, Sonja (dir.) (1995) *Gay Cuba*, Frameline Video.

Fernández, Pablo Armando (1995) 'Bridges of the heart', in R. Behar (ed.) *Bridges to Cuba/Puentes a Cuba*.

Frankenberg, Ruth and Mani, Lata (1993) 'Crosscurrents, crosstalk: race, "postcoloniality" and the politics of location', *Cultural Studies*, 7(2): 292–310.

Fusco, Coco (1989) 'The border art workshop/Taller de arte fronterizo: Interview with Guillermo Gomez-Peña and Emily Hicks', *Third Text*, 7: 53–76.

Gil, Lourdes (1995) 'Pilgrimage to France: the Cuban painters', in R. Behar (ed.) *Bridges to Cuba/Puentes a Cuba.*

Hicks, Emily (1991) *Border Writing: The Multidimensional Text*, Minneapolis: University of Minnesota Press.

Larson, Neil (1991) 'Foreword', in E. Hicks *Border Writing: The Multidimensional Text*, Minneapolis: University of Minnesota Press.

Lavie, Smadar and Swedenburg, Ted (1996) 'Between and among the boundaries of culture: bridging text and lived experience in the third timespace', *Cultural Studies*, 10 (1): 154–79.

Leiner, Marvin (1994) *Sexual Politics in Cuba: Machismo, Homosexuality, and AIDS*, Boulder, CO: Westview Press.

Manzor-Coats, Lillian (1995) 'Performative identities: scenes between two Cubas', in R. Behar (ed.) *Bridges to Cuba/Puentes a Cuba.*

Muñoz, Elias Miguel (1995) 'Strange planet', in R. Behar (ed.) *Bridges to Cuba/Puentes a Cuba.*

Pérez Firmat, Gustavo (1995) 'Three mambos and a son montuno', in R. Behar (ed.) *Bridges to Cuba/Puentes a Cuba.*

Pérez, Jr., Louis A. (1995) 'The circle of connections: one hundred years of Cuba–U.S. relations', in R. Behar (ed.) *Bridges to Cuba/Puentes a Cuba.*

Randall, Margaret (1992) *Gathering Rage: The Failure of Twentieth Century Evolutions to Develop a Feminist Agenda*, New York: Monthly Review Press.

Risech, Flavio (1995) 'Political and cultural cross-dressing: negotiating a second generation Cuban-American identity', in R. Behar (ed.) *Bridges to Cuba/Puentes a Cuba.*

Rivero, Eliana S. (1995) '"Fronterisleña," border islander', in R. Behar (ed.) *Bridges to Cuba/Puentes a Cuba.*

Ruiz, Teofilo F. (1995) 'Cubans and airports', in R. Behar (ed.) *Bridges to Cuba/Puentes a Cuba.*

Said, Edward (1978) *Orientalism*, New York: Pantheon.

—— (1986) 'Intellectuals in the post-colonial world', *Salamagundi*, 70–1: 44–64.

Shapiro Rok, Ester Rebeca (1995) 'Finding what had been lost in plain view', in R. Behar (ed.) *Bridges to Cuba/Puentes a Cuba.*

Smorkaloff, Pamela María (1995) 'Fragments from Cuban narratives: a portfolio by Eduardo Aparicio', in R. Behar (ed.) *Bridges to Cuba/Puentes a Cuba.*

Torres, María de los Angeles (1995) 'Beyond the rupture: reconciling with our enemies, reconciling with ourselves', in R. Behar (ed.) *Bridges to Cuba/Puentes a Cuba.*

West, Alan (1994) 'Music to live by (even far away)', *Michigan Quarterly Review*, 33(4): 657–64.

—— (1995) 'My life with Fidel Castro: a soap opera without transmitter', in R. Behar (ed.) *Bridges to Cuba/Puentes a Cuba.*

Williams, Brackette (1993) 'The impact of the precepts of nationalism on the concept of culture: making grasshoppers from naked apes', *Cultural Critique*, 24: 143–91.

Alvina E. Quintana

BORDERS BE DAMNED:
CREOLIZING LITERARY RELATIONS[1]

Abstract

Conventional literary practices have always been used to perpetuate an us/them binary that reduces potential discussions concerning diversity, transnationalism or hybridization to a simplified relationship between dominant and subordinate categories. This article proposes that in order to avoid this predicament, cultural critics should move beyond 'vertical' methods of analysis and instead employ intercultural models which lend themselves to a consideration of the horizontal affiliations that can be found among women writers of colour. By engaging the writings of Jessica Hagedorn, Hisaye Yamamoto and Sandra Cisneros, the article argues that multicultural analysis enables an understanding of these (social, cultural and political) affiliations between racialized women in the United States. Further, it suggests that by comparing, contrasting, and interfacing emergent literary practices within current theories of cultural and feminist studies, critics will develop a 'creolized' approach which will help facilitate new alliances and sensitivity among the disenfranchised.

Keywords

women of colour; creolization; multicultural literature; feminism; transnationalism; literary politics

> A movement is afoot to assert artists and thinkers to
> celebrate our histories, our rich and complicated ethnicities.
> (Hagedorn, 1993:ix)

IN THE INTRODUCTION to *Danger and Beauty*, Jessica Hagedorn suggests that her birth and childhood experiences in the Philippines have not only determined a particular racialized social position but have also provided a slate of artistic opportunities that afford her the choice of writing from the perspective of the colonial, the postcolonial or the creolized within a postmodern American context. However, as an 'assertive' artist and 'thinker', Hagedorn is keenly aware of the 'limitations' imposed by academic discourse and of the concomitant resistant practices that resonate among artists who 'write, perform, and collaborate with each other'. It is because of her positive experience working within a diversified literary community that she proposes that 'borders be damned'.

In rallying around the creative relationships of this budding alternative literary coalition, Hagedorn raises a number of important issues concerning emergent writing practices and the politics of representation. With a series of provocative questions ('Who are we? People of color? Artists of color? Gay or straight? Political or careerist? Decadent or boring? Or just plain artists?') she problematizes confining labels and the basic assumptions that drive critics to separate emergent literary-political traditions, by challenging the simplistic reasoning behind conventional literary categorizations that make it necessary to re-engage the culture wars (Hagedorn, 1993:ix). In different terms, Hagedorn's self-styled battle cry confronts and resists academic constructions of monolithic literary traditions which attempt to address complex social problems with the institutionalization of exclusive (some might argue 'essentialist') racial and ethnic compartmentalizations. She invites her readers to reflect once again on the productive value of local grass-roots organizations that allow marginalized creative writers 'of colour' to recover, reconcile, reconfigure and unite emergent racialized communities. At the same time, she provides a window into the types of 'outlaw' networks that are necessary for 'justice', 'survival' and 'creativity' within a society which, as we know, continues to marginalize and even dismiss writers of colour, notwithstanding the success of a number of high-profile literary figures. Clearly, Hagedorn's testimonial of her own experience within one of these networks speaks to the power and inspiration that comes from enabling horizontal affiliations (Lowe, 1996) as well as unpredictable – yet vital – 'creolized' genealogies that cultivate new 'complex' ethnic engagements between groups. Who are her teachers, peers and kindred spirits? Those who are participants in 'a new movement which is afoot', a movement that points to a 'rich' history and a 'complicated' ethnicity, including 'Al Robles, Ishmael Reed, Norman Jayo, Ntozake Shange, Victor Hernandez Cruz, Janice Mirikitani, Thulani Davis, David Henderson, Alejandro Murguia, Ed Dorn, Alta, Serafin and Lou Syquia, Kitty Tsui and on and on. . .'.

These writers are representative not only of her inspiration but also of the aesthetic/political community, a community empowered by an act of defiance which resists and transcends socially constructed barriers. Flaunting this racially diverse community of writers, she highlights an oppositional platform that consciously builds coalitions between collectivities. What makes Hagedorn's subversive, resistant move so engaging is that her passionate defiance erupts with celebration of the 'pleasure' emerging from outwitting those patterns of social and literary association dictated by hegemonic academic institutions.

Most importantly for my purposes, Hagedorn's 'manifesto' also brings to light a significant question that often haunts those critics who are involved in the critical recovery of multicultural literary projects that also partake in this type of resistance: What types of literary affiliations and analyses are warranted or not warranted by these critical approaches, warranted or unwarranted by these 'pleasurably' subversive cultural productions?

It is my proposition that we, as cultural critics, should follow the lead of resistance narratives which move beyond an 'us/them' tactic. Within the feminist and cultural studies practices of people of colour the usefulness of this tactic has been questioned because, in the final analysis, it has been used to bolster conventional academic practices which view variations from the mainstream (i.e. alternative emergent literary productions of people of colour) as 'curious' or 'deviant' expressions from the 'norm', while within the 'alternative sector' this approach encourages singular nationalist recovery projects that deploy a monolithic 'separatist' approach based on race, gender or ethnicity. Interestingly, these opposing approaches are similar in that they both fail to address the 'militarized' inter/national and inter-ethnic barriers that police, discipline and ultimately separate artistic endeavours and ethnically 'complex' communities.

In the spirit of the type of coalition building and literary alliance that Hagedorn passionately evokes, I will re-engage the writings of two racialized women of colour – Hisaye Yamamoto and Sandra Cisneros – through an intertextual literary and cultural practice that congregates these writers and attends to the similarities as well as the differences that allow 'creolized' forms of social and political affiliation between them to take root. Admittedly, my enterprise differs from Hagedorn's because, unlike her, these writers are not affiliated with the same sort of literary community she describes; in fact, on the surface the dissimilarities between these two writers appear to dramatically overshadow any affinities.

Aside from their differing ethnic/racial affiliations, the year of each author's birth and their subsequent (regionally defined) socialization magnify their distinctions. Yamamoto, a second-generation Japanese American (Nisei), was born in 1921 in Los Angeles whereas Sandra Cisneros was born thirty-three years later in Chicago, Illinois to a Mexican father and a Chicana mother. Yamamoto's internment during the Second World War in Poston, Arizona contrasts sharply with Cisneros' experience growing up in the Midwest after a Supreme Court decision ('Brown vs. Board of Education', 1954) which initiated a series of legal battles and civic protests that later became known as the Civil Rights Movement. Whereas Yamamoto (with a Mexican husband and four children) is primarily affiliated with Asian American literature, Cisneros is associated with Chicana/o literature. Both writers are seen as 'representative' of divergent social and political objectives and are credited for different types of literary contributions. For example, King-Kok Cheung points out that 'Yamamoto was one of the first Japanese American writers to gain national recognition after the war, when anti-Japanese sentiment was still rampant' (Cheung, 1988:xiii), whereas *Newsweek* has suggested that Cisneros' 'feminist, Mexican American voice is not only playful and vigorous, it's original – we haven't heard anything like it before'.

However, even amidst their differences each writer has produced literary works that articulate issues relevant to gender relations and the interaction among various ethnic and racial groups in America, and for this reason they are independently recognized as important to the 'third wave' of the feminist movement. As I will demonstrate in this intertextual analysis, the spirit of this feminist practice is illustrated in their respective works *Seventeen Syllables* (Yamamoto, 1988) and *The House on Mango Street* (Cisneros, 1984), both of which inscribe women as complex central characters while at the same time advancing a multifaceted challenge of cultural tradition(s).

Significantly, both texts are composed of short stories which address the realities of cultural, political and geographical or social displacement and the inscription of femaleness in 'traditional' racialized American culture.[2] Both of these narratives can be read as novel stories of initiation – they not only involve coming to terms with the female role of submission and subordination but also with frightening social realities and sharp generational differences among racialized women. Finally, it is worth noting that they implement a similar strategy: Cisneros' and Yamamoto's narratives, although seemingly simple upon a first reading, illustrate in very real terms the limited understanding of racialized Americans just before their political awakening. Although cast as naive, the narrators themselves accentuate a sophisticated authorial intervention that challenges and resists the myth of the American 'melting-pot'. These are not simply female rite-of-passage narratives, but rather stories that reveal the complex relationship between race, class and gender in an American context.

It is not surprising, then, that the title stories ['Mango Street' and 'Seventeen Syllables'] of these writers conjure up a child's first person narration, ultimately creating a strain between the innocence of the child's point of view and the harsh realities she represents. In 'Mango Street', for example, the story opens by introducing this representation of the house(s).

> We didn't always live on Mango Street. Before that we lived on Loomis on the 3rd floor, and before that we lived on Keeler. Before Keeler it was Pauline, and before that I can't remember. But what I remember most is moving a lot. The water pipes broke and the landlord wouldn't fix them because the house was too old. We had to leave fast. We were using the washroom next door and carrying water over in empty milk gallons.
>
> (Cisneros, 1984: 7)

Cisneros' protagonist conveys an unsophisticated yet understandably pessimistic commentary on her marginal and precarious social position. As readers, we are struck by her reality – a life of poverty, inequality and a constant search for 'adequate' housing, a reality that this child translates into 'moving a lot', and an inability to 'remember' her address but a vivid recollection of leaving quickly, 'using the washroom next door and carrying water' because the 'landlord wouldn't fix' the broken water pipes. This opening incorporates the central conflict of the story: on the one hand, the child yearns for a house of her own, and on the other, social and economic circumstances make this type of stability difficult – if not impossible – to achieve. But as a Chicana feminist production 'in the making', Esperanza's story is much more complex than this, even if such a house were available to her; the child yearns for a house of her own, a (girl's/woman's) house that is unlike the patriarchal households that she describes in graphic detail, those that confine and stifle the creative energy of the other Mexican women in her neighbourhood.

In contrast to 'Mango Street' Yamamoto's 'Seventeen Syllables' opens by resonating the more subtle method of understatement. However, it none the less draws the reader's attention to yet another form of alienation: the kind of social, cultural and linguistic displacement that was exacerbated with Japanese internment during the Second World War.

> The first Rosie knew that her mother had taken to writing poems was one evening when she finished one and read it aloud for her daughter's approval. It was about cats, and Rosie pretended to understand it thoroughly and appreciate it no end, partly because she hesitated to disillusion her mother about the quantity and quality of Japanese she had learned in all the years that she had been going to Japanese school every Saturday. . . . Even so, her mother must have been skeptical about the depth of Rosie's understanding, because she explained afterwards about the kind of poem she was trying to write.
>
> (Yamamoto, 1988: 8)

With subtlety and exquisite precision Yamamoto highlights the overlapping plots and cultural tensions between two generations, the Issei and the Nisei, who are living the affects of internment. With two dialectically opposed views concerning the importance of language and culture, the author illustrates a harsh reality that literally tears families apart.[3] The modern American setting in which this narrative is set exacerbates the cultural predicament; Rosie's American socialization, lacking in terms of Japanese tradition, limits her understanding of the nuances of her heritage and precludes any 'facile' communication with her mother.[4] Yet it is clear that Rosie's alienation from her mother is not complete; she none the less feels the need to 'pretend to understand' and is reluctant to disillusion her mother even though she is aware that the Japanese language class isn't enough to bridge the differences between herself, a Japanese American and her mother, a Japanese immigrant. But the daughter's interpretation is not privileged here. From the other side of her generational divide, it is clear that Rosie's mother is able to 'discern' her daughter's deception and for this reason is sceptical and 'understands' the need to 'explain the kind of poem she was trying to write'. In this way Yamamoto uses generational and cultural differences as a way to call attention to the fact that, in a post-internment US context, the relations between Japanese women (here mother and daughter) must be negotiated. There is, in this sense, no intact cultural history or representation that does not require dialogue or clarification and possibilities of 'unity' are evidenced through a recognition of difference.

In 'My Name' Cisneros illuminates a generational rift and the pain and estrangement between women of the same family who are subject to racial and ethnic subordination, but from quite a different perspective. Cisneros links this estrangement to her protagonist's Spanish name, Esperanza:

> In English my name means hope. In Spanish it means too many letters. It means sadness, it means waiting. It is like the number nine. A muddy color. It is the Mexican records my father plays on Sunday mornings. When he is having, songs like, sobbing. It was my great-grandmother's name and now it is mine. She was a horse woman too, born like me in the Chinese year of the horse – but I think this is a Chinese lie because the Chinese, like the Mexicans, don't like their women strong . . . I would like to baptize myself under a new name, a name more like the real me, the one nobody sees. Esperanza as Lizandra or Maritza or Zeze the X. Yes. Something like Zeze the X will do.
>
> (Cisneros, 1984:12)

In *Mango Street* as in other ethnic American literature, the grandmother signifies the matriarchal handing down of cultural traditions. But in a somewhat ironic twist Cisneros' protagonist subverts the usual, stating, 'I have inherited her name, but I don't want to inherit her place by the window.' Contrary to the conventional nostalgic sentiment that associates grandmothers with an idealistic, cultural space of nourishment, Cisneros uses the sign of the great-grandmother to represent traditional cultural values as confining and debilitating. What is important about her casting of this predicament is that she does not limit her discussion to Mexicans, but engages in a decisive cross-cultural comparison with her child protagonist's suggestion that 'the Chinese like the Mexicans don't like their women strong'. Thus her protagonist voices a desire to christen herself under what she perceives to be a new, culturally uncoded name – Zeze the X, a new, feminist ethnicity that is 'creolized', removed from traditional gender constraints, and perhaps shared with other Chinese women like her, rebellious women who affirm their strength through emergent American identities that are as yet unnamed. Cisneros herself seemed to confirm this reading upon suggesting to me that this story, 'My Name', was in fact inspired by Maxine Hong Kingston's 'No Name Woman' from *The Woman Warrior* (1975). I find this type of inspiration especially important because it speaks to the type of literary alliance that Hagedorn proposes earlier on, an alliance that subverts inter-ethnic borders and boundaries.

In 'Seventeen Syllables' Yamamoto reveals a different cross-cultural awareness that foreshadows the impending trend of out-marriage in Japanese communities with a contrast between Rosie's concerns, especially her secret, romantic attraction to Jesus Carrasco (the son of the Mexican couple her parents employ) with those of her mother, whose creativity is stifled by a domineering Japanese husband. This generational mother/daughter conflict culminates at the end of the narrative when Rosie's mother forces the gender issue with an outburst of emotion:

> Suddenly, her mother knelt on the floor and took her by the wrists. 'Rosie,' she said urgently, 'Promise me you will never marry!' With few words, Yamamoto's 'traditional' antagonist attempts to caution the younger 'modern' generation about the dangers of patriarchal control, whatever the ethnic context.

In conclusion, in these stories Yamamoto and Cisneros do more than catalogue a child's impressions; they invite us to confront the implications of 'racialized' cultural subordination and rejection, and they relate how young women struggle to reinvent themselves and transcend socially imposed gender and cultural limitations, including their own patriarchal baggage. As third wave feminist writers Yamamoto and Cisneros have employed a form of creolization; that is, 'a syncretic process of traverse dynamics' that 'reworks and transforms the cultural patterns of social and historical experiences and identities'.[5] And they shed 'some light on the elusive and ominous social, political and even economic underpinnings of emerging American identities' (Balutansky and Sourieau, 1998: 1). Finally, with literary allusions that subvert ethnic and gender boundaries, both writers undermine an academic or political aspiration for unitary origins and authenticity.

The challenge for critics writing in today's diverse culture is to engage creolization, heterogeneity and the development of models which will allow emergent texts to speak to one another. We have reached a new phase in our development wherein it has become necessary for us to reconsider the value of nationalist tactics that were strategically useful in the 1960s when racialized individuals were compelled to consciously assume a political identity that glossed over ethnic and cultural distinctions. By crossing cultural borders, comparing and interfacing emergent literary practices within current theories of cultural and feminist studies, critics can develop a creolized approach that will compliment the literary endeavours they discuss and help to cultivate new alliances and sensitivity among the disenfranchised. Reading literature in this way enables critics to connect political movements, avoiding reactionary compartmentalizing aesthetic practices that merely serve to suppress the political lines of affiliation between women writers of colour, reducing them instead to essentialized, one-dimensional cultural subjectivities.

Clearly for Yamamoto and Cisneros, writing is a vital necessity which, as Audre Lorde puts it, helps to 'give name to the nameless so that it can be thought' (Lorde, 1984:36). But beyond that, Yamamoto and Cisneros creatively subvert the gender boundaries set by their respective cultures within the pervasive confines of the US national frame, subtly exposing dominant ideology and the institutional barriers that have limited our appreciation and comprehension of their work. These are defiant and passionate writers, writing to enhance awareness and 'multicultural' understanding. They are, without a doubt, 'teachers and peers, kindred spirits, borders be damned!'

Notes

1   I would like to thank Angie Chabram-Dernersesian for her unwavering editorial support.
2   Because women writers of colour write from a perspective that draws from at least two origins – the long-standing culture they are born into and the culture of social and political forces of their immediate environment – they often advance multifaceted non-horizontal critiques that explore new ethnic, social and political terrain.
3   One need only to consider the ongoing controversy related to the official 'American' language; to revisit the national ebonics debate and the recent legislation passed in California against bilingual education to understand the ongoing relevance of Yamamoto's critique.
4   The depiction of Mrs Hayashi, Rosie's mother, is crafted beautifully in order to convey the complexity of the Japanese immigrant woman's position in the United States. Yamamoto represents this position by weaving two conflicting perspectives that simultaneously portray the mother as out of touch with her present modern American reality – celebrating cultural values that are set in direct opposition to those of modern Japanese American youth with that of the conflicted woman, torn between her role as a mother and wife and that of Ume Hanazono (the pen-name she takes as a blossoming poet). Consequently, readers begin to understand the feminist critique she advances with her presentation of (gender and cultural) generational conflicts.
5   Here I am modifying Kathleen Baluntansky's (1997) definition.

References

Balutansky, Kathleen (1997) 'Appreciating C. L. R. James, a model of modernity and creolization', *Latin American Research Review*, 3(2): 233–44.

Balutansky, K. and Sourieau, M.A. (1998) *Caribbean Creolization*, Gainsville: University Press of Florida.

Cheung, King-Kok (1988) 'Introduction', in Hisaye Yamamoto, *Seventeen Syllables and Other Stories*, Latham: Kitchen Table Press.

Cisneros, Sandra (1984) *The House on Mango Street*, Houston, TX: Arte Publico.

Hagedorn, Jessica (1993) *Danger And Beauty*, New York: Penguin Books.

Kingston, Maxine Hong (1975) *The Woman Warrior: Memoirs of a Girlhood Among Ghosts*, New York: Vintage Books.

Lorde, Audre (1984) *Sister Outsider*, New York: Crossing Press.

Lowe, Lisa (1996) *Immigrant Acts*, Durham: Duke University Press.

Yamamoto, Hisaye (1988) *Seventeen Syllables and Other Stories*, Latham: Kitchen Table Press. (Originally published 1949.)

Notes on Contributors

Frances R. Aparicio is Arthur F. Thurnau Professor and Associate Professor of Spanish and American Culture/Latino Studies at the University of Michigan, Ann Arbor. She is author of *Listening to Salsa: Gender, Latin Popular Music, and Puerto Rican Cultures* (Wesleyan, 1998) and has also published on linguistic hybridity, Latino and Latina literatures, and teaching Spanish to US Latinos. She is currently a member of the Smithsonian Institute's Latino Popular Music Initiative and is working on oral interviews with Latino and Latina musicians.

Angie Chabram-Dernersesian is an Associate Professor of Chicana/o Studies at the University of California, Davis where she is a member of the Cultural Studies Executive Committee. She is co-editor of 'Chicana/o cultural representations: reframing alternative critical discourses' (*Cultural Studies*, 4(3), 1990) and has published extensively on Chicana/o literature; criticism; cultural studies; feminism, ethnography, and the social construction of whiteness.

Tamara R. Dukes is a researcher/community educator in Sacramento, California. From 1992 to 1993 she helped organize community programmes on the US–Mexican border. For the past decade she has explored how gender, race and sexuality are negotiated across and within the context of Latino/a national cultures. She has a Master's degree in cultural anthropology at the University of California, Davis, and a Master's degree in Spanish from Middlebury College.

Rosa Linda Fregoso is an Associate Professor of Women's Studies at the University of California, Davis. She is author of *The Bronze Screen: Chicana/o and Chicana Film Culture*, 1993; co-editor of Mirada de Mujer, with Norma Iglesias; and editor of *The Devil Never Sleeps and Other Films by Lourdes Portillo* (University of Texas Press, forthcoming).

Michelle Habell-Pallán, on leave from an Assistant Professor position in the Department of American Ethnic Studies at the University of Washington, Seattle, is currently a University of California President's Postdoctoral Fellow in the Department of Literature at the University of California, San Diego. She is completing her manuscript on Chicana/o and Latina/o performance culture.

Beatrice Pita teaches in the Spanish section of the Literature Department at the University of California, San Diego. She has written on María Amparo Ruiz de Burton's novels *Who Would Have Thought it?* and *The Squatter and the Don*.

Alvina E. Quintana is an Associate Professor of English at the University of Delaware, where she chairs the department's concentration in ethnic and cultural studies. She is author of *Home Girls: Chicana Literary Voices.*

Sonia Saldívar-Hull is an Associate Professor of English at the University of California, Los Angeles, where she also teaches women's studies and Chicana/o studies. She is co-editor of the Latin America Otherwise book series for Duke University Press. Her book, *Feminism on the Border: Gender Politics, Geopolitics, and Transfronteriza Collectivities*, will be published later this year by University of California Press.

Rosaura Sánchez teaches Chicano/a and Latin American literature in the Literature Department of the University of California, San Diego. She is author of *Telling Identities* (Minnesota, 1995) and numerous articles.

Lisa Sánchez González teaches (trans-) American and ethnic/Third World literatures at the University of Texas at Austin, where she is an Assistant Professor of English. Her scholarship includes essays in *Emergencies* (1994/95) and *Recovering the U.S. Hispanic Literary Heritage* (Vol. II, 1996). She is currently finishing a manuscript entitled *AmeRícan Literature* (1898-1998), which explores narrative self-representation in the Puerto Rican colonial diaspora.

María Angelina Soldatenko holds a joint appointment as an Assistant Professor of Gender Feminist Studies and Chicana/o Studies at Pitzer College. She has conducted extensive ethnographic research among Latina workers and union organizers in Los Angeles. Her principal research interest is Latina immigrants and labour in the United States.

Yvonne Yarbro-Bejarano is Professor of Spanish and Chair of Chicana/o Studies in the Center for Comparative Studies in Race and Ethnicity Program at Stanford University. She is author of *Feminism and the Honor Plays of Lope de Vega* (1994); co-editor of *Chicano Art: Resistance and Affirmation* (1991); collected essays on Cherríe Moraga (forthcoming from the University of Texas Press, 1999). Her research concentrates on cultural representations of race, sexuality and gender, as well as the ongoing development of a digital archive of Chicana/o art accessible on the internet (www-asd.stanford.edu/Media 1/ChicanaARt).

Subject ■ Fellowship Announcement

The Privatization of Culture

Fellowship Residencies Available

The Privatization of Culture project offers fellowship residencies for research on cultural policy. The project encourages transdisciplinary work that takes into account both formal and informal markets, institutional participation, and dominant and alternative cultural practices. Rockefeller residencies will bring together scholars, foundation officers, corporate funding specialists, curators and educators, artists, and community cultural advocacy professionals to assess existing arrangements and to propose new ways to democratize cultural participation in local, national and transnational settings.

Description

The past decade has witnessed an acceleration in policies to privatize support for culture throughout North and Latin America, and East and West Europe. In some countries, government has abdicated what traditionally was its responsibility to the citizenry. In others, new intermediary institutions are attempting to pick up the lack. In still others, governments are entering partnerships with the corporate sector. The result is that it is increasingly difficult to distinguish between public and private, and that diverse groups are affected unequally by the emerging arrangements. What are the guarantees for democratic access to culture? Who determines participation and by what criteria? These and related questions are the focus of research in the Privatization of Culture project. Based in New York University's American Studies Program, it is a collaborative project with the Sociology Program at the New School for Social Research and the Center for Cultural Studies at the Graduate Center for the City University of New York.

Themes of Residency Fellowships

1999–2000: current changes in systems of support in the arts and humanities. This year focuses on the political and economic reasons for these changes and the ways in which cultural practices work with, against or independently of these systems. Deadline: 15 February 1999.

2000–2001: minority participation. This year focuses on the forms of exclusion, inclusion and marginalization of certain groups, as well as creative strategies to transform public spheres and to foster multicultural collaborations. Deadline: 1 February 2000.

Terms of Awards

Each year, the Privatization of Culture project will offer either one two-semester residency and two one-semester residencies, or four one-semester residencies. A one-semester residency carries a stipend of $17,500; a two-semester residency carries a stipend of $35,000. These stipends may be combined with sabbatical pay. There is also an allowance for medical insurance, although fellows make a small contribution as well. In 1999–2000, the project expects to offer either four one-semester residencies or one two-semester and two one-semester residencies at New York University, The New School or the CUNY Graduate Center.

Fellows will be expected to (1) conduct research on a project, as per their proposals; (2) participate in a bi-weekly seminar; (3) participate in a major conference sponsored by the project; (4) meet with other faculty and students who are interested in their work.

Application

People interested in a one- or two-semester residency fellowship should send, by 15 February 1999: (1) a cover letter; (2) a five-page project proposal; (3) a curriculum vitae; (4) sample work; (5) three letters of recommendation. Send applications to:

George Yudice, Director
Privatization of Culture Project
American Studies Program
New York University   Tel: 212-998-3725
285 Mercer St, 8th Floor   Fax: 212-995-4371
New York, NY 10003   Electronic mail: <priv.culture@nyu.edu>

Steering Committee

Barbara Abrash, Center for Media, Culture, and History, NYU
Stanley Aronowitz, Co-Director, Center for Cultural Studies, CUNY Graduate Center
Judith Balfe, Sociology, Staten Island College and CUNY Graduate Center
Faye Ginsburg, Center for Media, Culture, and History, NYU

Toby Miller, Cinema Studies, NYU
Andrew Ross, American Studies Program, NYU
Mary Schmidt-Campbell, Dean Tisch School of the Arts, NYU
George Yudice, Director, American Studies Program, NYU
Vera Zolberg, Co-Director, Sociology, The New School for Social Research

Advisory Network

John Brademas, President Emeritus, NYU Craig Calhoun, Sociology, NYU Vincent Crapanzano, Comp Lit, CUNY Manthia Diawara, Africana, NYU

Sondra Farganis, Director, Vera List Center for Art and Politics, New School Judith Friedlander, Dean of the Graduate Faculty, New School Jeffrey Goldfarb, Sociology, New School Flora E. S. Kaplan, Director, Museum Studies, NYU

Barbara Kirschenblatt-Gimblett, Performance Studies, NYU

Joel Lester, Dean of the Mannes College of Music, New School

James Lipton, Dean of the School of Dramatic Arts, New School

Randy Martin, Social Science and Management, Pratt Institute

Catherine McCarthy, Center for the Study of Philanthropy, CUNY

Dorothy Nelkin, Sociology, NYU

Pier C. Rogers, Robert J. Milano Graduate School of Management and Urban Policy, New School

Bob Stam, Cinema Studies, NYU

Catherine Stimpson, Dean, Arts and Humanities, NYU

John Kuo Wei Tchen, Director, Asian-Pacific-American Studies, NYU

Daniel Walkowitz, Director, Metropolitan Studies, NYU

Sharon Zukin, Sociology, CUNY

TV Living

Television, Culture and Everyday Life

David Gauntlett, University of Leeds, UK and
Annette Hill, University of Westminster, UK
TV Living presents the eagerly-awaited findings of the BFI Audience
Tracking Study in which 500 participants completed detailed
questionnaire-diaries on their lives, their television watching,
and the relationship between the two over a five year period.

April 1999: 234x156: 336pp
Hb: 0-415-18485-1: **£45.00** Pb: 0-415-18486-X: **£14.99**

Television and Common Knowledge

Edited by **Jostein Gripsrud**, University of Bergen, Norway
Television and Common Knowledge Knowledge considers how
television can facilitate well-informed citizenship in a fragmented
modern society.
Comedia
March 1999: 234x156: 224pp: illus. 20 b+w photos
Hb: 0-415-18928-4: **£45.00** Pb: 0-415-18929-2: **£13.99**

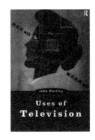

Uses of Television

John Hartley, University of Wales, Cardiff, UK
**'An immensely innovative, thought-provoking,
iconoclastic and ambitious book on the history and
meaning of television and television studies it both
expands and clarifies the academic field.'**
- Mica Nava

January 1999: 234x156: 256pp: illus.20 b+w photos
Hb: 0-415-08508-X: £45.00 Pb: 0-415-08509-8: **£13.99**

order direct on
Tel: +44 (0)1264 342939
Fax: +44 (0)1264 343005.
For further information or a *free*
1999 Media catalogue
please contact:
Aine Duffy, Routledge,
11 New Fetter Lane,
London EC4P 4EE, UK
or email:
infomedia@routledge.co.uk

The Nationwide Television Studies

David Morley, Goldsmiths College, London, UK and
Charlotte Brunsdon, University of Warwick, UK
This book brings together for the first time David Morley
and Charlotte Brunsdon's classic texts, *Everyday Television:
Nationwide* and *The Nationwide Audience*.

Routledge Research in Cultural and Media Studies 6
January 1999: 234x156: 336pp
Hb: 0-415-14879-0: **£55.00**

Frantz Fanon

Critical Perspectives

Edited by **Anthony C. Alessandrini**, Rutgers University, USA

Addresses Fanon's extraordinary, often controversial writings, and examines the ways in which his work can shed light on contemporary issues in cultural politics.

January 1999: 234x156: 304pp
Pb: 0-415-18976-4: **£14.99**

Home, Exile, Homeland

Film, Media, and the Politics of Place

Edited by **Hamid Naficy**, Rice University, USA

This book brings together a transnational array of distinguished critics, including Thomas Elsaesser, George Lipsitz, Margaret Morse, David Morley and Ella Shohat, to discuss the ways in which film, television, music, computer and electronic media are shaping identities and cultures in an increasingly globalized world.

AFI Film Readers

January 1999: 229x153: 256pp :illus.10 b+w photos
Pb: 0-415-91947-9: **£12.99**

Scattered Belongings

Cultural Paradoxes of Race, Nation and Gender

Jayne O. Ifekwunigwe, University of East London, UK

'An empowering and healing book that will make you laugh and cry. It is guaranteed to make you seriously rethink the perversity of our simplistic bi-racialized ways of thinking and talking.'

- Heidi Safia Mirza, editor of Black British Feminism

January 1999: 234x156: 240pp
Pb: 0-415-17096-6: **£15.99**

Ethnic and Racial Studies Today

Edited by **Martin Bulmer**, University of Surrey, UK and **John Solomos**, University of Southampton, UK

This important collection addresses recent developments in the teaching, studying and presentation of race across many disciplines, including sociology, politics, social geography, cultural studies and philosophy.

February 1999: 234x156: 216pp
Pb: 0-415-18173-9: **£14.99**

order direct on
Tel: +44 (0)1264 342939
Fax: +44 (0)1264 343005.
For further information or a
free catalogue please contact
Aine Duffy, Routledge, 11
New Fetter Lane, London
EC4P 4EE, UK
or email:
infomedia@routledge.co.uk

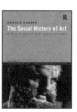

Differencing the Canon

Feminism and the Writing of Arts Histories
Griselda Pollock, University of Leeds, UK
In this major new book, renowned art historian Griselda Pollock makes a compelling intervention into a debate at the very centre of feminist art history: should the traditional canon of the Old Masters be rejected, replaced or reformed?
Re Visions: Critical Studies in the History and Theory of Art
February 1999: 246x174: 368pp: illus.100 images
Pb: 0-415-06700-6: **£13.99**

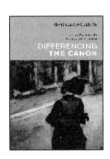

Native American Art in the Twentieth Century

Makers, Meanings, Histories
Edited by **W. Jackson Rushing III**,
University of Missouri - St Louis, USA
'This collection reveals the complexity of Native American art, speaking from and to a multiplicity of voices with a sensitivity and implicit respect for the topic that prevents the colonizing discourse of the academic world from taking over' - *Richard Shiff*
February 1999: 246x189: 252pp
illus.8pp colour section: 19 colour photos, 41 b+w photos
Pb: 0-415-13748-9: **£18.99**

The Photography Handbook

Terence Wright, Oxford University, UK
The Photography Handbook provides an introduction to the principles of photographic practice and theory and offers guidelines for the systematic study of photographic media.
Media Practice
February 1999: 234x156: 208pp: illus.72 b+w photos
Pb: 0-415-11594-9: **£14.99**

order direct on
Tel: +44 (0)1264 342939   Fax: +44 (0)1264 343005.
For further information or a *free catalogue* please contact Aine Duffy,
Routledge, 11 New Fetter Lane, London EC4P 4EE, UK
or email: infomedia@routledge.co.uk